Routledge Library Editions

MONEY, INCOME AND EMPLOYMENT

ECONOMICS

Routledge Library Editions – Economics

ECONOMIC THEORY & ECONOMETRICS

In 6 Volumes

I	Fiscal Policy & Business Cycles	*Hansen*
II	Macrodynamics: Fluctuations and Growth	*Hénin*
III	Optimisation in Economic Analysis	*Mills*
IV	Economic Theory	*Richardson*
V	Money, Income and Employment	*Schneider*
VI	Pricing and Equilibrium	*Schneider*

MONEY, INCOME AND EMPLOYMENT

ERICH SCHNEIDER

Routledge
Taylor & Francis Group
LONDON AND NEW YORK

First published in 1962

Reprinted in 2003 by
Routledge
2 Park Square, Milton Park, Abingdon, Oxon, OX14 4RN
or
270 Madison Avenue, New York, NY 10016

First issued in paperback 2010

Routledge is an imprint of the Taylor & Francis Group

British Library Cataloguing in Publication Data
A CIP catalogue record for this book
is available from the British Library

Money, Income and Employment
ISBN 978-0-415-31318-6 (hbk)
ISBN 978-0-415-60712-4 (pbk)
ISBN 978-0-415-31318-6 (set)

Miniset: Economic Theory & Econometrics

Series: Routledge Library Editions – Economics

MONEY, INCOME AND EMPLOYMENT

BY

DR. ERICH SCHNEIDER
Professor at the University of Kiel

Translated by

KURT KLAPPHOLZ
Lecturer in Economics
The London School of Economics

London

GEORGE ALLEN & UNWIN LTD

RUSKIN HOUSE MUSEUM STREET

FIRST PUBLISHED IN 1962

The German Original

GELD, KREDIT, VOLKSEINKOMMEN UND BESCHAEFTIGUNG

is Volume III, first published in 1953 of Prof. Schneider's

EINFUEHRUNG IN DIE WIRTSCHAFTSTHEORIE

Verlag J. C. B. Mohr (Paul Siebeck)

TRANSLATOR'S NOTE

This translation is based on the fifth German edition (1959) but incorporates the major improvements of the sixth German edition (1961).

The only changes from the original German occur in chapts. I and II, where some statistical tables have been omitted and several footnotes have been added. The footnotes were provided by Mr. R. G. Opie, Lecturer in Economics at the London School of Economics, and are initialled R. G. O.

One of the risks of translating is that one's style may be strongly influenced by the original language. This can be particularly unfortunate when one is translating from German into English. I have endeavoured to minimize this risk by asking friends to check various parts of the manuscript. Their generous help has greatly improved the readability and clarity of this translation.

Here I should like to thank my colleagues, Mr. L. P. Foldes and Mr. J. Thomas, for their kind assistance. I am especially indebted to Miss Gwyneth Miles, who has read the entire manuscript more than once and suggested numerous stylistic improvements, and who helped me at all stages of the tedious process of checking and cross checking.

I alone am responsible for the final form of this translation.

K. K.

PREFACE

The present volume concludes my *Introduction to Economic Theory.*[1] What it offers is set forth in the Introduction, and can be seen at a glance from the Table of Contents. I obviously had to limit myself in selecting material for this book; one cannot expect an encyclopaedic introduction to the present state of economic theory. Nevertheless, it is the function of an introduction to make the reader familiar with all those tools of theory which are necessary for the analysis of economic reality. Since this work attempts to acquaint the reader with the contents of the tool-box of theory, this box must contain all the indispensable tools. In this respect I have striven after completeness and thoroughness; and in this sense this third volume concludes the *Introduction.* Beyond this, I think that this work as a whole not only introduces the reader to the mode of thinking and working in modern theory, but also offers a general view of its main problems, and, in this connection, shows how the tools of theory may be employed to deal with concrete problems. Anyone who has mastered the method of thinking developed in this work will also have at his disposal tools for the analysis of problems not treated here.

In the preparation of this volume I have been guided by the same considerations as in the case of the first two volumes. Professional criticism has confirmed in a friendly manner that the method I have adopted has proved useful. It gives the student the insight into theoretical thought and work without which neither an understanding of economic events, nor a fruitful study of contemporary domestic and foreign technical literature, is possible.

I have again made use of simple algebra and geometry which can be understood without any more knowledge than that acquired in the course of higher secondary education. A thorough understanding, especially of the theory of income determination, is impossible without simple mathematics; experience also shows that it assists the beginner considerably.

This work is the fruit of long teaching experience, and the result of my striving to facilitate the student's understanding of modern economic theory. I owe sincere thanks to all my colleagues who have stimulated and encouraged me in my endeavours. I also owe thanks to my students who, through questions and discussion, have drawn my attention to those points which students find particularly difficult to understand and which therefore require particularly careful exposition.

E. SCHNEIDER

(1) Vol. II is published in English under the title *Pricing and Equilibrium* (completely revised version based on the 6th German edition, Allen and Unwin, 1961). All subsequent references are to this English edition of Vol. II.

CONTENTS

INTRODUCTION

We have seen in the preceding volumes that the course of the economic process through time is determined by the manner in which economic units (i.e. households, firms, banks and the government) dispose of their scarce resources. The way in which an economic unit disposes of its scarce resources in various circumstances may be called the *dispositions* of that economic unit. It is the task of economic theory to discover how these dispositions are determined, and how given dispositions will influence the course of the economic process. Substantial parts of this range of problems have been investigated in Vol. II. We described, in the framework of an analysis of the economic plans of households and firms, how their dispositions are determined. Then, using partial equilibrium analysis, we described the equilibria corresponding to various dispositions and the effects of changes in dispositions. Finally, we gave an exposition of the problem of general micro-economic equilibrium in a stationary economy.

The inquiry must now be broadened and supplemented in several directions. First, we must show what part financial and credit institutions play in the economic process. The inclusion of this range of problems at once raises the whole complex of questions relating to "monetary influences" on the course of the economic process. Those who have studied the earlier volumes carefully will be familiar with our approach to these questions. As we saw in our previous inquiries, dispositions relating to sales and purchases of goods and services have an important influence on the course of the economic process, and are decisive for the determination of income. In the terminology of Walb these transactions influence both the "sales-purchases" and the "expenditures-receipts" accounts of firms. However, in addition to dispositions which create income directly there are others which only affect the "expenditure-receipts" columns, and thus have no immediate influence on the level of income. Examples of such transactions are sales and purchases of securities by households or firms, and the creation and extinction of debts between banks and firms. Although these transactions affect directly only the "expenditures-receipts" accounts, they may have substantial indirect effects on the formation of income. We shall have to investigate these interconnections. To do this, it will be necessary to analyse in detail the process of the creation and destruction of the means of payment. The reader already knows that the means of payment in the present-day economy consist of claims. Thus we shall have to show how such claims come to be created and destroyed in the course of the economic process, and what economic effects flow from the processes of the creation and destruction of money. We shall deliberately restrict ourselves to the analysis of an economy of the present-day type, i.e. one in which claims alone are used as means of payment.

Our previous exposition must be extended in yet another direction. In the first volume we presented an *ex-post* analysis of the national income. Now we must inquire how the level of national income in a future period is determined by the prevailing dispositions of the economic subjects, and how we may explain fluctuations in income and, in connection with this, fluctuations in employment. The theory must uncover the determinants of any prevailing level of national income.

It is possible to undertake such a total analysis on a micro-economic basis, i.e. by considering *the behaviour of every single economic unit individually*. This, in fact, was done in the second volume, in connection with the general equilibrium analysis of a stationary economy. The treatment of the problem of income formation, however, is considerably simplified if we carry out the analysis on a macro-economic basis, i.e. by employing macro-economic variables obtained by the aggregation of micro-economic ones. The assumptions and implications of this sort of analysis will have to be specified precisely. Depending on the problem we shall, in the course of our inquiry, make use of static, comparative-static or dynamic modes of analysis.

We shall also have to examine how government activity and the balance-of-payments affects the level of income. The analysis will be restricted solely to the aspects relevant to this problem. A complete exposition of public finance theory lies outside the scope of this book, as does an exhaustive analysis of all balance-of-payments problems.

CHAPTER I

The Means of Payment in the Present-Day Economy

The means of payment, or money, are those assets which may be used everywhere and at any time in the settlement of claims arising from the economic process. Let us consider the balance sheets of individual economic units (households, firms, banks and the government) and see which items among the assets are to be regarded as money at any given moment of time.

1. Let us first consider an inventory of the means of payment of a household at a given moment of time. As was shown in Vol. I, the assets (gross wealth) of a household consist of its real wealth and of claims against other economic units. In general these claims consist of claims against (a) other households, (b) firms, (c) banks and (d) the state. Only some of these have the characteristics of money, namely: (1) the claims against the central bank, held in the form of notes and coins,[1] and (2) current accounts (demand deposits) kept with the commercial banks. Time deposits and savings deposits (i.e. deposits which can be withdrawn only after agreed notice is given) are not money, since their owner has relinquished the right of free disposal for a fixed period of time. However, they may easily be turned into money by giving the required notice. Similarly, any bills of exchange, shares and bonds in the possession of a household are not money.

If, for the sake of simplicity, we regard coins as bank notes printed on metal (as we did in the first volume) we may say that the means of payment of a household at any given moment consist of its stock of notes and its current accounts with banks. Notes are also called *legal tender* money, because every economic unit is obliged to accept them in settlement of debts.

For a household, a current account with a bank is equivalent to holding an equal amount in notes. The household can convert a part or the whole of the account into notes at any time, i.e. it can convert its claim against a commercial bank into a claim against the central bank. The ownership of a current account thus simply means that the household has requested the bank to look after part of its cash. This gives the household considerable advantages in making its

[1] For the sake of simplicity we assume that minting rights are vested in the central bank.

payments. For example, if a household H wishes to settle a claim held against it by an economic unit U, it may, instead of making payment in notes, give U a cheque, i.e. an instruction to its bank to pay U the sum stated on the cheque. If U is willing to accept the cheque (there is no obligation to do so) he may present it at the drawer's bank for payment in cash. If U owns a current account at the drawer's or another bank, he may give the cheque to his bank, and have the sum credited to his account. In the case where household H and economic unit U keep accounts with the same bank, the payment is made simply by the bank's debiting the account of H and crediting that of U. In the case where U keeps an account with another bank, the process of payment is somewhat different and will be discussed shortly. In every case, however, payment is made by debiting the account of H and crediting that of U with the same sum. Instead of giving U a cheque, household H may simply instruct its bank to credit the account of U. In this case payment is made in the same way, by the bank making the appropriate transfer from one account to the other. *In all these cases, the means of payment consist of current accounts, parts of which are transferred to other accounts by means of instructions to the banks* (*by cheque or banker's order*). Since these means of payment consist of entries in the banks' books, they are often called *book money*.

2. A consideration of the balance sheets of firms does not shed any new light on our original question. We merely need to note that some large firms keep current accounts not only with the commercial banks but also with the central bank. The firms' stock of money at any one moment thus consists of (a) their stock of bank notes (b) their current accounts with the commercial banks, and (c) their current accounts with the central bank. Both bank notes and current accounts with the central bank represent immediately realizable claims against the central bank, and may be called *central bank money*. We may say, therefore, that *the stock of the means of payment at any one moment consists of the amount of central bank money plus the amount of book money held with the commercial banks.*

3. We designate the sum of the means of payment held at any one moment by all firms and households *as the stock of money of the private sector of the economy.*

4. Let us now consider the stock of money held by a commercial bank at any one moment of time. A bank holds at any one moment a given amount of money in the form of (a) bank notes, (b) current accounts with the central bank and (c) current accounts with other banks. The sum of bank notes (including coins) and of current accounts with the central bank is called the bank's *cash reserve*.

A bank's current accounts with the central bank fulfil the same function as do the public's current accounts with the commercial banks. They may be exchanged for bank notes at any time, and are thus potential bank notes. Moreover, they serve as means of payment for financial transactions among banks. For example, if bank A has to make a payment to bank B, it does this usually by issuing appropriate transfer instructions to the central bank. The central bank then credits the account of bank B, and debits that of bank A. Such payments occur, for example, when bank A, on the instructions of a client, makes a payment to a client of bank B. In this case, bank A debits the account of its client, instructs the central bank to debit its own account and to credit the account of bank B in favour of B's client. Bank B then credits the amount to the account of its client. Payments among banks may, of course, be made by using the accounts kept by one commercial bank with another.

Since the commercial banks' current accounts with the central bank serve as means of payment in transactions among the commercial banks, these accounts are also called *central bank book money. Central bank book money must be sharply distinguished from commercial bank book money.* This will be discussed in detail in the next chapter.

If we neglect the fact that some large firms keep current accounts with the central bank, we may say that the central bank plays the same part in the process of payments among the commercial banks as do the commercial banks in respect of payments among members of the private sector.

5. In a closed economy the balance sheet of a central bank does not contain any items representing money.(1) Only in an open economy does it contain such items, in which case they represent stocks of foreign currencies and current accounts held with foreign banks.

6. Finally, the balance sheet of the government shows a stock of money consisting of (a) a stock of bank notes and coins, (b) current accounts with commercial banks and (c) current accounts with the central bank.(2)

7. Let us divide the economy into the following sectors: (a) the private sector, consisting of households and firms; (b) the banking sector, consisting of the commercial and savings-banks; (c) the

(1) The balance sheet of the Bank of England is an apparent exception to this rule. The weekly bank-return does contain both notes and coins. This is because the Bank, for historical reasons, is still divided into an Issue Department and a Banking Department. (R. G. O.)

(2) The United Kingdom Government has no accounts with any banks other than the central bank, the Bank of England. (R. G. O.)

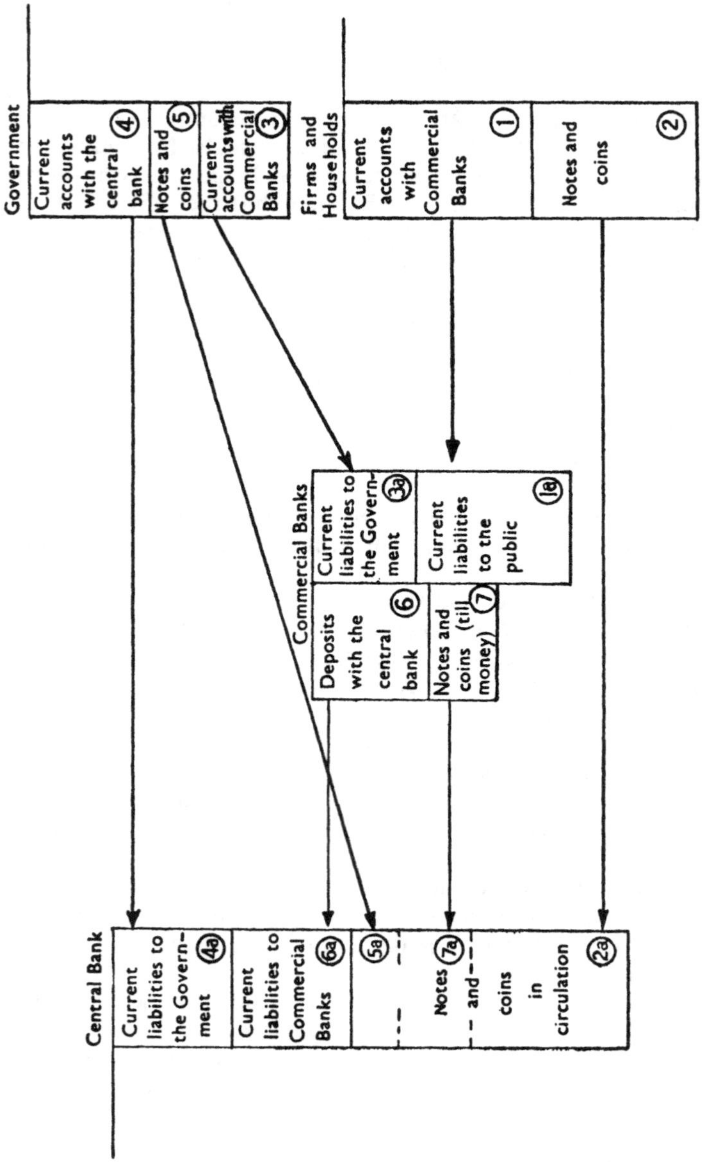
Government
Current accounts with the central bank 4
Notes and coins 5
Current accounts with Commercial Banks 3
Firms and Households
Current accounts with Commercial Banks 1
Notes and coins 2
Commercial Banks
Current liabilities to the Govern-ment 3a
Current liabilities to the public 1a
Deposits with the central bank 6
Notes and coins (till money) 7
Central Bank
Current liabilities to the Govern-ment 4a
Current liabilities to Commercial Banks 6a
5a
7a
Notes and coins in circulation 2a

Fig. 1

government sector. In a closed economy, at any one moment, we shall have the following overall picture of the kinds of money and of its distribution among the three sectors:[1]

(a) the private sector holds a stock of notes and coins (cash), as well as current accounts kept with the commercial banks;[2]

(b) the government sector holds a stock of notes and coins, a certain amount of current accounts kept with commercial banks, and current accounts kept with the central bank;

(c) the banking sector, taken as a whole, holds a stock of notes and coins, and current accounts kept with the central bank.

If we restrict ourselves to stocks of money, the balance sheets of the individual sectors can be represented in the form shown in the adjoining chart (Fig. 1). The sum of the debit amounts, 2a, 4a, 5a, 6a, 7a, in the central bank's balance sheet represents the entire amount of central bank money held by the private, government and banking sectors, and consists of the notes (including coins) in circulation, and of the current accounts kept with the central bank. The sum of the debit items 1a and 3a of the consolidated balance sheet of the commercial banks equals the amount of commercial bank book money held by the private and government sectors.

The chart shows clearly that the means of payment in the modern economy consist of claims held against banks. Central bank money consists of claims against the central bank, whereas book money kept with the commercial banks consists of claims against the commercial banks.

Furthermore, our chart shows immediately that the amount of money held at any one moment by the banking and non-banking sectors may be ascertained in two ways:

(a) by adding the amounts of money shown on the assets side of the balance sheets of these sectors; or

(b) by adding the liabilities which represent money shown on the debit side of the balance sheets of the commercial banks and the central bank.

The quantity of money in the non-banking sector (cash and current accounts) may be called for short the *volume of money in the economy*. This quantity is of special importance for our inquiry.

8. Since the existence of a claim is always the expression of a relationship involving credit, we may say that modern money is a

[1] The "private" and "government" sectors are often called the *non-banking sector*.

[2] For the sake of simplicity we neglect the fact that some large firms keep current accounts with the central bank.

feature of the credit system. Its character and nature cannot be understood without inquiring into the nature of credit. The reader, therefore, should once more recall the account of credit which we gave in the first volume.

9. Present-day money consists of claims, but the converse of this is not true. Not all claims in our economy are money; for example, debts owed by one man to another, and claims such as bills of exchange, shares and bonds. Although these represent claims on national wealth they are not money. The majority of such claims can, however, be exchanged for money. The more easily any such claim may be exchanged for money, or used as the basis for the creation of money, the more liquid it is.[1]

10. The quantity of money in the economy, or in any sector of the economy, relates to one moment of time; it is, therefore, a stock quantity. Experience shows that the size of this stock, as well as its distribution among individual economic units, varies from time to time. It follows that claims which are money are continually being created and destroyed in the course of time. In order to understand the variations in the quantity of money which take place in the course of time we must examine carefully the process by which the economy is supplied with its means of payment. Since our money consists of claims on the commercial banks and the central bank, we shall have to pay attention to the role of banks in the process of creating and destroying money. Our analysis will show that the banks "are in fact the heart and centre of the modern currency system".[2]

[1] Compare R. v. Keller, "Ausstattung, Konsolidation und Tilgung staatlicher Arbeitsbeschaffungs—und Investitionskredite", *Weltwirtschaftliches Archiv*, Vol. 53, 1941, p. 482.

[2] K. Wicksell, *Lectures on Political Economy*, Vol. II, p. 73.

CHAPTER II

The Creation and Destruction of Money

§1. Model of a System with One Bank in Which Payments Are Made without Using Cash (Wicksell's Ideal Bank)

1. When examining the process of the creation and destruction of money it is useful to start with the model which is simplest theoretically. Let us therefore assume an economy in which there is only one bank, and in which all payments are made without using cash. The stock of money at the disposal of economic units thus consists solely of current accounts kept with this single bank, and all payments are made by means of book-transfers from one account to another. With the aid of this model we can demonstrate clearly certain important aspects of our problem.

2. Let us consider some of the transactions that arise in the course of the bank's business.

(a) The bank buys a piece of land from X at a price of £1000, and pays X by crediting his account with £1000. This transaction will be reflected in the bank's balance sheet by a rise in the bank's assets equal to the value of the land and a rise in its liabilities equal to the amount paid to X. This, in turn, may be expressed by saying that both sides of the bank's balance sheet, i.e. total assets and total liabilities, have increased by £1000. The bank has acquired the piece of land and paid for it with a claim on itself which represents money. When the bank purchases the land, it creates at the same time £1000 of new money; i.e. the quantity of money increases by £1000.

(b) The bank buys foreign currency from Y to the value of £1000. This purchase also leads to an increase on both sides of the bank's balance sheet, since the bank has acquired a new asset in the form of foreign currency and has paid for it with a claim on itself, by crediting Y's account with £1000. The purchase of the currency has once again entailed the simultaneous creation of new money to the value of £1000.

(c) The bank discounts a bill of exchange drawn by A on B in the course of selling some goods. As we saw in the first volume, the discounting of a bill of exchange leads to the substitution of an indirect for a direct credit relationship, in that the bank places itself between the last debtor and the last creditor. Instead of the credit chain

$$A \rightarrow B$$

we now have the lengthened credit chain

$$A \rightarrow \text{Bank} \rightarrow B.$$

The bank now holds a bill of exchange, and A holds a current account with the bank which the bank created in the process of discounting the bill. This transaction also leads to a rise on both sides of the bank's balance sheet.

(d) The bank grants credit of £1000 to firm E for productive purposes. What happens is that the bank acquires an asset in the form of a claim on the firm, and credits the firm's account with £1000. We now have the following fictitious credit chain:

$$E \xrightarrow{1000} \text{Bank} \xrightarrow{1000} E$$

whose first link consists of a claim which represents money, while the second link consists of a claim which does not. Once more the bank's acquisition of a claim has led simultaneously to the creation of money and to a rise in the bank's assets and liabilities.

From these examples we derive the following basic proposition:

In the one-bank model money is created by the bank acquiring assets which are not money in the home country and paying for them by claims on itself which are money. We may also describe this process by saying that *the bank creates new money by monetizing assets which are not money.*

The creation of money which results from the bank monetizing the assets considered in examples (a) and (b) differs significantly from that which occurs when the bank turns into money the assets mentioned in examples (c) and (d). In cases (a) and (b) the seller receives money from the bank which is freely at his disposal, and without incurring any future liabilities to the bank. He does not become the bank's debtor. Cases (c) and (d) are different. Here the bank also creates money, in the course of monetizing the bill of exchange or the I.O.U., which is at the free disposal of its customers. However, the customer has now incurred a debt to the bank to the value of the money put at his disposal.[1] The difference between an economic unit's credit with the bank and its debts to the bank may be called its net credit with the bank (and may be positive or negative). Thus the bank's acquisition of assets of the first kind (cases (a) and (b)) leads to a rise in the seller's net credit with the

[1] When discounting a bill he incurs a contingent liability towards the bank.

bank. Let us call assets of this kind *primary assets.*[1] By contrast, the acquisition by the bank of an asset of the second kind (cases (c) and (d)) does not lead to a rise in the customer's net credit with the bank, since the rise in his credit with the bank is matched by an equivalent rise in his debts to it. Let us call assets of the latter kind *secondary assets.* It is clear that the monetization of assets of the first kind confers greater freedom on the recipient than does the creation of money on the basis of the second kind of asset.

Since a debt must be repaid at some future time, each creation of money based upon secondary assets leads to an automatic destruction of money at the time of repayment.

3. The process by which money is destroyed is the exact reverse of the process by which it is created. *Means of payment are destroyed by the bank selling assets.*

Examples:

(a) The bank sells foreign currency to an economic unit X, and as a result the assets in the bank's balance sheet are reduced by the amount of the foreign currency sold. At the same time the diminution in the buyer's current account reduces the bank's liabilities. Thus there is a reduction on both sides of the balance sheet.

(b) Economic unit X redeems a bill of exchange. The bill of exchange disappears from the bank's assets, and the bank's liabilities are reduced by the same amount through the fall in X's current account. Money is therefore destroyed.

(c) Firm E repays the credit which had been granted to it by the bank. The claim against E disappears from the bank's assets, and on the liabilities side there is an equal reduction in E's current account. Once again money has been destroyed.

4. From what has been said it follows that new means of payment can be created only by the bank, *but they may be created at the initiative of either the bank or the public or the government.* For example, if a firm takes an overdraft from the bank, or a trader discounts a bill with the bank, or the government places securities with the bank, the initiative comes from the public or the government, as the case may be. If however the bank buys securities from the public, the initiative comes from the bank. Yet, wherever the initiative may originate, *money cannot be created* (i.e. both sides of the bank's balance sheet increased) *unless the bank is willing to create it.* At any one time there are claims on the bank on the liabilities side of its balance sheet, while there are corresponding

[1] Jorgen Pedersen calls assets of the first kind assets which confer liquidity (*Pengeteori og Pengepolitik*, 2nd ed., Copenhagen 1948, p. 65).

assets on the credit side, on the basis of which the claims on the bank were created. By its ability to influence the composition of its assets the bank can increase or decrease the volume of money. The bank can always decrease the quantity of money; for example, it need only recall some loans. But it cannot always create credit, since it cannot force firms or the government to become its debtors. The quantity of money can be increased only if, given the bank's willingness to extend credit, there are some economic units willing to incur debts.

5. It can be seen immediately that transactions among the bank's customers only affect the liabilities side of the bank's balance sheet. If X pays Y £1000, the bank debits X's current account and credits that of Y. This kind of transaction does not change the quantity of money in the economy.

The quantity of money is changed, however, if X transfers £1000 from his current account to his savings account. Since the transfer renders £1000 idle for a certain period, the quantity of money is reduced by this amount. *The bank's creditors can affect the quantity of money in the economy in this way, but only in this way.* It is their decisions alone which determine the distribution of the bank's liabilities between current accounts and savings accounts.[1]

6. It follows from what we have said that in a closed economy the bank can never become insolvent. This is so because the bank itself creates the claims which represent money. For the bank there is no such thing as "cash". Moreover, there are no limits to the bank's ability to create credit. In the course of granting new credit the bank can create as many claims on itself as it likes, provided of course, that there are economic units willing to incur debts. The only limits to the bank's ability to extend new credit are those it sets itself. The above can be expressed simply by saying that *the bank is always liquid.*

When speaking of the *liquidity of a bank* we have to distinguish clearly between *two concepts of liquidity: liquidity in the sense of the bank always being able to meet current liabilities, and liquidity in the sense of the ability of the bank to grant new credit, i.e. to accept new*

[1] In the English banking system too, savings accounts can be excluded from the quantity of money as here defined. Withdrawals can, however, be made from deposit accounts with only seven days' notice. It thus seems more sensible to include both current and deposit accounts in the quantity of money in England. Hence, if the public shifts its funds from current to deposit accounts or in the opposite direction, this will not affect the quantity of money.

The situation in the United States is similar to that in Germany because the minimum legal reserve ratios for the two types of accounts are different. Given the reserves of the banking system, the public can thus affect the quantity of money by switching funds from one type of account to the other. (R. G. O.)

liabilities. In a closed economy our bank is always liquid in both senses.

In an open economy the situation is different. In this case the bank also has to make payments in foreign currency, i.e. in currency which it cannot create. The bank's liquidity (in both senses) is now limited by the available stock of foreign currencies and by the possibilities of acquiring foreign currencies. *A bank always faces a liquidity problem if it has to make payments in a form of money which it cannot create.* This problem will shortly have to be considered in detail in another context.

7. The conclusions so far established are not affected if the bank also issues notes. For example, if the owner of a current account wishes to have part of it paid in notes all that happens in the bank's balance sheet is a transfer on the liabilities side from the item: current accounts, to the item: note-issue. The reverse happens when a customer pays notes into the bank: there is a reduction in the item: note-issue, and an equal increase in the customer's current account. Thus no one can become a new creditor of the bank by paying in notes, and no one can cease being a creditor of the bank by converting current accounts into notes. This could happen only if payments into the bank, and payments by the bank, were made in a form of money which the bank cannot create, and in our model such payments do not occur.

8. Finally, let us consider the relationships between the creation of money by our bank and the creation of credit.[1] The existence of such relationships follows from the fact that the means of payment are themselves claims.

The following four cases are possible:

(a) *Creation of Money on the Basis of Prior Credit Creation*

Example: Merchant B sells goods on credit to A. B's claim on A is in the form of a bill of exchange. The creation of the new credit-chain B → A entails a rise in the total amount of credit in the economy, and thus represents credit creation.

If B discounts the bill with the bank, the bank places itself between the last creditor and the debtor: B → Bank → A, and the direct credit relationship between B and A now becomes an indirect one. The volume of credit in the economy does not alter as a result of the bank's participation but the quantity of money does. This is so, because the first link in this chain of credit represents a claim by B

[1] Credit creation takes place when the total amount of credit in the economy rises. See Vol. I, 7th ed., 1958, p. 32.

on the bank which is payable on demand, i.e. it is money. In this case the creation of money takes place on the basis of prior credit creation.

(b) *Creation of Money without Prior Credit Creation*

Example: Firm E obtains credit from the bank to the value of £1000. The bank acquires a claim of £1000 on E and credits E's current account with £1000. We now have a fictitious credit-chain: E → Bank → E, whose first link represents money. Thus money is created without any change in the volume of credit in the economy. An increase in the volume of credit, i.e. credit creation, takes place only when the firm buys goods and pays for them with the loan obtained from the bank.

(c) *Money Creation and Simultaneous Credit Creation*

Example: The bank grants a firm an overdraft of £1000 (i.e. £1000 is put at the firm's disposal without being credited to the firm's current account). If the firm now buys goods worth £500 from X, the bank will debit the firm by £500 and credit X's account with £500. Now a genuine credit-chain arises: X → bank → E whose first link represents newly created money. In this case money creation and credit creation take place simultaneously.

(d) *Credit Creation without Money Creation*

Example: Direct credit between two private individuals.

The model of a universal bank discussed in this paragraph also explains the process of the creation and destruction of money in an economy with a state bank where both the bank's book money and its notes are used as means of payment.

§2. Model of a System with Several Banks in Which Payments Are Made without Using Cash

1. We may now drop the assumption that there is only one bank, and consider an economy which has several banks. However, we still retain the assumption that all payments are made without using cash. For the sake of simplicity we shall consider an economy with only two banks, but the conclusions we shall reach are valid for a system with more than two banks.

We wish to consider how the process of money creation takes place in this kind of banking system, and we are particularly interested in the question whether there are limits to the process of money creation in a system of several banks, in which all payments are made by cheque (i.e. without using cash).

The process of money creation takes place in the same way as in the single-bank system. Each of the banks create new money by buying assets, and crediting the seller's current account. Conversely, the destruction of money takes place when a bank sells assets. The problem, however, is complicated by the fact that customers of one bank usually have to make payments, not only to other customers of that bank, but also to customers of the other bank. This gives rise to credit links between the two banks which, although they do not alter the process of money creation itself, do influence the limits to which each individual bank can create money.

Let us consider a simple example. An economic subject X is granted credit of £1000 on current account by bank A. In the books of bank A the account of X is credited, and the account "credits granted" is correspondingly debited. (Transaction 1 in the following table.)

Bank A

Credits granted		Account "X"	
(1) 1000		(2) 400	1000 (1)
		(3) 600	

Account "Y"		Account "Bank B"	
	400 (2)		600 (3)

Bank B

Account "Z"		Account "Bank A"	
	600 (4)	(4) 600	

X uses the £1000 put at his disposal to make a payment of £400 to Y and one of £600 to Z. Let Y be a customer of bank A and Z a customer of bank B. The payment to Y leads to the entries (2). The payment to Z leads to the entries (3) in the books of bank A: X's account is debited and that of bank B credited. But this is not the end of this transaction. Bank A still has to request bank B to credit Z's account with £600 at the expense of bank A. In the books of bank B this leads to the entries (4). Bank B has a claim on bank A corresponding to Z's credit with bank B. The payment by X to Z thus presupposes that bank B is willing to allow bank A to incur a debt of £600 to it. If bank B were unwilling to do this, bank A would be forced either to reduce the credit granted to X, or to refuse payment to Z. Bank A can continue to extend new credit to its customers, without fearing payment difficulties, if bank B is willing to go on being its creditor. Alternatively, bank B may be willing, if bank A has "acceptable" assets, to receive assets from bank A in settlement of debt. The possibilities of money creation on the part of bank A are thus limited by the willingness of bank B to accept bank A as debtor or to accept assets from bank A in the settlement of debts.

Thus the continued granting of new credits by only one bank presupposes the acquiescence of the remaining banks in the system.

Generally both banks will be engaged in granting loans to their customers. The payments which result from the granting of credits by bank B will include some by bank B to customers of bank A, as a result of which bank A will become a creditor of bank B. Unlimited credit creation by one bank independently of the other requires that the extent of credit creation by both banks be such that the resulting claims of one bank on the other cancel out. If this condition is fulfilled there is no limit to the possibility of money creation by the banking system. Otherwise one of the banks will acquire net claims on the other, and money creation by the debtor bank will depend on the acquiescence of the creditor bank.

If the banks always grant credit (create money) to such an extent that the claims of one bank on the other cancel out, we say that the banks *move in step*.[1] Thus there is no limit to the continued creation of money by the two banks so long as the two banks move in step. The limit to which each individual bank can extend credit depends on the behaviour of the other banks in the system.

Let us summarize: if each bank, independently, is to be able to create money as it likes, two conditions must be fulfilled:

(a) *credit granted to customers must never be in the form of cash*;

(b) *the banks must move in step.*

A single bank *alone* can never create money *ad libitum.* It should be noted that the "*principle of movement in step*" *is derived from the assumption that all payments are made without using cash*, and is valid only on this assumption. When we drop this assumption the principle of movement in step has no bearing on the limits to which the banking system can create money. This will be shown in the next paragraph.

§3. Model of a Single-Tier Mixed-Money Banking System (Single-Tier Mixed-Money System)

1. None of the banking systems discussed in the two preceding paragraphs correspond to the conditions prevailing in our economy. As we saw in the first chapter, the means of payment in our economy consist of central bank money, in the form of central bank notes and current accounts with the central bank (central bank book money); and of current accounts with the commercial banks (commercial bank book money). Our monetary system is thus a *mixed-money*

[1] C. A. Phillips, *Bank Credit*, New York, 1921.

system in which central bank money is the only legal tender. As a first model of such a mixed-money system we shall consider a credit system consisting of *one* central bank and a group of commercial banks. The non-banking sector, the commercial banks and the central bank are linked by the process of payments in the manner indicated in Fig. 1. The credit systems of the following countries, among others, correspond to this model: those of the Third Reich, the German Federal Republic after the passing of the Law of the 1.8.1957 regarding the Deutsche Bundesbank, England, France, Denmark, Sweden.

In this system payments within the private sector are made in two ways: either by using central bank notes (cash), which are claims on the central bank; or through transfers of commercial bank book money. Thus, payments within the private sector (and also by the government) are made partly by using cash, and partly without using cash. There is now a large volume of payments without cash (payments by cheque), especially in the business world. Nevertheless, a considerable volume of transactions is still settled in cash in the non-banking sector, for example, wage-payments, and the large number of small purchases made which require payment in cash.

Payments within the commercial banking system are usually made by transfers among the commercial banks' current accounts with the central bank, or sometimes by transfers among the accounts banks keep with each other.

Let us now consider the process of money creation and money destruction in this model of a mixed-money system.

2. Central bank money can be created only by the central bank, and commercial bank money only by the commercial banks. On the basis of the argument of §1 we know that the central bank creates central bank money by acquiring assets and paying for them with claims on itself which represent money. The central bank may acquire assets from the private sector, the commercial banks or the government.

The central bank may acquire both primary and secondary assets.[(1)] If the central bank acquires *primary assets*, for example, claims on foreigners, the sellers receive central bank money which is freely at their disposal. The assets and liabilities of the central bank increase while those of the seller remain unchanged, although his net claims on the central bank will have risen.

If the central bank acquires secondary assets, for example by making a loan to a commercial bank (or the government), there will

(1) See: pp. 24–25.

be an increase in the total assets and liabilities of *both* the central bank *and* the commercial bank. In the balance sheets this transaction will appear as follows:

Central bank		**Commercial bank**	
L	A	L	A
Current account of the commercial bank:	Loans: (claims on the commercial bank)	Liabilities to the central bank:	Central bank money:
+1000	+1000	+1000	+1000

The increase in central bank money in the commercial bank's balance sheet is matched by an equal increase in debt to the central bank. There is no change in the net credit position of the commercial bank *vis-a-vis* the central bank.

The category of secondary assets includes bills of exchange in the portfolio of a commercial bank which are eligible for re-discount with the central bank. When a commercial bank re-discounts a bill with the central bank its cash reserves increase; but since the bank has endorsed the bill its debts to the central bank rise by the same amount. The net credit position of the commercial bank *vis-a-vis* the central bank thus remains unchanged.[1] When the commercial banks have to re-discount bills with the central bank on a large scale in order to acquire central bank money, this is always a sign that money is "tight".[2] Conversely, when the banks have large net credits with the central bank (which never earn interest) this is always a sign of "easy money" within the commercial banking system. The commercial banking system's supply of central bank money can only be permanently increased if the central bank exchanges money for primary assets; only then does the central bank place central bank money unconditionally at the disposal of the commercial banks.

[1] Compare also p. 24–25.

[2] In the English system a tight monetary position at the clearing banks results first in funds being withdrawn from the discount houses. Usually this situation is relieved by the Bank of England making advances to the discount houses at the current bank rate for a period of seven days. Occasionally a discount house may choose to re-discount bills at the bank but this is unusual.

Funds may also flow from the Bank to the clearing banks directly. This occurs when the Bank buys bills from the clearing banks at rates very close to the going market rates. This procedure is often used when tightness occurs for some accidental reason at a time when the central bank has no wish to enforce an increase in short-term interest rates. Whether it is used or not is entirely a matter for the central bank to decide. (R. G. O.)

When the central bank sells primary or secondary assets the quantity of central bank money is reduced.

The central bank alone determines whether, when and in what quantities to buy or sell primary or secondary assets. The central bank decides whether any asset which is not money may be exchanged for central bank money (i.e. whether the asset is liquid). There is no such thing as inherent liquidity in an asset which is not money. Liquidity—exchangeability into central bank money—can be conferred on an asset only by the central bank. Thus, whether a commercial bill held by a commercial bank is a liquid asset depends on whether the central bank is willing to re-discount the bill. Even though the initiative for the creation of central bank money may come from the central bank, a commercial bank or the government, the decision whether or not the money is to be created lies solely with the central bank.

When the central bank creates money on the basis of acquiring secondary assets this creation of money, as was pointed out earlier (see pp. 25–26), is automatically followed by a corresponding destruction of money after a period of time (in the case of the re-discounting of three months' bills the period is three months). But if central bank money is created through the acquisition of primary assets there is no subsequent automatic destruction of money; this can only be brought about by deliberate decision on the part of the central bank. When money is created and destroyed on the basis of primary *and* secondary assets, the central bank has more flexibility in its policy of supplying the economy with central bank money than it would have if, for example, money were created solely on the basis of re-discounting three months' bills. Commercial bills are created in the private sector in the course of trade. The supply of bills and, given the re-discount policy of the central bank, the supply of central bank money to the economy would thus depend on the prevailing level of economic activity. In times of depression there would be a shrinkage in the quantity of central bank money, while in times of upswing there would be an expansion in it.

It follows from what has been said that in a closed economy there are no limits to the central bank's power to create money, except such limits as the bank may set itself, or as may be prescribed for it by law. It is clear that such limits can never be due to any inability on the part of the central bank to finance the purchase of assets, since it pays with claims on itself which constitute money. In a closed economy the central bank is always liquid, in the sense that it can never get into payment difficulties, and also in the sense that, if it wishes, it can always grant new credits to those willing to become its debtors. In an open economy the central bank does not enjoy such unlimited liquidity; it can get into payment difficulties, since it has to make some payments in foreign currency, i.e. in a form of money which it cannot create. Similarly, when granting new credits, the bank must take into account the possibility that a part might have to be made available in foreign currency. The bank thus encounters a limit to its power to create money which is determined by the available stock of foreign currency, and the possibility of acquiring it. The necessity of having to make payments in a form of money which it cannot create gives rise to a liquidity problem for the central bank. This case is of interest even in a closed economy, for it is relevant to the analysis of *the problem of money creation by the commercial banks in a mixed-money system.* In a mixed-money system the commercial banks have to make payments in central bank money, i.e. in a form of money which they cannot create. This explains the presence of a liquidity problem for the commercial banks in a closed economy. We now have to investigate this in greater detail, in connection with an analysis of the problem of money creation by the commercial banks.

3. A commercial bank creates money by acquiring assets from economic subjects and paying for them with claims on itself which constitute money. As we already know, the money thus created by commercial banks is called *commercial bank book money.*

Let us consider in greater detail the *process by which an individual commercial bank creates or destroys money.*

CASE 1: A customer pays £100 in central bank notes into his current account. This leads to the following changes in the bank's balance sheet: on the assets side there is an increase of £100 in central bank money, and on the liabilities side an increase of £100 in current accounts. In other words, there is an increase in the sum of assets and liabilities. The bank has created commercial bank deposits to the value of £100 in exchange for claims on the central bank in the form of bank notes.

Balance sheet

L	A
Customers' current accounts:	Central bank money:
+100	+100

The amount of commercial bank money in the economy has increased as a result of a customer exchanging a claim on the central bank, which constitutes money, for a claim on a commercial bank, which also constitutes money. Alternatively, we may say that the customer has purchased a current account at his bank. It is clear, however, that the paying of £100 into a current account has not, *ceteris paribus*, altered the quantity of money in the non-banking sector of the economy; a given amount of central bank money has been replaced by an equal amount of commercial bank money. However, there has been an increase in the stock of money in the commercial banking system. This is so because the stock of money in the commercial banking system consists, as we know, of the stock of central bank notes and of deposits with the central bank. In our example this stock has gone up by £100.

The reverse process occurs when a customer withdraws £100 in central-bank notes from his current account. The commercial bank's assets are reduced by £100 of central bank money and its current account liabilities are reduced by the same amount. The quantity of money in the non-banking sector remains unchanged, but the quantity of money in the commercial banking system is reduced. *Payments into the commercial banking system from the non-banking sector thus lead to the creation of commercial bank deposits, and payments into the non-banking sector from the commercial banks lead to the destruction of commercial bank deposits.*

In our example the initiative of the bank's customer determines whether commercial bank money is created or destroyed; the bank's role is purely passive. The economic subjects of the non-banking sector alone decide how they wish to distribute any given quantity of money in that sector between holdings of central bank money and commercial bank deposits. In the creation and destruction of commercial bank money which results from *these* decisions the role of the banks is entirely passive. The commercial bank money which is created or destroyed solely as a result of payments into, and payments out, of the commercial banking system may be said to be *passively created or destroyed* by the commercial banks. It must be stressed that the quantity of money in the non-banking sector is not affected when the banks passively create or destroy commercial bank deposits. For example, if the stock of money in the private and government sectors is £1 million, of which £300,000 consists of central bank notes and £700,000 of current accounts with the commercial banks, a decision to convert all the bank deposits into central bank notes obviously would not alter the stock of money in the non-banking sector. As a result £700,000 of bank deposits would be destroyed and the commercial banking system would lose the same amount of central bank money. As we shall see later on, the commercial banks as a group can never meet the demand for the payment in cash of *all* current accounts because their total deposit liabilities always far exceed their stock of central bank money. In this situation the central bank has to provide the commercial banks with the required amount of central bank money. It does this by monetising those assets of the commercial banks which do not constitute money. If the central bank refused to meet the wishes of the public, the result would be a severe shock to economic life.

CASE 2: Let us now consider the case in which a commercial bank offers economic subjects in the non-banking sector commercial bank money in exchange for non-monetary assets. For example, a bank may acquire a bill of exchange from a firm (acquisition of a secondary asset), or foreign exchange from a customer (acquisition of a primary asset), or it may grant a loan to a firm (acquisition of a secondary asset). These transactions are reflected in the balance sheet in the same way as when the central bank acquires assets. The only difference is that the commercial bank pays with commercial bank deposits while the central bank pays with central bank money created by it.

Example 1: A customer discounts a bill with his bank; the bank's assets rise by the value of the bill, and its liabilities by the (same) amount credited to the customer's account. The customer's stock of money and, *ceteris paribus*, that in the non-banking sector, increase, while the bank's stock of money and that in the commercial banking system remain unchanged.

Example 2: The bank grants a customer a loan of £1000.

(a) If the accounts are drawn up in the American manner, the bank immediately credits the full amount of the loan to the customer's current account. The bank's assets rise by the amount of its claim against the customer:

Balance Sheet

L	A
Current liabilities	Claims (loans):
+1000	+1000

(b) If the accounts are drawn up in the continental manner, the bank debits the customer only to the extent that he in fact uses the loan.[1] For example, the customer might use £800 in the first instance to pay a supplier who, we may assume, banks with the same bank. In this case the supplier's current account increases by £800, and the

[1] Translator's note: in England this is known as the "over-draft" method of granting credit and is very widely used.

bank acquires an asset of £800 in the form of its claim against the customer:

Balance Sheet

L	A
Current liabilities:	Claims: (loans)
+800	+800

Whichever method of drawing up the accounts is used there is an increase in the stock of money in the non-banking sector, while the commercial bank's stock of money remains unchanged. For our purposes it does not matter whether we assume that loans are entered in the books in the American or the continental manner. Since it simplifies exposition we shall adopt the American method.

There is a fundamental difference between the examples of case (1) and those of case (2). In both cases commercial bank money is created at the initiative of the bank's customer. But in case (2) the decision whether commercial bank money is to be created lies with the bank; the bank decides whether or not to discount the bill or to grant the request for a loan. The bank plays an active role in these transactions. A bank's transactions which fall within the categories of those of case (2) may be called *active transactions,* and the commercial bank money which is created in the course of active transactions may be called *actively created money. A commercial bank creates money actively whenever it monetises assets* (*mainly secondary assets*) *which are not money.* Each active transaction raises the quantity of money in the non-banking sector in exactly the same way as each active transaction by the central bank raises the quantity of central bank money. Conversely, the sale of assets by the banks (for example the redemption of a bill, or the repayment of a loan) reduces the quantity of money in the non-banking sector. The reader should bear in mind that the quantity of money in the non-banking sector is not altered as a result of passive transactions by the bank. All commercial banks continuously actively create and destroy commercial bank money. Active transactions by the banks will lead to an increase in the stock of money in the non-banking sector during any given period only if the sum total of money created exceeds the sum total of money destroyed. If the amount of money destroyed in the course of active transactions is larger than the amount created there will be a net reduction in the stock of money in the non-banking sector during the period.

4. Let us consider the balance sheet of a commercial bank on a given day. The main items on the liabilities side are current accounts

and deposits for varying periods of time. On the assets side we find the bank's claims on other economic subjects, among them the bank's cash in the form of central bank notes and deposits with the central bank. The bank's cash (the so-called cash reserve = bank notes plus deposits with the central bank) is only a small percentage of its current account liabilities. Since the cash reserve earns no interest the bank will obviously try to keep it as small as possible. Students new to the subject are often puzzled by the fact that the commercial banks are able to transact their business without any difficulty with a cash reserve so small in relation to their current liabilities. Let us inquire, therefore, why a commercial bank should require any central bank money.

5. A commercial bank clearly requires central bank money to make payments resulting from its passive transactions. Such payments have to be made to the bank's creditors who wish to convert their current deposits into central bank money. Payments in central bank money also have to be made to other banks; this happens when the bank's customers transfer money to economic subjects who hold deposits with another bank. As was explained earlier, a payment by a customer of bank A to a customer of bank B is effected in the following way: bank A instructs the central bank to debit its account and to transfer the given sum to the account of bank B, in favour of the payee. Bank A thus loses central bank money to bank B. It is easy to see that, as a rule, a commercial bank requires only a relatively small initial stock of central bank money to meet these payments during any period, because the bank continuously receives central bank money as a result of deposits by its customers. Indeed, it is conceivable that the size and timing of payments and receipts (of central bank money) might be such that the bank did not require any initial stock of central bank money. This, however, would be as exceptional a case as a run on the bank when all customers wished to convert their deposits into cash. To be able to meet the latter contingency the bank would have to keep its reserves of central bank money exactly equal to its liabilities. In fact, payments and receipts are roughly equal from day to day, and the bank requires only a relatively small initial stock of central bank money. Basically, this is the result of the working of the so-called law of large numbers.[1] It may happen that the dispositions of the bank's customers at certain times give rise to requirements for central bank money which exceed the bank's available stock. In this case the bank must obtain central bank money on a short-term basis, either from other

[1] The reader should consult the excellent exposition of these matters in K. Wicksell, *Lectures on Political Economy*, Vol. II. pp. 81–84.

banks who have a temporary surplus, or by discounting eligible assets at the central bank (the bank, for example, may do the former by taking up money at call on the money market, i.e. the market for central bank money where the banks appear as both suppliers and demanders,[1] or by passing on to other banks assets eligible for the money market).[2] Resort to the central bank is always necessary when cash payments out of the banking system exceed cash payments into the banking system. The situation remains the same when the banks adopt a clearing system to settle their transactions with one another. In this system the claims which arise among the banks are added up, and only the net claims are settled by transfers of central-bank money.

6. This is all we need say regarding the stock of central bank money which a bank requires to meet the payments arising out of its passive transactions. A commercial bank, however, also requires central bank money to meet the liabilities arising out of its active transactions. In practice it is difficult to distinguish the payments which arise from the bank's passive transactions from those which arise from its active transactions; yet it will facilitate the understanding of the theory of credit if we separate the two conceptually. Active transactions consist in granting credits, i.e. in monetising secondary assets. If a commercial bank grants a customer credit of £100 it creates commercial bank money to the same amount. The recipient of the credit may dispose of it as he likes; he may make payments by cheque to other economic subjects, e.g. suppliers, or withdraw part of the amount in notes, perhaps for wage-payments. If the suppliers hold deposits with other banks, our bank must transfer the amount to the other banks in central bank money. In granting the credit the bank also assumes the obligation to make payment available in bank notes on demand. Since the recipient of the credit will soon make use of it the bank must expect that the entire amount granted will be withdrawn in central bank money, either in the course of payments to other banks, or through direct cash withdrawals. We have now come to the point which is decisive in the investigation of the limits on the power of a commercial bank to create money. *The fact that, in the course of its active and passive transactions the bank has to make payments in central bank money, i.e., in a form of money which it cannot create, gives rise to a liquidity*

(1) "The money market is . . . nothing but a mutual exchange of cash surpluses and deficits among the banks, either through credit, or the purchase and sale of eligible assets". H. Gestrich, *Kredit und Sparen*, 3rd edn. 1957, p. 59.

(2) Assets eligible for the money market are those assets which are also eligible for discount with the central bank.

problem for the bank, both as regards its ability to meet current liabilities and as regards its ability to extend new credit. We have already discussed the liquidity problem in the sense of safeguarding the ability to meet current liabilities. We now have to discuss the liquidity problem which arises in the course of granting new credit. If the bank has to reckon that the credit it grants will be withdrawn entirely in cash, it can grant credit of, say, £100 only if it has either £100 of excess reserves, i.e. if its stock of central bank money exceeds the *otherwise* required stock by £100, or if it can acquire that amount by incurring a debt to the central bank, i.e. if it has at its disposal assets which the central bank is willing to monetise. The limit to which an individual bank can create deposit money is thus determined by its surplus cash (central bank money) and/or by the possibilities of acquiring central bank money. It follows that the central bank has a decisive influence on the extent to which a commercial bank can create money. Later on (§ 4) we shall discuss in detail the various ways in which the central bank can assert this influence.

Institutional considerations determine whether a commercial bank will grant a request for credit when it would have to incur a debt to the central bank in order to do so. As a rule a commercial bank does not like to incur debts to the central bank in the course of extending credit. The situation is different if, by granting the credit, the bank acquires a claim against the debtor, for example, a first-class bill of exchange which is eligible for re-discount with the central bank. The bank in fact becomes more liquid through the acquisition of the bill, since it can obtain central bank money to the amount of the bill (minus the discount) at any time. Although the bank's net claims against the central bank do not increase as a result of re-discounting the bill, the bank will be willing to extend new credit on the basis of eligible bills. The bank does incur a debt to the central bank by re-discounting the bill; but the nature of this indebtedness is different from that which occurs when the bank obtains credit from the central bank against securities from its own portfolio.[1] A bank will, of course, feel most free to grant credit when it has central bank money available without any corresponding liabilities whatever to the central bank.

7. We have seen that a bank requires some central bank money for settling its current transactions, and that this sum is small in relation to the bank's current liabilities. The ratio required between cash and current liabilities is determined by custom in some countries, in others by law.

[1] The liability which the bank incurs when re-discounting a bill is a contingent liability.

In England, for example, it is customary to keep current liabilities and cash in the ratio of 9 : 1.[1] This "... practice of bankers is a compromise between keeping the pool which they expect in fact to be large enough, and keeping the only pool (i.e. 100% reserves) which could possibly in all circumstances be large enough. And it seems to be a compromise based rather on habit, and on the necessity of giving depositors confidence in the strength of the bank, than on any nice calculation of what events are reasonably likely and what may be dismissed as 'unthinkable' ".[2] In Germany and the U.S.A. the law requires a commercial bank to keep a certain percentage of its current liabilities, and a certain percentage of its deposit liabilities, in the form of deposits with the central bank. The minimum amount which legally has to be kept on deposit with the central bank is called the minimum cash reserve and the corresponding percentages are called the minimum reserve ratios.[3] The bank has at its free disposal only the sum of cash in excess of the minimum reserve, the so-called *excess reserves* or *excess cash.*

The minimum legal reserve ratios are usually set at higher levels than are required to safeguard a bank's liquidity. The reason for setting the minimum legal reserve ratios at these higher levels thus cannot be explained in terms of the desire of legislators to safeguard the liquidity, and hence the creditors, of the bank. There must be other reasons to explain the setting of minimum legal reserve ratios, which we shall discuss shortly.

8. In what follows we shall assume that the commercial banks are required by law to maintain minimum reserve ratios in the form of deposits with the central bank. Let us suppose that a commercial bank has excess reserves of £100 at a given time, and that the minimum legal reserve ratio for current accounts is 10%. In this case the bank is in a position to grant new credits up to £100. The excess reserves determine the *lending potential* of the bank, and it cannot lend beyond this *without the support of the central bank*. If the bank wishes to increase that potential by re-discounting bills or by borrowing from the central bank against securities, it must rely on the acquiescence of the central bank. The bank will, of course, try to lend up to the limits set by its excess reserves, to avoid the loss of earnings due to idle reserves. It must also decide in what form to lend: whether to buy bills, lend to the money market, purchase securities,

(1) This was the situation until 1946 when window-dressing was still practised by the clearing banks. Since then, the ratio aimed at and closely approached has been 8%, i.e. 12½ : 1. (R. G. O.)

(2) D. H. Robertson, *Money*, 4th edition, 1948, p. 55.

(3) It should be noted that notes held by the banks (so-called till-money) are not counted as part of the minimum cash reserve in Germany and the U.S.A.

or lend to customers. As a rule, the interest yield on loans to customers is higher than that on securities and bills. However, bills and securities are more liquid than loans to customers. Thus the bank must always weigh the relative profitability of the assets it may acquire against their relative liquidity.

Let us assume the bank succeeds in lending up to the limit of its lending potential, i.e. in granting new credits to the value of its excess reserves. After the credit is granted the bank's balance sheet will look as follows:

Balance Sheet

L	A
Current accounts:	Excess reserves:
+100	100
	Loans:
	+100

The quantity of commercial bank money held by the non-banking sector has increased by 100, and the bank's claims on the non-banking sector have increased by the same amount. Our wording here should be carefully noted: we are *not* saying that the bank lends its excess cash reserves. To put it this way would be false. *The bank itself creates the money with which it credits the debtors' accounts.* The bank is in a position to create new money, because its excess reserves enable it to meet demands for the conversion of the newly created commercial bank money into notes. The bank thus grants new credits, i.e. creates new commercial bank money, on the basis of its excess reserves. This is the state of affairs which is so often misunderstood.

The recipients of the credit will use it partly to make withdrawals in cash, partly to make payments to customers of the same bank and partly to make payments to customers of other banks. In the case of withdrawals in cash and payments to other banks the bank loses central bank money. For purposes of illustration let us consider the most unfavourable case from the point of view of our bank, namely when the recipient of the loan uses it in such a way that our bank loses all of its excess reserves. As far as our bank is concerned this ends for the time being the process resulting from the creation of credit, until the bank one more acquires excess reserves. As far as the banking system as a whole is concerned, however, the effect is by no means exhausted. This brings us to yet another point which is of fundamental importance to the understanding of the credit mechanism in a modern single-tier mixed-money system: *it is essential to distinguish clearly between the creation of credit by an individual bank and the repercussions of this credit creation on the banking system as a whole.* We shall see that the relationships which apply to the banking system as a whole are different from those which apply to an individual bank.

9. Let us assume that all the cash which the first bank (bank 1) loses in the course of withdrawals by its debtors returns to the banking system. For the sake of simplicity let us assume that the entire amount of cash, £100, is deposited in bank 2, either through payments by cheque or through cash deposits. Bank 2 now creates a total of £100 commercial bank money in the couse of its passive transactions while its stock of cash rises by £100. The increase of £100 in its current liabilities forces bank 2 to raise its minimum reserves by £10. The balance sheet of bank 2 will thus show the following changes:

Bank 2

L	A
Current liabilities:	Minimum reserves:
+100	+10
	Excess reserves:
	+90

As a result of these deposits bank 2 acquires £90 of excess reserves and is now in a position to grant new loans up to £90. In the real world the inflow of cash would not be concentrated on one bank, but would be distributed over several banks, among which might be bank 1 which started the process. All these banks together could then grant new loans up to £90. The argument thus remains unaffected by our simplifying assumption that all the cash which bank 1 loses accrues to bank 2. If bank 2 succeeds in granting credit up to £90, it will have actively created £90 new commercial bank money, and the new claims against its debtors will have increased its assets by the same amount. When bank 2 has fully used the increase in its lending potential its balance sheet will show the following changes:

Bank 2

L	A
Current liabilities:	Loans:
+90	+90

The debtors now use the credit they have acquired. Let us again assume that any amounts withdrawn in cash remain in the banking system, and that all deposits are made with bank 1 either through payments by cheque or through cash deposits. Bank 2 now loses its excess reserves of £90 to bank 1. Bank 1 now passively creates £90 in current accounts, while its stock of cash increases by the same amount. Bank 1 must legally keep additional minimum reserves of £9 against the increase in its current liabilities; the remaining £81 of its newly acquired cash represents excess reserves, which it can use freely. On the bais of its new excess reserves bank 1 may now grant new loans up to £81, and the process is repeated in the same way as before. Thus a process of deposit creation is set in motion solely as a result of the original credit creation by bank 1. We have assumed that any cash which flows out of the banking system in the course of credit creation returns to it, and that each bank is able to lend up to the limits of the increase in its lending potential. On these assumptions, this *multiple expansion of commercial bank money* occurs in the sequences indicated in the following table:

	Excess Reserves (1)	New Credits (2)	Increase in Minimum Reserves (3)
1st round	+100	+100	—
2nd round	+90	+90	+10
3rd round	+81	+81	+9
4th round	+72·9	+72.9	+8·1
5th round	+65·61	+65·61	+7·29
↓ ∞	:	→	↓
		+1000	+100

As can be seen, in the course of the multiple expansion of commercial bank money due to a change in the excess reserves of the banking system the participating banks can grant a *total* of credit and thus create a *total* of deposits which is given by the sum of the following geometric series:

$$100 + 90 + 81 + 72{\cdot}9 + 65{\cdot}61 + \ldots$$
$$= 100 + 100 \,.\, \tfrac{9}{10} + 100 \,.\, (\tfrac{9}{10})^2 + 100 \,.\, (\tfrac{9}{10})^3 + \ldots$$

The sum of this infinite geometric series is:

$$100 \,.\, \frac{1}{1 - \frac{9}{10}} = 1000$$

The total amount of commercial bank money which the banking system as a whole can create is £1000, i.e. ten times as much as can be created in the first round by the bank which starts the process. The total increase in minimum reserves is:

$$10 + 9 + 8{\cdot}1 + 7{\cdot}29 + \ldots$$
$$= 10 + 10 \cdot \tfrac{9}{10} + 10(\tfrac{9}{10})^2 + 10 \cdot (\tfrac{9}{10})^3 + \ldots$$
$$= 10 \cdot \frac{1}{1 - \frac{9}{10}} = 100$$

When the process of deposit expansion is completed there is an increase of £100 in minimum reserves—spread over all the participating banks—against the total of newly created deposits.

The results we have derived from a numerical example can be easily generalized. Let ΔZ denote the excess reserves of the banking system, and r[1] the minimum legal reserve ratio against current accounts. *If we assume that there are no permanent leakages of cash from the banking system in the course of credit expansion, the banking system as a whole can, without recourse to the central bank, create new credit in the course of the multiple expansion of deposits to an amount ΔK_r which is given by the equation*:

$$\Delta K_r = \frac{\Delta Z}{r}. \tag{1}$$

Given r and ΔZ, this equation gives the limit to which the banking system can actively create deposits. The equation shows that this limit depends on ΔZ, i.e. on the excess reserves of the banking system, and on r, i.e. the minimum legal reserve ratio. ΔK_r is directly proportional to ΔZ and inversely proportional to r. We shall shortly investigate these relationships in greater detail.

Barring recourse to the central bank, an individual bank which has excess reserves of ΔZ can grant new credit only up to the amount of its excess reserves. The banking system as a whole can grant new credit up to an amount several times the size of ΔZ. On our assumptions the "*money creation multiplier*" or "*money creation co-efficient*" is equal to the reciprocal of the minimum reserve ratio.

10. So far we have assumed that any cash which leaked out of the banking system in the course of credit extension returned to it. We shall now drop this assumption. The non-banking sector may wish to increase its holdings of central bank notes in the course of a

[1] When the minimum reserve ratio is 10% $r = 0{\cdot}1$.

credit expansion. This, for example, is always the case if the public and the government are accustomed to distribute their money balances (cash plus current accounts with the commercial banks) in a given ratio between cash and current accounts. In this case there is a permanent leakage of cash from the banking system which puts a brake on the amount of new credit extension by the banking system. We now have to examine the strength of the effect due to the leakage of cash.

Let us again assume that the minimum reserve ratio is 10% and that the leakage of cash in the course of new credit extension is 50%. Bank 1, which grants new loans of £100 on the basis of £100 excess reserves, loses all of its excess reserves through payments into bank 2 and through withdrawals in cash. Since we have assumed that £50 remain in the non-banking sector in the form of notes, the deposits at bank 2 increase by £50 in the course of passive transactions. Bank 2 must keep £5 of its newly acquired £50 cash as additional minimum reserves against the increase in its current liabilities. Bank 2 now has excess reserves of £45, on the basis of which it may grant new loans up to £45. While in the first round an extension of credit up to £100 was possible, in the second round new credit can be extended only up to

$$\begin{aligned} & 100 - \tfrac{1}{2} \,.\, 100 - (100 - \tfrac{1}{2} \,.\, 100) \,.\, \tfrac{1}{10} \\ &= 100 \,.\, (1 - \tfrac{1}{2}) \,.\, (1 - \tfrac{1}{10}) \\ &= 45 \end{aligned}$$

Similarly, in the third round bank 1 can extend new credit up to:

$$100 \,.\, (1 - \tfrac{1}{2})^2 \,.\, (1 - \tfrac{1}{10})^2$$

and so on.

On the basis of £100 excess reserves the banking system as a whole can extend a total of new credit in the course of the multiple expansion of deposits of:

$$100 + 100(1 - \tfrac{1}{2}) \,.\, (1 - \tfrac{1}{10}) + 100 \,.\, (1 - \tfrac{1}{2})^2 \,.\, (1 - \tfrac{1}{10})^2 + \ldots$$

The sum of this infinite geometric series is:

$$100 \,.\, \frac{1}{1 - (1 - \frac{1}{2}) \cdot (1 - \frac{1}{10})} = 100 \,.\, \tfrac{20}{11} = 181{\cdot}82.$$

The limit up to which the banking system can now extend new credit is £181·82, which is a considerably lower limit than the one obtained on the assumption that there are no leakages of cash from the banking system.

The result we have just obtained from a numerical example can be easily generalized. Let ΔZ again denote the excess reserves of the banking system (= the sum of the excess reserves of the individual banks), r the minimum reserve ratio ($0 < r < 1$) and c the fraction of new credits which debtors withdraw in notes and which remains in the non-banking sector ($0 < c < 1$). On these assumptions the limit to the expansion of credit by the banking system, ΔK_r, is given by

$$\Delta K_r = \frac{\Delta Z}{1 - (1 - r) . (1 - c)}$$

or

$$\Delta K_r = \frac{\Delta Z}{r + c . (1 - r)} . \tag{2}$$

11. If we neglect the process (which theoretically involves an infinite number of credit extensions) through which the system finally reaches this limit, and concentrate on the final result, i.e. on the limit to credit expansion, we can derive (2) quite simply.

We introduce the following abbreviations in addition to the notation already used:

- ΔN for the part of ΔK_r which is withdrawn in cash and which remains in the non-banking sector;
- ΔD for the part of ΔK_r which is kept in the form of current accounts with the commercial banks;
- ΔZ_b for the part of the excess reserves which remain in the banking system (i.e. the cash reserve which must be kept against ΔD).

We have the following four relationships between these variables and ΔZ, r and c.

$$\Delta N = c . \Delta K_r \tag{3}$$

$$\Delta K_r = \Delta D + \Delta N \tag{4}$$

$$\Delta Z_b = r . \Delta D \tag{5}$$

$$\Delta Z = \Delta Z_b + \Delta N \tag{6}$$

We wish to know what values ΔK_r, ΔD, ΔN and ΔZ_b must assume, given the values of ΔZ, r and c. That is to say, we wish to know the maximum volume of credit and deposits which can be created when excess reserves, the payment habits of the public, and the minimum reserve ratio are given, and how the initial excess reserves are distributed between the banking and non-banking sectors, assuming the banks fully exploit their lending potential.

Substituting (3) in (4) we have:

$$\Delta D = (1 - c) . \Delta K_r . \tag{7}$$

Similarly, from (6) we obtain:

$$\Delta Z_b = \Delta Z - c \,.\, \Delta K_r. \tag{8}$$

It now follows from (5) that:

$$r = \frac{\Delta Z - c \,.\, \Delta K_r}{(1 - c) \,.\, \Delta K_r} \,. \tag{9}$$

Solving (9) for ΔK_r we obtain:

$$\Delta K_r = \frac{1}{r + c \,.\, (1 - r)} \,.\, \Delta Z. \tag{10}$$

According to (3) we obtain ΔN:

$$\Delta N = \frac{c}{r + c \,.\, (1 - r)} \,.\, \Delta Z. \tag{11}$$

According to (7) ΔD is:

$$\Delta D = \frac{1 - c}{r + c \,.\, (1 - r)} \,.\, \Delta Z. \tag{12}$$

A numerical example may help to clarify these relationships.

Let $\Delta Z = 110, \quad r = 0{\cdot}1 \quad \text{and} \quad c = \frac{1}{2}$.

The credit potential of the banking system then is:

$$\Delta K_r = 200.$$

The relation (2) or (12) may be written in another form if we introduce the expression

$$k = \frac{\Delta N}{\Delta D} \qquad (k > 0)$$

i.e. the ratio of the additional note circulation in the non-banking sector to the additional volume of deposits. Since

$$c = \frac{\Delta N}{\Delta K_r} = \frac{\Delta N}{\Delta D + \Delta N}$$

it follows immediately that:

$$c = \frac{k}{1 + k} \,. \tag{13}$$

If we insert this expression for c in (10) and (12), (10) becomes:

$$\Delta K_r = \frac{1 + k}{r + k} \,.\, \Delta Z \tag{14}$$

and (12) becomes:

$$\Delta D = \frac{1}{r + k} \,.\, \Delta Z. \tag{15}$$

It can easily be seen that the "deposit multiplier" $\frac{1}{r+k}$ in (15) can assume any positive value.[1]

According to (14) and (15) the ratio between the maximum volume of deposits and the credit potential is:

$$(16) \qquad \frac{\Delta D}{\Delta K_r} = \frac{1}{1+k} = 1 - c.$$

The ratio of ΔD to ΔK_r thus depends solely on k or c (*not* on the minimum reserve ratio) and is smaller, the larger k.

12. It is important to note that the limit to credit expansion given by (2) is completely independent of whether or not the individual banks move in step.[2] Movement in step affects the limit to which a banking system can expand credit only when no cash is used in the system. *In a mixed-money system, the limit to potential credit expansion by the banking system, barring recourse to the central bank, is determined solely by the size of excess reserves, by the minimum reserve ratio, and the payment habits in the non-banking sector expressed by the size of c in (2).* The commercial banks are unable to increase the lending potential of the banking system through mutual agreement regarding the pace and extent of credit extension. It is true that if the banks move in step, no bank will lose cash to any other; but this does not increase the *total* reserves of the banking system, on the basis of which commercial bank money is created. Thus the banks cannot increase the lending potential of the banking system as a whole through movement in step. The limit to credit expansion given by (2) is also valid for a banking system which consists of one central bank and of only one single commercial bank. In this case the single bank would create all commercial bank deposits; and it could at once proceed to extend credit up to the limit indicated by (2) while in a commercial banking *system* this limit (theoretically) is reached only after an infinite number of credit extensions.

Before we proceed to draw further conclusions from equation (2) it must be emphasized that *equation (2) only gives the limit to which the commercial banking system, in a single tier mixed-money system, can extend credit without recourse to the central bank. This does not mean that, given ΔZ, r and c, credit will in fact be extended to this limit.* The banks cannot force their loans on anyone. The extent to

(1) The deposit multiplier was first stated in this form by J. H. Rogers, "The Absorption of Bank Credit" (*Econometrica*, Vol. I, 1933, p. 63ff.).

(2) See § 2 of this chapter for the concept of movement in step.

which the lending potential of the banking system is utilized depends not only on the policy of the banks (i.e. on their lending terms), but also on the behaviour of their customers. If no-one wishes to incur debts to the banks their lending potential will remain unused, however large it might be. The lending potential of the commercial banks, however, can be extended by recourse to the central bank, to an extent indicated by equation (2).

13. The central bank alone determines the extent to which the commercial banks can have recourse to it. If we further remember that the lending potential of the commercial banks, as given by (2), depends on:

(a) available excess reserves,

(b) the minimum reserve ratio,

(c) the payment habits in the non-banking sector, as expressed by c, it is clear that, given the payment habits in the non-banking sector,[1] the total lending potential is determined solely by the behaviour of the central bank. The minimum reserve ratio is fixed by the central bank; and the central bank also has the power to alter the size of the banks' excess reserves, as we shall explain later.

An increase in the lending potential of the banking system is possible only if the commercial banks acquire additional cash. This *may* happen if, given r and c, the central bank acquires assets and thus makes new cash available to the commercial banks. This case will be discussed in detail in the following paragraph. It can also happen in the following ways. First, if the central bank reduces the minimum reserve ratio and thus makes available to the commercial banks cash which was hitherto required as minimum legal reserves. Second, if the banks acquire eligible assets (compare pp. 40–41); finally, it can also happen without any action by the central bank, if there is a change in the payment habits of the private sector in the direction of increased payments by cheque. If economic subjects in the non-banking sector decide to settle more payments by cheque than hitherto, the quantity of cash in the non-banking sector will usually diminish in favour of the commercial banking system, so that a larger proportion of the existing amount of central bank money will now permanently remain in the banking system. This in turn means that the commercial banking system becomes more liquid, and its lending potential increases. If the banking system acquires an additional amount of cash $\Delta Z'$ in this way, equation (2) will be slightly modified. The permanent drain of cash from the non-banking sector takes place in the following way: the commercial

[1] The distribution of government accounts between the commercial banks and the central bank is included in the payment habits.

banks acquire cash from the non-banking sector and in return incur current liabilities to the non-banking sector. The banks incur new current liabilities of $\Delta Z'$ in the course of passive deposit creation, against which they must keep minimum reserves of $r \,.\, \Delta Z'$. The amount of cash which can serve as a basis for credit expansion is only $\Delta Z = (1 - r) \,.\, \Delta Z'$, so that the limit to credit expansion is now given by the equation:

$$\text{(2a)} \qquad \Delta K_r = \frac{(1 - r) \,.\, \Delta Z'}{r + c(1 - r)}$$

But this modification in no way alters the conclusions we have so far drawn from equation (2), nor those we still have to point out. Moreover, it should be observed that payment habits change only very slowly.[1] Credit expansion on this basis is thus impossible in the short run. Any growth in the volume of deposits, in periods in which payment habits do not change, or in economies in which payment by cheque is widespread, can be explained only in terms of the behaviour of the central bank which makes such growth possible.

Figure 2 shows how the money-creation multiplier, i.e. the expression:

$$\frac{1}{r + c(1 - r)}$$

in (2), varies with r and c. It can be seen that, given c, the multiplier declines with rising r, and given r, the multiplier declines with rising c.

Our analysis also shows that the possibility of multiple deposit expansion in a single tier mixed-money system depends on the existence of payments by cheque. If each debtor withdrew his loans in cash, and if the withdrawn cash remained in the non-banking sector, multiple expansion of deposits by the banking system would be impossible. On the basis of excess reserves of ΔZ the banking system could only grant new credits up to ΔZ. The same would be the case (irrespective of the size of c) if minimum legal reserves were equal to current liabilities (if $r = 1$).

Finally, we must mention yet another possible way in which the public can provide the banks with additional excess reserves (assuming unchanged behaviour on the part of the central bank). As a rule, the minimum legal reserve ratios against deposit accounts are lower than those against current accounts. Thus, whenever customers transfer money from current accounts to deposit accounts this will free some cash which until now was required as minimum reserves, on the basis of which the banks can grant new loans. As we know,

[1] Compare pp. 56–58.

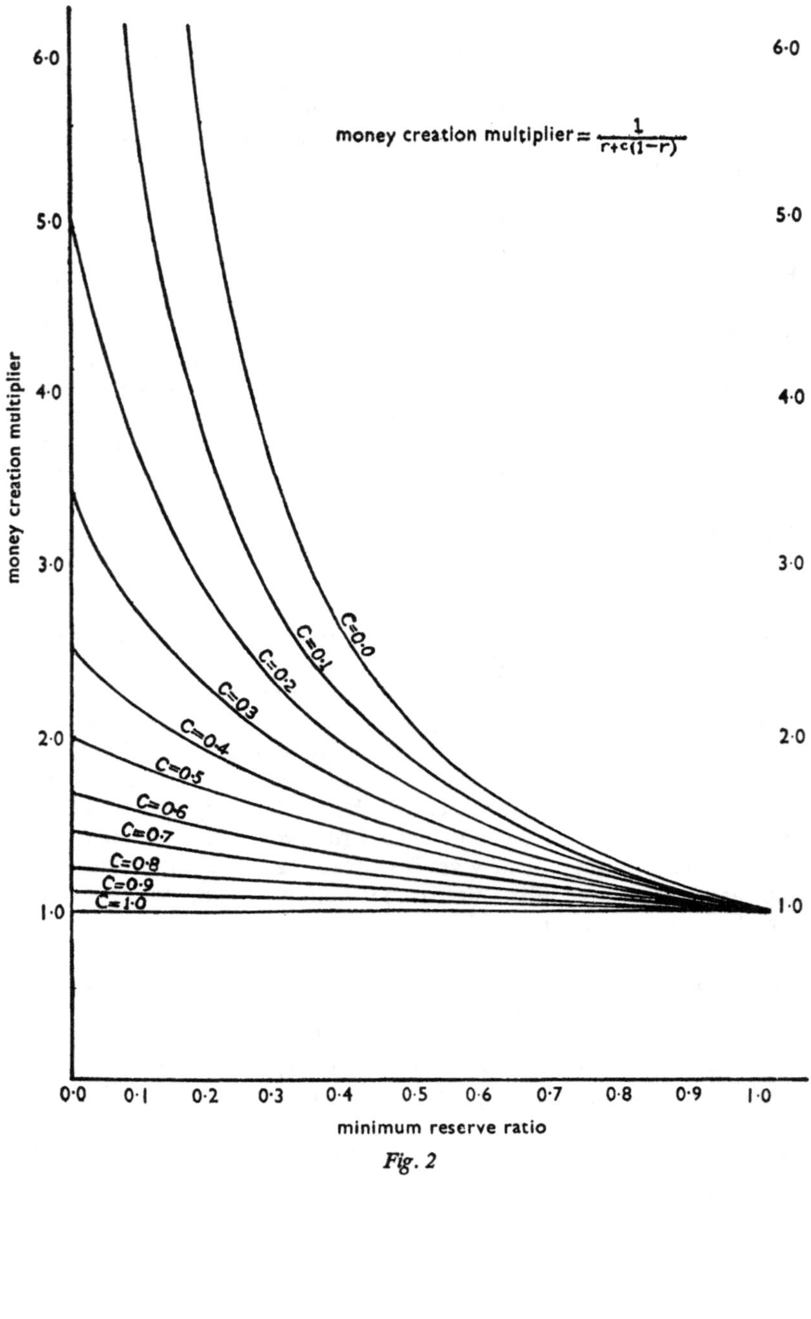
money creation multiplier = $\frac{1}{r+c(1-r)}$
money creation multiplier
minimum reserve ratio
6·0
5·0
4·0
3·0
2·0
1·0
0·0
0·1
0·2
0·3
0·4
0·5
0·6
0·7
0·8
0·9
1·0
C=0·0
C=0·1
C=0·2
C=0·3
C=0·4
C=0·5
C=0·6
C=0·7
C=0·8
C=0·9
C=1·0

Fig. 2

the banks' creditors alone decide how to distribute their money-holdings between current accounts and deposit accounts.

14. Several attempts have been made to measure the variables c or k, which are important in determining the lending potential of the commercial banking system. In his *A Treatise on Money*[1] Keynes states that Governor Strong, in his evidence before the U.S. Congress Committee on stabilization, estimated that in the United States the increase in note circulation was approximately 20% of the increase in demand deposits, and that reserves amounted to 10% of the demand deposits. This gives a money creation multiplier of 4.

Corresponding estimates for Germany were made by J. Marschak and W. Lederer[2] in 1932. They found that approximately 50% of payments were made by cheque.

According to an estimate for England made by J. E. Meade[3] the average value of c for the years 1925–1930 was between 0·14 and 0·16.

In appraising these measurements an important point must be borne in mind. In order to determine the maximum amount of credit which the commercial banks can grant on the basis of any given excess reserves, we need only know how the additional quantity of money created in the non-banking sector is divided as between cash holdings and current accounts. The size of c (or k) here refers to the ratio between marginal, not between total amounts. It would thus appear that only Strong's estimate meets our requirements, while the estimates of Meade and Marschak, which refer to the ratios between total quantities, would appear to be irrelevant in estimating the lending potential. Such a conclusion, however, would be premature. In Fig. 3 let the N-curve represent observed cash holdings over time, and the $(N + D)$ curve the observed total volume of money (cash plus current accounts). The ratio $\frac{N}{D}$ shows how the non-banking sector distributes its money holdings at each point of time. The ratio $\frac{N}{D}$ shows what proportion of money-balances in the non-banking sector is held in notes and what proportion is held in the form of current accounts. Thus the ratios $\frac{N}{D}$ or $\frac{N}{N+D}$ reflect the preferences at any given time between the two possible

[1] Vol. II, p. 51.

[2] J. Marschak and W. Lederer, "Grössenordnungen des deutschen Geldsystems", *Archiv fur Sozialwissenschaft und Sozialpolitik*. Vol. 67, 1932, p. 385ff.

[3] J. E. Meade, "The Amount of Money and the Banking System", *Economic Journal*, Vol. 44, 1934.

ways of holding money. In an economy where payment by cheque is widespread the ratio $\frac{N}{D}$ will be smaller than in one where payment by cash is more usual. Thus there can be no doubt that payment habits are reflected in the ratios $\frac{N}{D}$ and $\frac{N}{N+D}$. For instance, if at a certain point of time $\frac{N}{N+D} = \frac{3}{4}$ it is reasonable to assume that

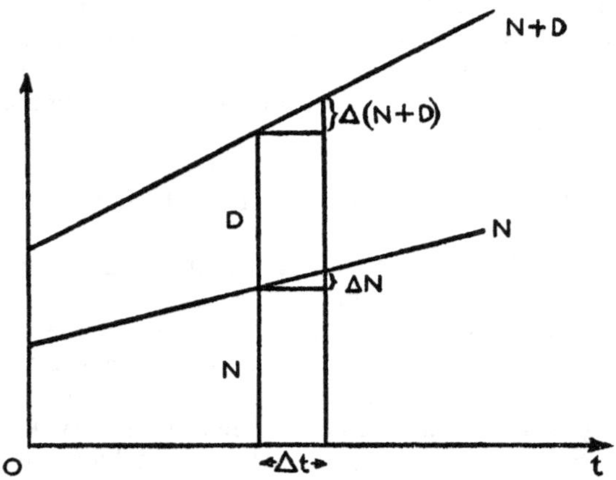

Fig. 3

credits granted at about that time will in aggregate be held in roughly the same proportions. However, the same cannot be said of the ratio $\frac{\Delta N}{\Delta(N+D)}$, where ΔN is the *change* in the quantity of cash and $\Delta(N+D)$ the *change* in the quantity of money held by the non-banking sector in a short period Δt. It is obvious that this ratio cannot reflect habits of payment in the period Δt. To see this, one need only think of the case in which the quantity of money rises continuously while cash holdings remain constant. The ratio $\frac{\Delta N}{\Delta(N+D)}$ would remain constant at zero which would seem to indicate constant habits of payment (at the margin), whereas the preferences of the non-banking sector have in fact changed in favour of making payments by cheque. If, in this case, $\frac{\Delta N}{\Delta(N+D)}$ were taken as representing the value of c, this would mean that the additional payments resulting from the new credits would be made exclusively by cheque—a conclusion which does not follow from the fact that the time series give a value of zero for $\frac{\Delta N}{\Delta(N + D)}$ in a particular period. It follows that the ratio between the total amounts N and D, or N and $N + D$, as measured statistically, must be regarded as giving the only acceptable estimate for k or c.

On pages 56–57 the values of c and k for the German Federal Republic for the years 1949–1954 are computed by the method just explained. Column 1 of the table shows the circulation of notes outside the banking system, and column 2 the current accounts held by the non-banking sector, all in monthly figures.[1] Columns 3 and 4 contain the calculated values for c and k. Column 4 of the table, which is represented graphically in Fig. 4, shows that the size of c in the German Federal Republic deviated only slightly from the value 0·4 during the period September 1948–December 1954. We can say, therefore, that on the average $\frac{4}{10}$ of the money holdings of the non-banking sector is held in cash (notes) and $\frac{6}{10}$ in the form of current accounts with the banks. Compared with the results obtained by Marschak and Lederer for 1932, a small increase in the preference for current accounts as against notes has taken place. Furthermore, as regards the German Federal Republic, the distribution of money holdings between cash and current accounts, and hence the value of c, may be regarded as practically constant for the period under consideration. Thus changes in the lending potential of the commercial banks must be traced mainly to changes in excess reserves and in the minimum reserve ratio.

15. We have seen that, in the course of multiple deposit expansion, individual banks continuously receive payments which raise the liquidity and hence the lending potential of the banks concerned. In our example, bank 2 received £100 in the first round as a result of active money creation by bank 1. Of this £100, bank 2 had to keep £10 as minimum reserves against the passively created deposits of £100. On the basis of its excess reserves of £90 bank 2 could grant new loans to the amount of the excess reserves, that is, it could actively create new deposit money up to this amount. Bank 2 is unaware that the additional cash deposited with it is the result of active money creation (the granting of loans) by bank 1. Since all banks continuously receive deposits which, given unchanged payment habits in the non-banking sector, are the result of active money creation by other banks, it is understandable that each *individual* bank should believe that it only lends the cash it has received in the course of

[1] Source: Bank deutscher Länder (Monthly Report).

Estimates of *c* and *k* for the German Federal Republic

Year	Month	Note circulation outside the banks in mill. DM (*N*) (1)	Current accounts of Non-banks in mill. DM (*D*) (2)	$\frac{N}{D}$ (*k*) (3)	$\frac{N}{N+D}$ (*c*) (4)
1949	January	5,903	8,261	0·72	0·42
	February	5,962	8,487	0·70	0·41
	March	5,935	8,637	0·69	0·41
	April	6,077	8,930	0·68	0·41
	May	6,093	8,972	0·68	0·41
	June	6,287	9,360	0.67	0.40
	July	6,417	9,430	0·68	0·41
	August	6,536	9,605	0·68	0·41
	September	6,763	9,617	0·70	0·41
	October	6,769	10,149	0·67	0·40
	November	6,670	10,269	0·65	0·39
	December	7,058	10,541	0·67	0·40
1950	January	6,902	10,214	0·68	0·41
	February	7,000	10,134	0·69	0·41
	March	7,148	10,201	0·71	0·42
	April	7,279	10,330	0·71	0·42
	May	7,168	10,712	0·67	0·40
	June	7,440	10,552	0·71	0·42
	July	7,494	—	—	—
	August	7,409	—	—	—
	September	7,627	11,311	0·68	0·41
	October	7,512	—	—	—
	November	7,487	11,431	0·66	0·40
	December	7,682	11,479	0·67	0·40
1951	January	7,209	11,200	0·64	0·39
	February	7,222	11,409	0·63	0·39
	March	7,292	11,258	0·65	0·39
	April	7,451	11,122	0·67	0·40
	May	7,395	11,423	0·65	0·39
	June	7,781	11,773	0·66	0·40
	July	7,946	11,743	0·68	0·41
	August	8,331	12,090	0·69	0·41
	September	8,656	11,955	0·72	0·42
	October	8,562	12,491	0·69	0·41
	November	8,778	13,083	0·67	0·40
	December	8,801	13,701	0·64	0·39
1952	January	8,685	12,909	0·67	0·40
	February	8,977	12,758	0·70	0·41
	March	9,054	12,855	0·70	0·41
	April	9,157	12,750	0·72	0·42
	May	9,365	12,688	0·74	0·43

Year	Month	Note circulation outside the banks in mill. DM (N) (1)	Current accounts of non-banks in mill. DM (D) (2)	$\frac{N}{D}$ (k) (3)	$\frac{N}{N+D}$ (c) (4)
1952	June	9,440	13,137	0·72	0·42
	July	9,484	13,191	0·72	0·42
	August	9,766	13,479	0·73	0·42
	September	9,838	14,158	0·70	0·41
	October	10,003	14,066	0·71	0·42
	November	10,129	14,210	0·71	0·42
	December	10,217	14,963	0·68	0·41
1953	January	10,089	14,406	0·70	0·41
	February	10,323	14,469	0·71	0·42
	March	10,310	14,564	0·71	0·42
	April	10,535	14,521	0·73	0·42
	May	10,501	14,912	0·70	0·41
	June	10,564	15,236	0·69	0·41
	July	10,791	15,074	0·72	0·42
	August	10,859	15,649	0·69	0·41
	September	11,017	15,892	0·69	0·41
	October	11,149	15,783	0·71	0·41
	November	11,126	16,464	0·68	0·40
	December	11,972	17,206	0·70	0·41
1954	January	11,667	17,093	0·68	0·41
	February	11,885	17,188	0·69	0·41
	March	11,791	17,707	0·67	0·40
	April	12,035	17,625	0·68	0·41
	May	11,886	18,147	0·65	0·39
	June	11,930	18.498	0·65	0·39
	July	12,158	18,363	0.66	0·40
	August	12,076	18,524	0·65	0·39
	September	12,358	19,296	0·64	0·39
	October	12,581	19,056	0·66	0·40
	November	12,556	19,833	0·63	0·39
	December	12,781	21,169	0·60	0·38

deposits. Yet, we must stress once again that is it *not true to say that a bank lends its excess cash when granting credit*. The bank monetises claims which do not constitute money, and *itself creates the money, in the form of new current liabilities, which it puts at the disposal of its debtor*. Thus, the new credits are not drawn from any existing money, but are put at the debtor's disposal in the form of deposit money, newly created by the bank itself. The bank assumes the obligation to exchange the created deposit money into cash at any time; and it can do this if it has excess reserves to the value of the created deposit money, or if it can procure the required cash.

The bank also does not lend its deposits. Deposits are liabilities of the bank to its customers; clearly, the bank cannot lend its liabilities! When a bank endeavours to receive as much in deposits as possible, it does so, not in order to acquire deposits which it might lend, but in order to acquire cash on the basis of which it can grant new credit.

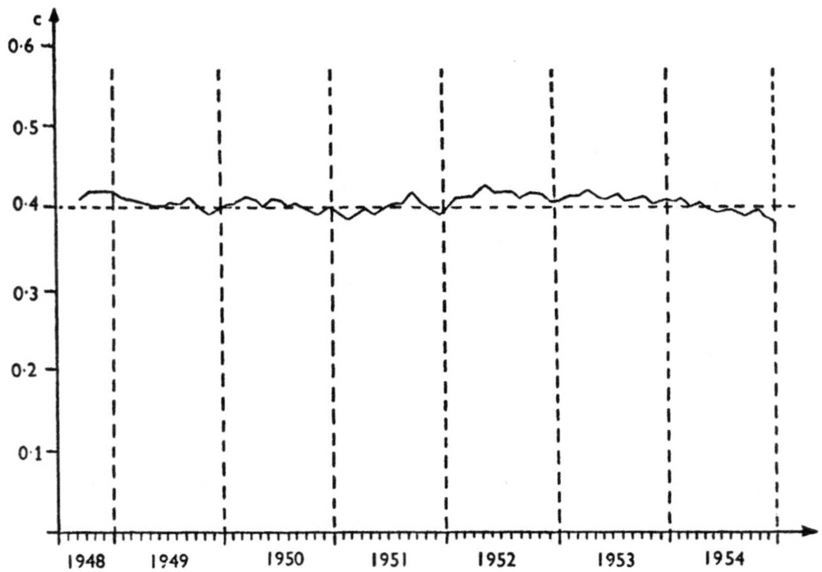

Fig. 4

A bank also does not lend savings; savings accounts kept with a bank represent the bank's liabilities to the savers. Liabilities cannot be lent, but the bank can grant new loans on the basis of the cash received in the course of savings deposits. That is, the bank can actively create new deposit money, although it does not lend the cash. Whenever credit is granted new deposit money is created; whenever loans are repaid deposit money is destroyed (assuming the debtor pays in deposit money). *It follows that deposit money creation by the commercial banks in no way depends on, or is limited by, the level of savings. An increase in savings is thus not a necessary condition for an extension of credit.* It is important to understand this clearly.[(1)]

(1) The reader is urged to consult the work of E. Preiser "Der Kapitalbergriff und die neuere Theorie" in *Die Unternehmung im Markt*, essays in honour of Wilhelm Rieger, Stuttgart, 1954. Further: H. Gestrich, loc. cit., pp. 79–101.

As we have seen, deposit money is also continuously created and destroyed in the course of the banks' passive business. But if payments habits in the non-banking sector remain unchanged this can never lead to a growth in the total volume of deposit money. *Growth in the total volume of deposit money is possible only if the central bank makes available new cash to the commercial banks.*[1] In the next paragraph we shall discuss the means whereby the central bank can bring this about.

16. So far we have been concerned exclusively with the process of credit expansion by an individual bank and by the banking system. In our discussion we have established a proposition which is of fundamental importance to the understanding of the modern credit mechanism, namely that the banking system as a whole can do something which an individual bank cannot do: on the basis of excess reserves of ΔZ the banking system can undertake an expansion of credit which is a multiple of ΔZ, the expansion multiplier depending on the minimum reserve ratio and the payment habits of the public. In conclusion, let us consider the *process of credit contraction*. In order to be able to consider it in its pure form, let us assume that the banking system has fully utilized its lending potential. Suppose that in the initial situation the consolidated balance sheet of the commercial banking system shows a given volume of deposits and of minimum reserves which are just sufficient for that volume of deposit money. The banking system has no excess reserves. A process of credit contraction can now be initiated either by the central bank withdrawing cash from the commercial banks (by means to be discussed in the next paragraph) or raising the minimum reserve ratio; or by a change in the payment habits in the non-banking sector towards increased payments by cash. The only way in which the

[1] This state of affairs is described as follows in "*The Federal Reserve System: Its Purpose and its Functions*", published by the Board of Governors of the Federal Reserve System (Washington, D.C., 3rd edition, 1954): "Taking the banking system as a whole deposits originate in bank loans and investments, but each individual bank's ability to lend and invest arises largely from deposits brought to it by its customers" (p. 21). In this context "investments" refer to the acquisition of assets by the banks which do not arise from loans to customers (for example, purchases of securities on the Stock Exchange). Loans, in this context, refer to the claims which a bank acquires in the course of its active business. In the famous *Macmillan Report* (Report of the Committee on Finance and Industry, London 1931) the same state of affairs is explained as follows: "It is not unnatural to think of deposits of a bank as being created by the public through the deposits of cash .... But the bulk of the deposits arise out of the action of the banks themselves, for by granting loans, allowing money to be drawn on an overdraft, or purchasing securities a bank creates a credit in its books which is the equivalent of a deposit" (loc. cit., p. 34.)

banking system can acquire the additional cash needed is by recalling loans and reducing the volume of bank credit. There is no other possibility. Let us inquire by how much the volume of bank credit has to be reduced when an amount of cash ΔZ is withdrawn from the commercial banking system. Instead of tracing the process, as we did in our analysis of credit expansion, we shall restrict ourselves to ascertaining the end result. The reader might analyse the process for himself.

Let us consider a simple example. The following table shows the state of the consolidated balance sheet of the commercial banking system before the process of contraction starts. In it we only indicate the entries relevant to our problem, and we assume a minimum reserve ratio of 10%.

Consolidated Balance Sheet

L	A
Current Accounts 100	Reserves: 10 Investments and loans: 90

The central bank now withdraws £5 cash from the banking system in such a way that the current liabilities of the banking system are simultaneously reduced by the same amount. In the next paragraph we shall discuss how the central bank can do this. There are now current liabilities of 95 against reserves of 5. As the required minimum reserves are 9·5 (given a minimum reserve ratio of 10%) the banks must attempt either to increase their cash reserves by 4·5, or to reduce their volume of credit appropriately. The banks cannot get the cash from the central bank, nor can they acquire it by selling assets within the banking system. A *single* bank can acquire cash by selling securities to other banks; but the banking system as a whole cannot obtain additional cash in this way.

In order to understand the economy's credit mechanism it is of decisive importance to distinguish clearly between the processes relating to single economic units and those relating to the economy as a whole. *Theorems which apply to individual economic units*—in this case to an individual bank—*cannot simply be applied to all economic units taken together*—in this case to the commercial banking system. If one man climbs on a chair in a hall full of people he can see better than the others; but when everybody climbs on chairs, this is no longer true. The ability to think in economic terms (i.e. in terms applicable to the economy as a whole) consists in recognizing how theorems which relate to individual economic units are modified when they are applied to the economy as a whole. Many false conclusions in economic arguments stem from the fact that theorems relating to individual economic units are simply applied to the economy as a whole. We pointed this out in connection with the analysis of multiple credit expansion, we see it again here, and in the course of our subsequent enquiries we shall meet many more examples demonstrating the importance of this proposition. We explained in the first two volumes that in order to gain a proper understanding of economic relationships we have to refer back to the economic dispositions made by individual economic units. The theorems derived from the study of individual economic units, however, only form the basis for the analysis of the relationships in the economy as a whole; they cannot simply be applied to the whole economy. The reader may find it interesting to try to find theorems which are valid for individual economic units, but not for the economy as a whole.

The only way in which the banking system can overcome the shortage of reserves is by recalling loans and (or) selling securities to the non-banking sector. The banks will attempt to exercise restraint in the recalling of loans, because each premature demand for repayment may, and usually does, involve the debtors in considerable financial difficulties. For this reason the banks will attempt to rely on the repayment of loans which fall due. Each repayment of credit has the following effect on the bank's balance sheet: on the assets side the claim against the debtor disappears and, if the debtor pays by cheque, current liabilities are reduced by the amount repaid. If the debtor pays partly in cash and partly by cheque, current liabilities are reduced by the amount repaid by cheque, and on the assets side cash increases by the amount repaid in cash. In both cases the repayment reduces the shortage of reserves. If we assume that all repayments are made by cheque, then repayments of loans of 10 reduce the shortage of reserves of the banking system by 1. Sales of securities to the public have the same effect. We thus have to ask to what extent the banking system has to recall credits and (or) sell securities to the public if the reserves are once more to meet legal requirements. Given the minimum reserve ratio (r), the extent to which the banking system has to recall loans and/or sell securities will depend on the payment habits in the non-banking sector (c). Let us assume that the public pays for securities and repays loans by cheque ($c = 0$). Let ΔD denote the amount by which the public's deposits have to be reduced. Given a minimum reserve ratio r, the following equation must then hold:

$$r \,.\, \Delta D = \Delta Z$$

or

$$(17) \qquad \Delta D = \frac{1}{r} \cdot \Delta Z$$

The minimum reserves corresponding to a volume of deposits D are $r \cdot D$; and a change in the volume of deposits of ΔD correspondingly requires a change in minimum reserves of $r \cdot \Delta D$, irrespective of whether this change is an increase or a decrease. If the central bank reduces the commercial bank's cash by ΔZ, deposits must be reduced by the amount ΔD given in equation (17)[1]. With a minimum reserve ratio $r = \frac{1}{10}$, deposits must be reduced by an amount ten times the reduction in cash. In our numerical example the minimum legal reserve ratio will be re-established only when the banking system has reduced its current liabilities to 50. A comparison of (17) with (1) shows immediately that the money-creation multiplier $\frac{1}{r}$ is identical with the money-destruction multiplier. The quantitative extent of the process is thus the same in both the upward and downward direction. This important proposition, however, needs to be qualified. If the banking system acquires an additional amount of cash ΔZ then, given the assumptions underlying equation (1), the lending potential of the banking system will increase by an amount indicated by (1). Whether the banks in fact wish or are able to utilize the increased lending potential is another matter. If the central bank partly or wholly reduces the excess reserves of the banking system its lending potential will diminish without, however, forcing the banks to reduce their current liabilities. Yet, the central bank is always able to bring about a shortage of reserves in the banking system, and in this case the banks are *forced* to reduce the volume of deposits. *The central bank's influence on the volume of deposit money is thus much stronger in a downward than in an upward direction.* This important fact will concern us in the next paragraph, and also in our subsequent discussions.

So far we have assumed that the non-banking sector paid by cheque for the assets disposed of by the banking system in the course of credit contraction. If the non-banking sector pays only partly by cheque, formula (17) will be altered. It will be replaced by the previous formula (2) which is also valid both for expansions and contractions of credit. If, in the course of credit contraction $c = \frac{1}{2}$, this means that the non-banking sector pays half by cash and half by cheque

[1] Equation (17) can also be derived from the following relation. Clearly,

$$D \cdot r - \Delta Z = (D - \Delta D) \cdot r,$$

from which (17) follows directly.

for the assets disposed of by the commercial banks. Otherwise our analysis remains unaffected. If the non-banking sector pays only partly by cheque the contraction will be weaker than when all payment is by cheque ($c = 0$). If $\Delta Z = 100$, $r = \frac{1}{10}$ and $c = \frac{1}{2}$, we have according to (2):

$$\Delta K_r = \frac{100}{\frac{1}{10} + \frac{1}{2}(1 - \frac{1}{10})} = 181{\cdot}82,$$

while for $c = 0$ we have:

$$\Delta K_r = 1000$$

In the first case only 181·82 of credits must be recalled, while in the second case 1000.

§4. The Rôle of the Central Bank in a Single-Tier Mixed-Money System

We have seen that the lending potential of the commercial banking system depends on:

(a) the size of excess reserves,
(b) the availability of eligible assets,
(c) the minimum reserve ratio,
(d) the payment habits in the non-banking sector.

If we take the payment habits in the non-banking sector as given, (a), (b) and (c) determine the size of the credit potential of the banking system. The institution which controls the factors mentioned under (a), (b) and (c) thus controls the commercial banking system's lending potential, i.e. its ability to create deposit money. We have explained that the minimum legal reserve ratio is set by the central bank, and we have also suggested in passing that the central bank has the power to regulate the size of excess reserves. In this paragraph we shall have to show in detail the means by which the central bank can increase or decrease the cash of the commercial banks. *The essential function of the central bank is to regulate the volume of money and credit and the terms on which credit is available.*[1]

(i) CENTRAL BANK MINIMUM RESERVE POLICY

Central bank minimum reserve policy consists in influencing the commercial banks' volume of credit (their ability to create deposit-money) by alterations in the minimum reserve ratio, *given the stock*

[1] "Central banks exist because we are not willing to allow the total supply of money and of credit, and the cost of credit, to be determined by the unregulated forces of private supply and demand". (L. V. Chandler in "United States Monetary Policy: Recent Thinking and Experience", *Hearings before sub-committee on economic stabilization*, 83rd Congress, 1954, p. 46.)

of cash. Ceteris paribus, a change in the minimum reserve ratio can influence the commercial banks' volume of credit. This follows directly from equation (2) which we derived in the previous paragraph. If the commercial banking system has excess reserves of a given amount, an increase in the minimum reserve ratio will reduce its lending potential. Figure 2 shows how the lending potential varies with an increasing minimum reserve ratio. In the absence of excess reserves, an increase in the minimum reserve ratio forces the commercial banking system to reduce the quantity of deposit money by means of recalling loans and (or) selling securities to the non-banking sector. Conversely, if the minimum reserve ratio is reduced the commercial banking system acquires additional excess reserves which make an expansion of credit possible. Central bank minimum reserve policy is thus a powerful means of regulating the commercial banks' volume of credit.[1] But it is obvious that frequent changes in the minimum reserve ratio are not feasible, since this would introduce constant disturbances and uncertainty into the business of the commercial banks.[2] For this reason minimum reserve policy is important principally "for longer-run operations and in particular situations".[3]

Paragraph 16 of the Act (cf. 26.7.1957)[4] relating to the Deutsche Bundesbank contains the following provisions regarding minimum reserve policy:

> "(1) For the purpose of influencing the circulation of money and the supply of credit, the Deutsche Bundesbank may require the credit institutions to maintain with it, on giro account, balances (minimum reserves) equal to a specified percentage of their liabilities arising from sight, time and savings deposits and from short and medium term borrowings, with the exception of

[1] Minimum reserve policy "... goes straight to the root of the matter ... If the member banks are lending too much ... or if, on the other hand, they are lending too little, the variation in their reserve proportions puts on them the directest possible pressure to move in the desired direction." (J. M. Keynes, *A Treatise on Money*, Vol. II, p. 261.)

[2] The following apposite comment is made in the booklet of the Board of Governors of the Federal Reserve System mentioned above: "This method of influencing bank reserve positions and the flow of credit and money is usually employed only when large scale changes in the country's available bank reserves are desired. For day-to-day operations in influencing the flow of credit and money, the Federal Reserve depends principally on the more flexible instruments of discount and open market operations". (loc. cit., p. 52.)

[3] Report of the Bank Deutscher Länder for 1954, p. 23.

[4] On 26.7.1957 the Länderzentralbanken and the Berliner Zentralbank were amalgamated with the Bank deutscher Länder. The Bank deutscher Länder became the Deutsche Bundesbank.

liabilities to other credit institutions required to maintain minimum reserves. The rates fixed by the Bank shall not exceed thirty per cent for sight liabilities, twenty per cent for time liabilities, and ten per cent for savings deposits. Within these limits the Bank may fix the rates at various levels in accordance with general principles, in particular for individual groups of institutions, and may exclude certain liabilities from the computation.

"(2) The average monthly balance of a credit institution with the Deutsche Bundesbank (actual reserve) must not be less than the percentages, fixed in accordance with par. (1), of the monthly average of that institution's liabilities subject to the reserve requirement (required reserve). The bank shall issue detailed regulations concerning the computation and establishment of the actual reserve and of the required reserve."

The Federal Reserve System of the U.S.A. obtained the power to operate minimum reserve policy in 1933. According to current legal provisions minimum reserve ratios can be set within the following limits:

Time Deposits	from 3 to 6%
Demand Deposits	
For New York and Chicago	from 13 to 26%
For other districts with a Reserve Bank	from 10 to 20%
For other districts	from 7 to 14%

(ii) CENTRAL BANK OPEN MARKET POLICY

(ii_1) *Central bank open market policy consists in the purchase and sale of primary assets*, i.e. *of gold, foreign exchange and fixed interest securities on the open market*. Open market policy thus consists of all measures which are aimed at changing the amount of primary assets held by the central bank. *Nowadays, however, the concept of open market policy is generally restricted to the central bank's open market sales and purchases of short, medium or long term fixed interest securities* (*e.g. of government securities*). But the purchase and sale of other primary assets has the same effect on the stock of central bank money in the economy. When the central bank buys gold or foreign exchange, it makes central bank money available unconditionally to the seller; and the same happens when the central bank buys securities on the stock exchange. Conversely, when the central bank sells primary assets on the open market central bank money flows back to the central bank.

E

(ii_2). *By open market policy the central bank can influence the lending potential of the commercial banking system through the resulting changes in the size of the cash reserve.* As in the case of minimum reserve policy, this influence is exercised at the initiative of the central bank. Whereas open market policy affects the *size* of the commercial banks' cash reserves (in an upward or downward direction), in the case of minimum reserve policy the stock of central bank money remains unchanged and only the required minimum reserves are altered. The influence exercised on the cash reserves of the commercial banks by open market policy is known as the *quantity effect* of open market operations.

Let us consider a few examples:

(a) The central bank buys £1 million of government securities on the stock exchange. These securities are bought from the commercial banks.

This transaction will have the following effects on the balance sheet of the central bank and on the consolidated balance sheet of the commercial banking system:

Central Bank		**Commercial Banking System**	
L	A	L	A
Current liabilities (to banks): + 1 million	Government securities: + 1 million		Central bank deposits: + 1 million Government securities: −1 million

The central bank has acquired primary assets of £1 million and paid for them by crediting the sellers' accounts. The banks have sold government securities in return for additional deposits with the central bank. There has been an increase in the assets and liabilities of the central bank; but there has only been a change in the composition of the assets of the commercial banks. There has been an increase in the quantity of cash in the commercial banking system, which is made available unconditionally by the central bank. The banks can grant new credit on the basis of the newly acquired cash if they find transactors willing to take it. If the banks owe debts to the central bank they can also use their new deposits with the central bank to repay these debts.

(b) The central bank buys £1 million of government securities on the stock exchange. These securities are sold by the public.

Since payment to the public is made through the banks, the central bank credits the deposits of the commercial banks. The banks in turn credit the accounts of their customers who sold the securities. The balance sheets will show the following changes:

Central Bank		Commercial Banking System	
L	A	L	A
Current liabilities to banks: + 1 million	Government securities: + 1 million	Current liabilities: + 1 million	Central bank money: + 1 million

This transaction increases the assets and liabilities of the central bank as well as those of the commercial banking system. The quantity of money in the commercial banking system and in the non-banking sector has increased.

If the central bank sells government securities the reverse process takes place. If these securities are bought by banks, the banks lose cash and acquire government securities. If these securities are bought by the public the quantity of money in the non-banking sector and in the commercial banking system is reduced. The ability of the central bank to reduce the quantity of central bank money in this way is clearly limited by the central bank's stock of fixed interest securities.

In December 1938 the commercial banks in the U.S.A. had excess reserves of $5·2 billion. Since the central bank only held government securities to the value of $2·5 billion, the Federal Reserve Banks could at best have reduced the quantity of central bank money by $2.5 billion through open market operations.

Open market policy supplements minimum reserve policy admirably, since minimum reserve policy cannot deal with short-run fluctuations in the liquidity of banks, and affects all banks without regard to their differing liquidity positions. By contrast, open market policy can ". . . absorb substantial amounts of liquid funds—at the points where such funds initially accumulate—in a way which is both highly flexible and makes considerable allowance for the credit institutions' need to earn a profit." (Report of the Bank deutscher Länder, 1954, p. 24). For this reason, open market policy is of decisive importance in achieving a short-run central bank policy which operates quickly and smoothly.

Finally, we have to ask whether the commercial banks can defend themselves against the loss of cash resulting from a contractionary open market policy. If payment habits in the non-banking sector remain unchanged the banks clearly cannot get additional cash from the non-banking sector; nor can they acquire it through the sale of securities to one another. The only way in which the banks can get cash is by incurring debts to the central bank. The central bank, however, can stipulate the terms on which it will lend; and these may be such as to deter the banks who, in any case, do not like to be in debt to the central bank. If central bank credit is easily available the banks may be able to frustrate the contractionary policy of the central bank. We shall discuss this further in connection with discount policy.

(ii_3) We now turn to another important aspect of open market policy. When the central bank enters the open market as buyer or seller of fixed interest securities it not only influences the stock of central bank money in the commercial banking system, and hence the availability of credit, but it also influences the price,(1) or in other words, the effective rate of interest on these securities.(2) Open

(1) In the kind of open market policy so far practised in the German Federal Republic there is no such effect on the price of securities. There, the central bank fixes the purchase and sale price of money market paper, so that no price risk attaches to it. Herein lies the essential difference between the open market policy of the Deutsche Bundesbank and the open market policy in, for example, England, the United States, Sweden and Denmark. In these countries open market policy is carried out through the sale and purchase of certain securities on the open market, and hence these securities are subject to price fluctuations. In these countries, the price of these securities (the effective rate of interest) is determined by the interplay of buyers and sellers on the stock exchange, and the central bank can influence the price (the rate of interest) only by entering the market as buyer or seller. In this case the central bank either fixes the quantity of money which has to be absorbed or created, or the quantity of securities which have to be sold or bought.

In the United States the authorities generally operate only in short term government securities, whose price is thus determined on the open market by the interplay of supply and demand. "These securities are the most liquid in the market, and, because of their role as operating and liquid assets of financial institutions and business corporations, are subject to a large daily volume of trading. Moreover, open market operations in these securities are rapidly communicated throughout the credit market by the mechanism of the market itself, as well as through their effect on bank reserves". (*The Federal Reserve System . . . loc. cit.*, p. 40.) In Denmark, on the other hand, open market operations are undertaken chiefly in long term government securities.

(2) If we denote the price of a fixed interest security by k, the nominal rate of interest (per cent) by z, the effective rate of interest (the yield) r will be:

$$(*) \qquad r = \frac{z}{k} \cdot 100$$

For example, if $k = 80$ and $z = 4$, $r = 5$; if the price is at par, i.e. $k = 100$, then $r = z$; if the price is above par, i.e. $k > 100$, $r < z$; if the price is below par, i.e. $k < 100$, $r > z$.

With a given nominal rate of interest the yield is inversely proportional to the price.

The above equation enables us to state all changes in the price of the security in terms of changes in the effective rate of interest.

market operations thus not only have a *quantity effect* but also a *rate of interest effect* and hence influence the demand for credit. We have referred to these relationships briefly in Vol. II, when we discussed the liquidity preference theory of interest,[1] and now have to discuss them in greater detail.

The price of a fixed interest security on any given day is determined by the prevailing supply and demand for it. In Fig. 5, *DD'* is the demand curve, *SS'* the supply curve of a long-term security,

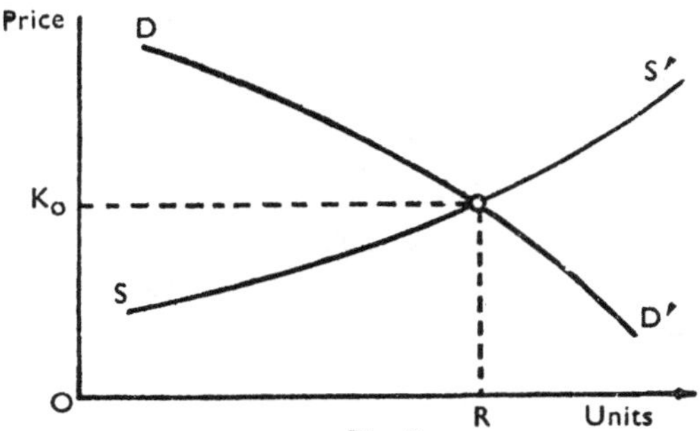

Fig. 5

k_0 the corresponding equilibrium price, and *OR* the number of securities traded at that equilibrium price. The suppliers wish to trade the security for money, that is, to exchange a less liquid claim for a highly liquid one; the buyers wish to do the opposite. The suppliers have a preference for money and the buyers a preference for the security—the strength of these preferences will naturally vary with the price of the security. The fact that transactors wish to change the composition of their assets in this way means that they are not satisfied with the present composition of this part of their assets. There may be various reasons for this. For example, a household might wish to sell a security in order to acquire money to finance a large purchase, or because it expects such a fall in the price of the security that it appears advantageous to hold money (an interest-free claim) instead of the security. Another household might buy securities in order to invest its excess cash holdings. A commercial bank might buy securities in order to acquire interest-earning assets, or sell securities for speculative reasons, or in order to acquire cash. In all these cases the dispositions of the public and of the commercial banks reflect their relative preference for money and for interest-yielding securities, that is for liquid and less liquid claims.

We have shown in Vol. II that the prevailing preferences for a fixed

(1) See Vol. II, Ch. IV, Section B, § 4.

interest security of *both* buyers *and* sellers may be expressed in one single demand curve, which is composed by adding the curve of new demand to the curve of reserve demand. Using this *single* demand curve—which expresses both supply *and* demand conditions—we can obtain the equilibrium price of the security from the following theorem, which we also derived in Vol. II:

The price of a security on any day is determined by the prevailing preferences—as expressed by the summation of the curve of new

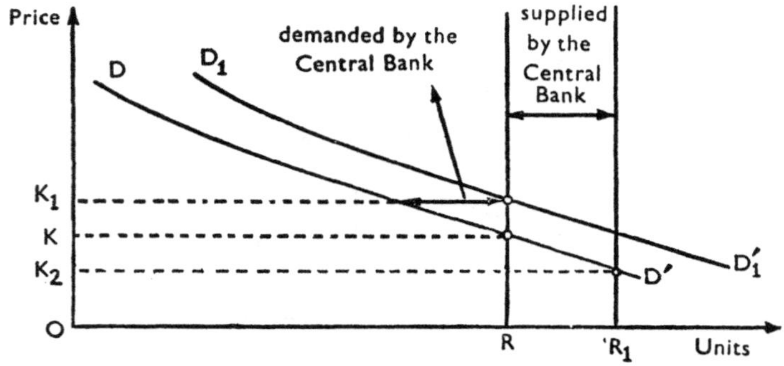

Fig. 6

demand and the curve of reserve demand—together with the quantity (units) of the security available.

Let us assume that on a given day only the commercial banks and the public enter the market as buyers and sellers of the security. According to the theorem just stated a certain price of the security would be established. In Fig. 6 DD' denotes the sum of new and reserve demand of the public and the commercial banks on a particular day. OR is the quantity of the security held by the public and the commercial banks. The equilibrium price of the security, and hence the long term rate of interest, will be given by OK.

If the central bank, pursuing an expansionary open market policy, enters the market on that day as a buyer, new demand will be increased by the amount the central bank demands. The curve DD' will shift upwards and assume a position such as D_1D_1'.[1] As can be seen

[1] If the central bank buys a certain number of securities (irrespective of their price) the curve DD' will shift parallel to the right by the number of units demanded by the central bank. However, if the central bank intends to buy securities for a total sum of £a, its demand curve will be of the form:

$$k \,.\, x = a,$$

where k is the price and x the number of securities demanded. In this case the central bank's demand curve will be of unit elasticity, and the curve DD' will also shift to the right but the shift will not be a parallel one.

from Fig. 6, the purchase of securities by the central bank raises the equilibrium price to OK_1, and thus correspondingly reduces the yield. The central bank's open market policy has not only increased the liquidity of the banks and the public, but at the same time has brought about a reduction in the long term rate of interest.

Conversely, if the central bank, pursuing a contractionary open market policy, enters the market to sell a given amount of securities, the result will be as follows: the quantity available on the market increases by RR_1 (Fig. 6) and as a result the equilibrium price of the security falls to OK_2, i.e. the long-term rate of interest rises (assuming unchanged preferences on the part of the public and the commercial banks for the security in question). Besides reducing the quantity of cash in the commercial banking system, the central bank has brought about a rise in the long term rate of interest. It is important to understand that the central bank is in a position to influence the level of the rate of interest *without suspending the free determination of prices on the security market*. The central bank can do this simply because it can enter the market as buyer or seller, and because it is not subject to any limitations regarding the size of its sales and purchases.

These changes in the long term rate of interest affect in the first instance those securities which are the subject of open market operations. The yields on other long term securities will, however, adjust to these changes as a result of arbitrage, so that we may speak of *the* (uniform) market rate of interest. Moreover, since there is a fairly close positive correlation between all kinds of interest rates as we shall see (Section (iii) of this paragraph), we may simply speak of a rate of interest which represents the *general level of interest rates*. This is equivalent to assuming that there is only *one* kind of interest-bearing claim in the economy.

On this assumption we can express the results so far established in yet another way which will be particularly useful in our subsequent discussion. Here our analysis will again link up with that in Vol. II.

$(ii)_4$. Consider the assets of a particular transactor, such as a household, a firm or a commercial bank. Among them we shall find at any one time a certain stock of money and a certain stock of interest-yielding securities. The ratio between the amounts of these two types of assets will vary through time. Now the question arises as to why a transactor should keep any money at all, i.e. why he should keep a stock of assets which yield no interest when he can always acquire interest-yielding claims. The next question is, what factors determine the prevailing distribution of monetary assets between interest-yielding and interest-free claims?

It is clear that each household, each firm and each commercial bank requires a certain stock of money to meet current transactions. The amount of money which an economic unit requires to settle its current transactions is called its *transactions balance*. The size of an economic unit's transactions balance depends on the time distribution and the size of its receipts and expenditures. The size of receipts and expenditures is related to the level of income. Assuming given payment habits and a given price level, we can, therefore, regard the size of transactions balances of all households, firms and commercial banks taken together, as a function of the level of national income (measured in money terms.)[1] Given constant payments habits, the higher the level of national income the higher will be the transactions holdings of the private sector. The amount of money L_T which the private sector wishes to hold for transactions purposes at any time is thus a rising function of national income Y:

$$L_T = L_T(Y) \tag{18}$$

In a stationary economy, the stock of money available at any time would always equal transactions holdings, since economic units would have no reason to hold money for any other than transactions purposes. The situation, however, is different in a non-stationary economy.

To begin with, in such an economy unforeseen expenditures may occur. Unexpected price increases, or changes in tastes, or the occurrence of other unforeseeable events, may give rise to expenditures which would not be included in an estimate of transactions holdings based solely on foreseeable expenditures and receipts. For this reason, transactors will wish to hold a certain additional amount of liquid assets, *as a precaution* against unforeseen expenditures. Here the question arises regarding the form in which transactors in the private sector will wish to hold these additional monetary assets, i.e. whether they will wish to hold them in the form of interest-yielding or interest-free claims. As a rule, transactors will prefer interest-free to interest-yielding (less liquid) claims, so as to be able to meet unforeseen expenditures immediately. It is also possible that they may wish to keep these assets wholly or partly in the form of interest-yielding claims, if they believe that a possible sale of these claims will not entail a capital loss. Precautionary holdings are thus intermediate between those kept purely for transactions purposes and those kept purely for speculative purposes. Without limiting the applicability of our analysis we can include both precautionary and speculative

(1) We now group all households, firms and commercial banks into one *private sector*.

holdings in one category of monetary assets, namely those kept in addition to the assets required for purely transactions purposes.

Let us now consider why transactors in the private sector of a non-stationary economy keep *monetary wealth for speculative purposes. If we exclude the possibility of speculation in goods,* the reason must lie in the expectations regarding interest rates, i.e. the price of the interest-yielding security. Depending on these expectations transactors will appear on the market as buyers or sellers of securities. The higher the rate of interest, i.e. the lower the price of securities, the more the public and the banks will be inclined to buy interest-yielding claims, i.e. to exchange speculative holdings of money for securities. In other words, their preference for securities increases and their preference for money, their so-called liquidity preference, decreases. Indeed, it is possible that some transactors will find it profitable to borrow short from the banks in order to buy securities, if the expected price rise is sufficiently great. When the rate of interest is low, i.e. the price of securities high, transactors will have a high *liquidity preference.* This is so, not only because the loss in interest incurred through holding cash is small, but also because they must take into account the possibility of a fall in price which may outweigh the earning of interest. If there are no expectations of a price fall, i.e. of a future rise in the rate of interest when the rate of interest is low, the desire to exchange cash holdings (which exceed transactions requirements) for interest-yielding securities will be greater than when there are expectations of a price fall.

Let us consider the state of affairs on a particular day. In the morning, each transactor in the private sector holds a certain amount of cash and (or) interest-yielding securities. If we subtract the amount held for transactions purposes from the total stock of cash we obtain the amount which is carried over from the preceding day and which was kept for speculative purposes. Depending on the prevalent subjective preferences for securities and money, some transactors will wish to sell interest-yielding securities on certain terms, i.e. demand cash; and others will wish to buy interest-yielding securities on certain terms, i.e. supply money.

The supply and demand conditions for interest-yielding securities, i.e. the supply and demand conditions for money, determine the rate of interest (the price of the security) on this particular day. We have shown that the supply and demand conditions for interest-yielding securities can be expressed in one single curve, which indicates the sum of new demand and reserve demand. This curve together with the total stock of securities available in the private sector determines the rate of interest (see pp. 69–70).

Instead of using the supply and demand conditions for interest-yielding securities we can also use the corresponding demand and supply conditions for central bank money. In other words, we can use the curve representing the sum of new demand and reserve demand for central bank money.(1) The theorem we have stated above (p. 70) can also be expressed in the following way:

The rate of interest is determined by the curve showing the sum of new demand and reserve demand for central bank money for speculative purposes, together with the amount of central bank money available for these purposes on the particular day.

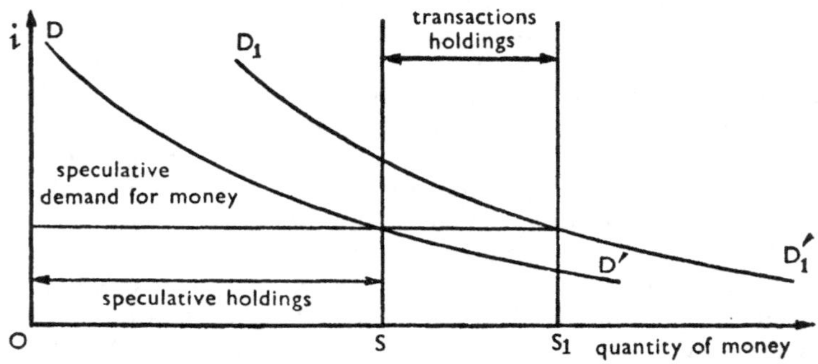

Fig. 7

If we denote the curve of the sum of new and reserve speculative demand for money as the *curve of liquidity preference proper*(2) we can also express the above theorem as follows:

the rate of interest on any day is determined by the private sector's curve of liquidity preference proper and the amount of central bank money available for speculative purposes;

or:

the rate of interest on any day will be such that the private sector's speculative demand for central bank money is just equal to the amount of central bank money available for these purposes (Fig. 7);

(1) In Vol. II we showed in detail how the demand curve (supply curve) for money can be derived from the corresponding supply curve (demand curve) for interest-yielding securities. (See Ch. IV, Section B, § 4.

Since we have grouped households, firms and commercial banks in one single "private sector", this sector can obviously generate a demand for central bank money only.

(2) So called by G. Haberler (*Prosperity and Depression*, 3rd edn. 1941, p. 210.)

or finally:

the rate of interest will always be such that transactors in the private sector willingly hold the total amount of "speculative" balances and the amount of interest-yielding securities available in the private sector.

If we add the transactions demand for central bank money (which depends solely on the level of national income) to the speculative demand, the curve *DD'* will shift to the right by the amount of the transactions demand (which is constant on any one day) (Fig. 7). If we further assume that actual transactions holdings are always equal to desired transactions holdings (which is a realistic assumption) the available quantity of money simultaneously increases by the amount of the transactions holdings, so that the rate of interest remains unchanged. Thus, on our assumptions it does not matter whether or not we include the transactions demand for central bank money in our analysis. Our theorem, therefore, can also be stated in the following way (*major theorem*):

the rate of interest is determined by the private sector's total demand for central bank money (for transactions and speculative purposes) together with the total amount of central bank money available in the private sector (Fig. 7);

or:

the rate of interest is determined by the total liquidity preference in the private sector together with the total quantity of money;[1]

or:

the rate of interest on any day will be such that transactors in the private sector willingly hold the available total quantity of central bank money, i.e. that no transactor has reason to engage in further exchanges of interest-yielding claims for interest-free claims, or vice versa.

The following propositions, which we also pointed out in Vol. II, follow directly from our analysis:

given the quantity of central bank money, a rise (fall) in liquidity preference leads to a rise (fall) in the rate of interest.

[1] When deriving these propositions in Vol. II we did not distinguish between the transactions and speculative demand for money, because this distinction was not necessary there.

Given liquidity preference, a larger (smaller) quantity of central bank money will be absorbed only at a lower (higher) rate of interest.

If there are several interest-yielding securities with differing yields the following proposition correspondingly applies:

the level of interest rates on any day is determined by the private sector's total demand for central bank money and the available quantity of money (or: by the demand for interest-yielding claims and the available quantities of the different kinds of claims.)

It is difficult to illustrate this theorem geometrically, and for this reason we shall maintain the assumption that there is only one rate of interest.[1]

(ii)$_5$. Our theorems yield a number of conclusions which are important in appraising open market policy. In order to establish these conclusions it is useful to state our major theorem in terms of an equation. Let L_s denote the private sector's liquidity preference proper (the demand for central bank money for speculative purposes), which depends on the rate of interest:

$$L_s = L_s(i), \tag{19}$$

where i denotes the rate of interest (as a fraction).

We obtain the private sector's total liquidity preference by adding (18) and (19):

$$L = L_T(Y) + L_s(i). \tag{20}$$

It is a function of national income and the rate of interest, which we can also write in the form:

$$L = L(Y, i). \tag{21}$$

If the quantity of central bank money in the private sector equals M, the rate of interest will be such as to satisfy the equation:[2]

$$L(Y, i) = M \tag{22}$$

[1] For further justification of this assumption, see pp. 87–88.

[2] If we postulate the existence of money illusion, we have

$$L = L(P, Y_r, i).$$

If Y_r denotes real income, equation (22) will take the following form in the absence of money illusion:

$$P \,.\, L(Y_r, i) = M$$

or:

$$L(Y_r, i) = \frac{M}{P}$$

in which P denotes the price index and $\frac{M}{P}$ the real value of the quantity of money.

We can easily state the form of the function (20) or (21). As we know, $L_s(i)$ is a rising function as i falls (Fig. 8). The transactions demand for money $L_T(Y)$ depends solely on the level of income;

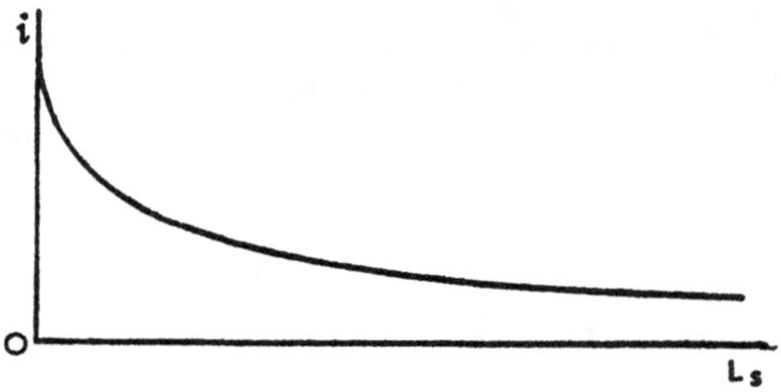

Fig. 8

it rises with the level of income. We assume $L_T(Y)$ to be completely interest inelastic.[1] Figure 9 shows the size of the demand for transactions balances at various levels of income, where $Y_1 < Y_2$

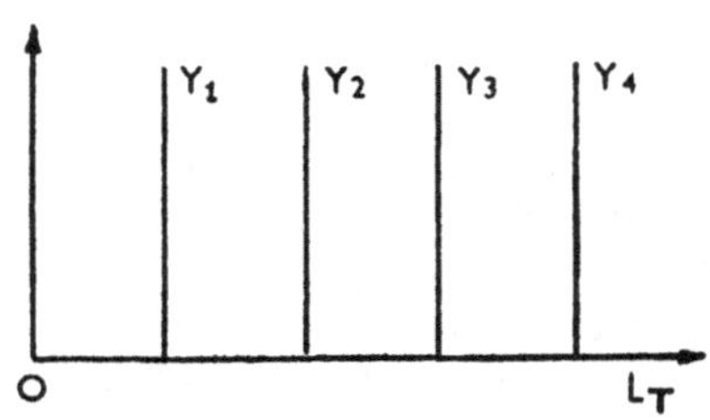

Fig. 9

$< Y_3 < Y_4$. If we add the demand for transactions holdings at various levels of Y to the demand for speculative holdings (L_s), i.e. to the curve shown in Fig. 8, we obtain the family of curves shown

(1) It is possible that at high rates of interest the transactions demand is no longer completely interest inelastic, but falls with a rising rate of interest. Even though the level of income remains unchanged, there may be attempts to "save" on transactions holdings, in order to invest in interest-yielding securities. This means that the same level of income is financed with smaller transactions holdings, which is identical to saying that the income velocity of circulation rises (see Vol. I). The curves drawn parallel to the interest axis in figure 9 would bend slightly to the left if the rate of interest reached a certain (high) level. In place of equation (18) we would then have the equation

$$L_T = L_T(Y, i).$$

in Fig. 10. These curves represent the total demand for money (demand for transactions and speculative holdings) as a function of the rate of interest at various alternative values of national income. As can be seen, the curvature of these curves is determined solely by the curvature of the demand curve for speculative holdings. Thus the form of the liquidity preference curve is determined by the elasticity of the speculative demand with respect to the rate of interest at various alternative rates of interest. Now, it is obvious that the

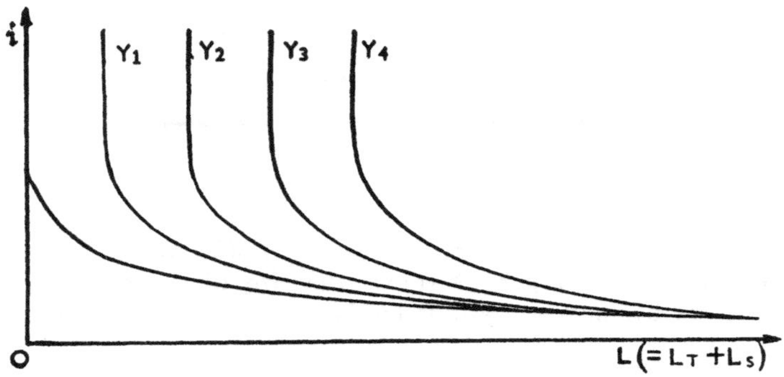

Fig. 10

speculative demand for central bank money will not only be very high at a low rate of interest, i.e. at a high price of securities, but will also be highly elastic with respect to that rate of interest. If the price of the securities is already high one must take into account the possibility of a fall in price which would greatly outweigh the interest yield.[1] Holders of the security will thus be inclined to sell, and holders of speculative balances will prefer to hold cash rather than buy securities. The new and reserve demand for speculative balances will thus be particularly elastic at a low rate of interest, and the curve representing the L_s function will generally have the form drawn in Fig. 8. Indeed, special cases are conceivable, which we shall discuss later, in which the speculative demand for central bank money becomes perfectly elastic at a certain low rate of interest, i.e. the L_s curve becomes parallel to the L_s-axis. In this case (Fig. 11) an increase in the quantity of central bank money from OM to OM_1, by way of expansionary open market operations, will not bring about a fall in the rate of interest. The private sector will simply absorb the whole

[1] If someone buys a 4% security at par price and the price falls to 80 after three years, the resulting capital loss of 20 exceeds the interest yield of 12 by 8. If he buys a 2% security at par price, and the price falls to 80 after two years, the resulting capital loss is 20, which exceeds the interest yield of 4 by 16.

additional cash MM_1 in its speculative holdings without any change in the rate of interest, and a relatively small fall (rise) in the rate of

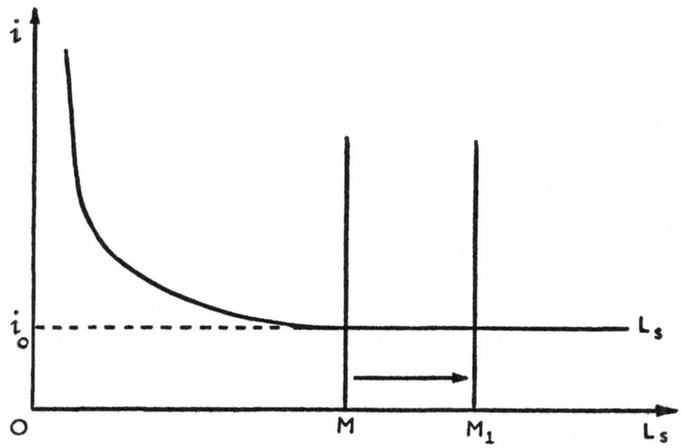

Fig. 11

interest may be associated with a considerable increase (decrease) in the available quantity of credit. When the liquidity function is perfectly elastic open market operations only have a quantity effect.

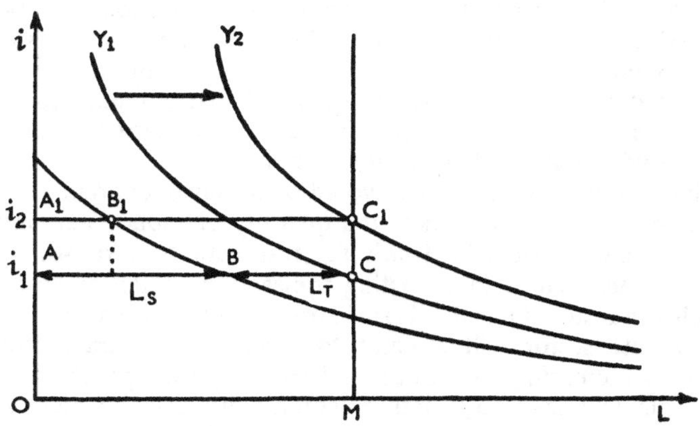

Fig. 12

Let us consider a given liquidity preference situation at a certain level of income Y_1. If the quantity of central bank money in the private sector is M, the rate of interest will be at i_1 (Fig. 12). AB of the total quantity of money will be held as speculative balances and BC as transactions balances.

Now let us assume that national income rises to Y_2 in the course of an expansionary process. Liquidity preference proper, i.e. the L_s curve, remains unchanged, but transactions demand in the private sector will rise, so that the total liquidity preference curve will shift upwards (to position Y_2 in Fig. 12). If the quantity of money remains unchanged, this shift will lead to a rise in the rate of interest to i_2, as can be seen immediately from Fig. 12. At this higher rate of interest transactors in the private sector wish to keep only A_1B_1 for speculative purposes; and the difference between the previous and present speculative demand ($AB - A_1B_1$) is made available for transactions purposes. This money is made available for transactions purposes as a result of transactors selling securities in order to acquire more cash for transactions purposes. However, given unchanged liquidity preference proper, they can only sell these securities if they accept a lower price. The fall in the price of securities i.e. the rise in the rate of interest, thus induces a transfer of money from speculative to transactions balances. This re-shuffling of the stock of interest-yielding claims in the private sector will continue until their price is such that, from the given stock of money, the amount available for transactions purposes just meets the demand at the higher level of income Y_2. We can also express this in the following way: the rise in the level of income renders the previous transactions balances too small, and a "struggle" for additional transactions balances ensues. Given the quantity of money, these additional balances can only be obtained at the cost of speculative holdings, and this in turn requires that the buyers of securities be offered a higher rate of interest. The rate of interest will continue to rise until transactors willingly hold the available quantity of money.

It is interesting to analyse what would be the effect of an increased transactions demand for money, the quantity of money remaining constant, if money were held *only* for transactions purposes. For example, let us assume that existing transactions balances become too small as a result of a general rise in prices. In this case transactors in the private sector will attempt to increase their transactions balances by increasing their sales, and reducing their purchases, of goods. This will lead to a fall in commodity prices which will continue until transactions balances are regarded as adequate. In his classic work "*Interest and Prices*" (London, 1936), which is the origin of modern developments in monetary theory, K. Wicksell has described this process with unsurpassable clarity:

"Now let us suppose that for some reason or other commodity prices rise while the stock of money remains unchanged. . . . The cash balances will gradually appear to be *too small in relation to the new level of prices*. . . . I therefore seek to enlarge my balance. This can only be done—neglecting for the present the possibility of borrowing etc.—through a *reduction* in my *demand* for goods and services, or through an *increase* in the *supply* of my own commodity . . . or through both together. The same is true of all other owners and consumers of commodities. But in fact nobody will succeed in realising the object at which each is aiming—to increase his cash

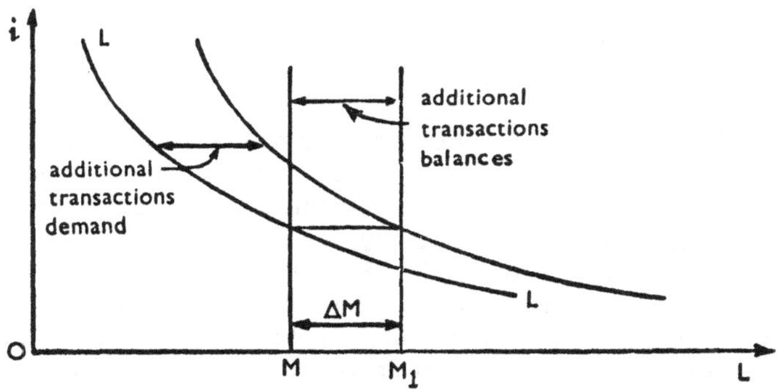

Fig. 13

balance; for the sum of individual cash balances is limited by the amount of the available stock of money, or rather is identical with it. On the other hand, the universal reduction in demand and increase in supply of commodities will necessarily bring about a continuous fall in all prices. This can only cease when prices have fallen to the level at which the cash balances are regarded as *adequate*".[1]

We have seen that, given unchanged liquidity preference proper and an unchanged quantity of central bank money, a rise in transactions demand leads to a rise in the rate of interest. It is obvious that the central bank can always prevent this rise in the rate of interest by means of an expansionary open market policy. All it need do is to increase the quantity of central bank money in the private sector by an amount equal to the additional demand for transactions holdings (Fig. 13). The bank can do this by buying the requisite amount of fixed-interest securities.[2] Now there is no need to transfer money from speculative balances, and there will be no rise

[1] K. Wicksell, loc. cit., pp. 39–40.

[2] The open market sale or purchase of fixed-interest securities by the government will have the same effect. For present purposes it is therefore useful to include the government and the central bank in one sector.

in the rate of interest, since the additional demand for money is exactly matched by an additional supply.

When an increase in the demand for transactions holdings is accompanied by a simultaneous reduction in liquidity preference proper, i.e. by a shift downwards of the L_s curve, the additional demand for transactions holdings might be met without any change in the rate of interest, even though the quantity of central bank money remains unchanged. Similarly, an increased demand for transactions holdings might be accompanied by an increase in liquidity preference proper. In this case the resulting rise in the rate of interest would be greater than when the L_s curve remains unchanged.

(ii)$_6$. We must draw attention to a number of important points which will be relevant to our subsequent considerations. The theorem—"The rate of interest is determined by liquidity preference in the private sector and the quantity of central bank money"—only indicates the *immediate* determinants of the rate of interest. These immediate determinants, i.e. the demand for money and the quantity of money, are indeed purely monetary. Yet it is important to observe that *it does not follow from this that the rate of interest, i.e. the reward for parting with liquidity, is ultimately a purely monetary phenomenon.* We have seen that liquidity preference in the private sector is a function of the level of income and the rate of interest and that, given the quantity of money, the level of income and the rate of interest must be such as to satisfy equation (22). But we obviously need two equations in order to determine two variables; the level of income and the rate of interest must be determined simultaneously. We have to know the nature of the second equation, and the factors determining it, before we can decide whether the rate of interest is a purely monetary phenomenon, in the sense of being determined by purely monetary magnitudes and factors. We shall return to this problem in Chapter III.

The second point is this: *given the quantity of central bank money*, equation (22) represents a relationship between national income and the rate of interest. Given liquidity preference proper and a given stock of central bank money, a rise in national income is associated with a rise in the rate of interest, as can be seen from Fig. 10.

Figure 10 shows that the curve describing the relationship between Y and i will have the form shown in Fig. 14. It is also obvious from (22) that the curve A_1B_1 which corresponds to a larger quantity of money will lie below the curve AB (Fig. 14).

In conclusion we must emphasize again that we grouped commercial banks, firms and households into one "private sector" when we derived the demand function for money. This sector's demand function thus related exclusively to central bank money. We could, of course, split up the private sector into smaller aggregates, e.g. into commercial banks and non-banks, and introduce the banks' and non-banks' liquidity functions explicitly. We should then have to take account the commercial banks' demand for central bank money for transactions and speculative purposes, and the non-banking sector's demand for central bank money and deposit money for the

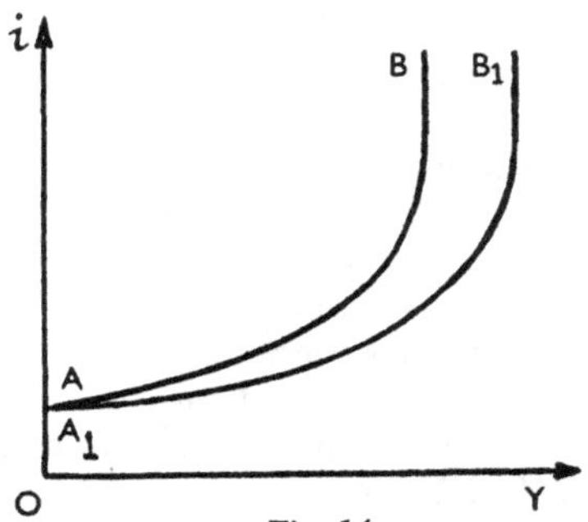

Fig. 14

same purpose. However, on the basis of the minimum reserve ratio we can derive the commercial banks' demand for central bank money from the non-banking sector's demand for deposit money. When discussing the rate of interest we can thus restrict ourselves to the demand for central bank money on the part of transactors outside the central bank.[1]

(iii) CENTRAL BANK DISCOUNT AND LENDING POLICY

(iii)$_1$. A commercial bank's customer can acquire money by discounting a bill with it. A commercial bank can similarly acquire central bank money by re-discounting bills with the central bank, provided (a) the central bank is willing to re-discount, and (b) provided the commercial bank is willing to pay the re-discount rate demanded by the central bank (*the so-called bank rate*). The terms

[1] Regarding this problem see especially the discussion between Bent Hansen and Jörgen Pedersen in the Danish *Nationalökonomisk Tidsskrift* 1946, Vol. 84, p. 30 ff. and 150 ff.

See also, B. Kragh, *Prisbildningen på Kreditmarknaden*, Uppsala 1951 (an English summary of this author's main ideas is now available in Vol. V of *International Economic Papers*, London 1956), and R. Turvey, "Consistency and Consolidation in the Theory of Interest", *Economica*, Vol. 21, 1954.

on which the central bank is willing to re-discount bills comprise *central bank discount policy*. Discount policy thus consists in (a) setting the discount rate, and (b) laying down what bills are to be eligible for re-discount.

The terms on which the central bank is willing to lend to the commercial banks comprise *central bank lending policy*. For example, the central bank determines what sort of paper it will accept as security for loans.

(iii)$_2$. When a commercial bank re-discounts a bill with the central bank, it sells the bill on the terms laid down by the central bank, but it remains liable to the central bank until the bill is redeemed. Thus, as was pointed out earlier, the re-discounting of a bill gives rise to a debt to the central bank just as does the taking of a loan. In both cases the commercial bank incurs debts to the central bank. *The re-discounting of a bill leaves the bank's net credit with the central bank unchanged just as does the taking of a loan.*

(iii)$_3$. It is clear from what has been said that the nature of discount and lending policy is entirely different from that of minimum reserve and open market policy. In the case of minimum reserve and open market policy, the central bank exercises a direct influence on the cash reserves, and hence on the lending potential, of the commercial banks. When the central bank buys gold, foreign exchange or securities from the banks and (or) from the public, the banks obtain central bank money *unconditionally*, and their net credit with the central bank increases. If the central bank reduces the minimum reserve ratio the banks obtain additional excess reserves unconditionally. *In these cases the amount of central bank money in the commercial banking system is altered solely at the initiative of the central bank.* In the case of discount and lending policy the central bank only stipulates the *terms* on which it will grant short term credit to the banks. *The commercial banks alone decide whether, and to what extent, they will take up credit on these terms and thus increase their holdings of central bank money.* The central bank can no more force the commercial banks to incur debts to it than the commercial banks can force the public to take loans from them. In the case of minimum reserve and open market policy the banks obtain excess reserves solely at the initiative of the central bank; in the case of discount and lending policy, the banks must turn to the central bank, which stipulates its own terms.

(iii)$_4$. Let us assume that discount policy is the only instrument of credit policy available to the central bank, as was the case with the German Reichsbank until 1933, and also in other countries earlier on. Since the commercial banks alone decide to what extent they wish to make use of the central bank's re-discount facilities, it would appear that the central bank loses all control over the quantity of money in the economy. In this connection Keynes made the following comment in his *A Treatise on Money* which appeared in 1930: "Since the Member Banks were not tied by reserve ratios and were not prevented from freely re-discounting with the Central Banks whenever they wanted to expand their resources, the control exercised over them by the Central Bank was very imperfect, the main limitation on credit expansion by the member Banks being set by their supply of bills eligible for re-discount . . . the Reichbank in particular . . . has an altogether inadequate control over its member Banks . . .".[1]

Let us consider these relationships in greater detail. Suppose the central bank is prepared to buy any amount of three months' bills at a certain discount rate, and that at this rate the commercial banks hand in more (fewer) bills for re-discount than the central bank regards as desirable. In such a case the central bank could raise (lower) the re-discount rate in order to deter (stimulate) borrowing and hence money creation by the commercial banks. In fact, it used to be believed that the central bank could reduce or expand the volume of credit simply by "turning the discount screw".[2] Yet it is clear that a change in the discount rate cannot have a *direct* influence on the volume of credit. Money is created in this case on the basis of prior credit creation in the private sector in the form of new three months' bills. The central bank, however, has no direct influence on the extent to which new bills are issued in the private sector and brought for discount to the commercial banks. The extent to which new bills are issued in the private sector depends solely on the extent to which firms are willing to incur short-term debts. The rate which firms take into account in this connection, however, is not bank rate, but the rate which commercial banks charge for short-term credit. If the proposition—"a high (low) bank rate deters (stimulates) the creation of money by the commercial banks"—is to have any validity at all there must be a direct connection between changes in bank rate and changes in the rates which commercial banks charge for short-term credits. The commercial banks must vary their short-term rates in sympathy with the central bank's discount rate. This is a *necessary* condition for the effectiveness

[1] J. M. Keynes, *A Treatise on Money*, Vol. II, pp. 233–34.

[2] "When the note issuing bank raises its discount rate, fewer bills will be discounted; when the discount rate is reduced, more bills will be brought for re-discount" (R. v. Strigl, *Einführung in die Grundlagen der Nationalökonomie*, Vienna 1937, pp. 135–36).

of discount policy. In Germany the banks behaved in this way. Figure 15 shows the close positive correlation between the Reichbank's discount rate and the rate for current account credits during the period 1924–1940. Essentially the same situation prevailed in other countries. Yet the reason for such behaviour on the part of the

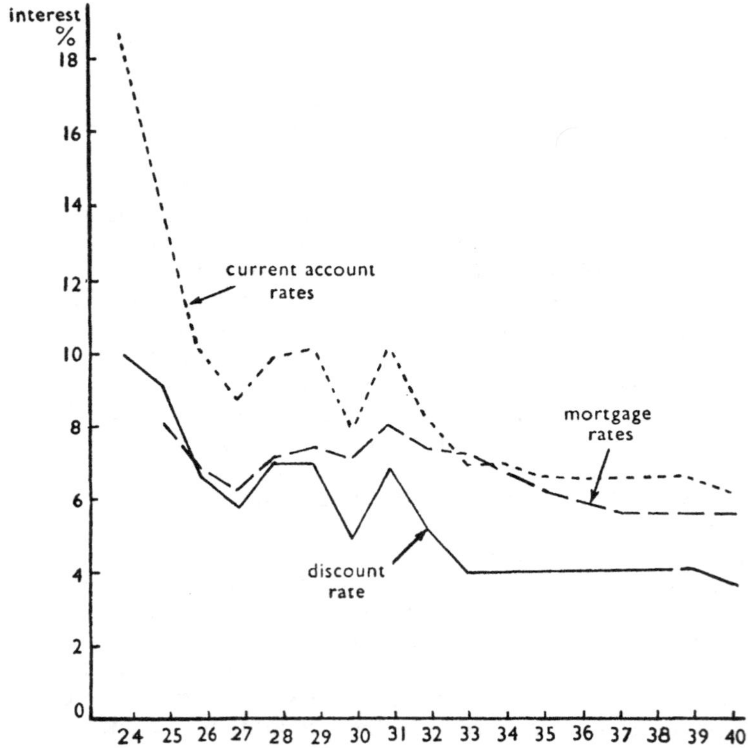

Fig. 15

banks is merely habit and convention. As regards England, D. H. Robertson observes:—"... the chief proximate cause impelling them to raise their rates seems to be the force of long-established custom—the knowledge that that is the course of action expected of them by the Bank of England, and our implicit confidence that the Bank of England does not act without good reason".[(1)] It must be emphasized that the banks are not forced to behave in this way. If the banks have

[(1)] D. H. Robertson, *Money*, 4th edition, p. 161.

sufficient free cash they *need not* raise their short-term rates when the central bank raises its discount rate. If they do so, they do it only for the reasons given in the quotation from D. H. Robertson.

There is also a very close relationship between bank rate and money market rates. Money market rates may lie below or above bank rate depending on the degree of ease or stringency in the money market. As was explained above[(1)], the size of the fluctuations of money market rates around bank rate can be mitigated by appropriate open market operations in money-market paper. Thus all short term rates move in sympathy with the central bank's discount rate.

The automatic reaction of banks and the money market to changes in bank rate is, nevertheless, not a *sufficient* condition for the effectiveness of discount policy as a means of bringing about an expansion or contraction in the quantity of money. A rise (fall) in the rates which banks charge for short-term credit need not automatically reduce (increase) the demand for credit by firms. Fluctuations of 1 or 2% in short-term credit rates will hardly influence the firms' short-run investment decisions. However, we must inquire whether a change in the short-term rate of interest may bring about a change in the same direction in the long-term rate of interest and in this way initiate an expansion or contraction in the volume of credit. This sort of relationship between changes in the short-term rate and changes in the long-term rate can in fact be observed, if the change in in the short-term rate is maintained for a certain length of time. Experience shows that in free credit markets the direction, although not necessarily the extent, of changes in the short-term rate is transmitted to the long-term rate. (The reader should compare the curve of mortgage rates with that of rates for current account credits in Fig. 15.[(2)]) This fact can easily be explained, but we shall merely refer the reader to Keynes' detailed treatment of this problem.[(3)] For

(1) See p. 67.

(2) He might also compare the curves of short- and long-term interest rates in the United States reproduced by J. M. Keynes in his *A Treatise on Money*, Vol. II, pp. 352–54.

(3) J. M. Keynes, *A Treatise on Money*, Vol. II, chapter 37. See also: "*The Federal Reserve System . . .*", *loc. cit.* pp. 40 and 144. "Long-term rates generally rise when short-term rates rise and decline when short-term rates decline. The tighter or easier credit conditions that accompany changes in business activity are generally felt directly in both long and short-term fields. The reason is that, for some lenders, the long-term markets for credit are competitive with the short-term markets. While short- and long-term rates generally move together, the change in long-term rates is ordinarily smaller than that in short-term rates. Lenders generally expect extreme levels of short-term rates to prevail for only a short period of time. Since the current yield on

our purpose it is sufficient to indicate the relevant historical experience. Yet, it should be noted that these facts in no way express a necessary relationship, but are the result of a particular kind of behaviour on the part of the commercial banks. In our theoretical analyses, as in our treatment of the liquidity theory of interest in the previous section, we speak of changes in *the* rate of interest instead of referring to changes in interest *rates*. The positive correlation between short and long-term interest rates justifies this procedure.[(1)]

The fact that a fall (rise) in the short-term interest rate affects the long-term rate in the same direction does not mean that a fall (rise) in the long-term interest rate necessarily leads to an expansion (contraction) in the volume of credit. Firms take up long-term credits in order to carry out long-term investments. The extent to which long-term credits are taken up thus depends on the firms' inclination to invest. However, as we showed in volume II in our discussion of the long-term plans of firms, the long-term rate of interest is only one of many factors which affect the investment decisions of firms. Experience shows that there are conditions in which a high rate of interest does not deter, and a low one does not stimulate, investment by firms.

It follows from what has been said that, *by itself, central bank discount policy is a most inadequate means of regulating the volume of credit.* It is simply not the case that a low discount rate, via its effects on short-term rates charged by the banks and on the long-term rate, automatically leads to an expansion in the amount of money, or that a high discount rate automatically leads to a contraction in the quantity of money. *Unlike minimum reserve and open market policy, discount policy by itself does not guarantee the*

---

long-term securities will be received until the maturity of the security, a relatively small change in long-term rates will restore the competitive relationship".

Compare also R. S. Sayers, *Modern Banking*, 5th edition, Oxford, 1960, Chapter VII.

(1) The period from 1952 to 1954 in the U.S.A. offers an excellent example of how quickly movements in short-term interest rates can be transmitted to the rates in all other credit markets. "The movement in interest rates spread throughout the credit market affecting all types of credit paper and securities although in different degrees". ("United States Monetary Policy: Recent Thinking and Experience" p. 28.)

It is of course possible that for some reason a particular credit market may be affected only very slowly by movements in rates in other markets. In such cases the desired change in rates can be brought about quickly by means of open market operations in the paper of this market (loc. cit., pp. 25–26).

central bank's control over the commercial banks' lending potential.[1]

Nevertheless, *increases* in bank rate have usually led to reductions in the volume of credit; yet this cannot be explained in terms of the extent of the increase in bank rate. The reason rather is psychological. The banks regard a rise in bank rate as a signal that the central bank intends to pursue a policy of credit restriction; and the banks know that the central bank can always impose its will on them, although not necessarily by means of a further rise in bank rate. The bank can use other means. It can raise the requirements for bills eligible for re-discount or (and) impose re-discount ceilings.

(iii)$_5$. Discount policy can thus be made effective only in conjunction with other instruments of credit policy. In particular, discount policy can be used successfully *in support of a contractionary or expansionary open market policy*, and conversely, open market policy can be used in support of discount policy. A central bank which is able to employ open market policy can employ discount policy when it is pursuing a contractionary policy (i.e. reducing the amount of central bank money and simultaneously raising the long-term interest rate). In this case it can employ discount policy in order to prevent the commercial banks from frustrating its intentions by the re-discounting of bills. The Bank of England has successfully developed and employed the combination of discount and open market policy to bring about credit contraction. "The Bank of England uses both the weapons at its disposal in the following way: it employs open market policy to bring about greater stringency or ease in the money market. It only employs discount policy to prevent the banking system from undoing the effects of the Bank of England's open market policy, by recourse to the Bank's discount facilities. It does this by keeping the bank rate above market rates"[2]. "This pincer-like policy together with the bank's rigid cash ratios guarantees the power of the central bank in England".[3] Conversely, a reduction in bank rate can be used to support an expansionary open market policy. In this sense discount and open market policies are complementary.[4]

[1] "The experience of the last years . . . has clearly shown that an effective limitation of credit expansion in times of a strong boom is hardly possible unless the effect of raising interest rates is simultaneously supported by a certain pressure on the lending potential of the banks" (Report of the Bank deutscher Länder, 1955, p. 19.)

[2] F. Lutz, *Das Grundproblem der Geldverfassung*, Stuttgart and Berlin, 1936, p. 27. This work is especially recommended.

[3] F. Lutz, loc. cit., p. 29.

[4] See: O. Donner, "Über die Grundsätze der Geld- und Kreditpolitik in den Vereinigten Staaten", *Weltwirtschaftliches Archiv*, Vol. 69, 1952, p. 158 ff.

(iii)$_6$. The central bank can further influence the volume of credit by *announcements regarding credit policy*. For example, if the central bank announces that it intends at all costs to dampen an inflationary movement of prices by means of credit contraction, such an announcement will generally be effective. But in this case also there is only an indirect influence on the volume of credit, its extent depending on the behaviour of the commercial banks and the public.

(iii)$_7$. We have discussed the methods by which the central bank can influence the volume of credit. Of these the most powerful are minimum reserve and open market policy (supported by an appropriate discount policy) and the setting of re-discount ceilings. These instruments give the central bank unconditional control over the lending potential of the commercial banks and thus over the upper limit to the quantity of money in the economy. *Given payment habits, the central bank can determine this upper limit unequivocably.* As we have seen, discount policy *alone* does not give the central bank this control; it becomes effective only in conjunction with other instruments of credit policy.

(iii)$_8$. The central bank must not exercise arbitrary control over the quantity of money. Money is merely an instrument which facilitates the process of exchange in a market economy; hence the quantity available must be appropriate to the prevailing aims of economic policy. The central bank cannot by itself decide what quantity of money is appropriate or necessary at any given time. *Monetary-and-credit policy is merely a part of general economic policy. The central bank must provide that quantity of money required to attain the generally accepted aims of economic policy.* It follows, on the one hand, that the central bank must not be subject to restrictions which may impede or render impossible the attainment of the major aims of economic policy, whether these aims be price stability and a high level of employment, or others. On the other hand, the central bank must not have the power to prevent the adoption of measures required for the attainment of the major aims of economic policy. What would be, from this point of view, the most appropriate constitution for the central bank, is a question we cannot discuss here since it would require a thorough analysis of the appropriate relationship between the government and the central bank. All that needs to be said for our purposes has been admirably stated by D. H. Robertson:

"Among the half-truths left us as a legacy by the Great Muddle is the doctrine that a banking system must at all costs be "independent of the Government". If this means that a bank cannot be administered as if it were a tax-collector's office, or that a banker must not be pestered by daily questions in Parliament as to why he lent money to John Smith and not to William Brown, well and good. But if it means that the monetary policy of a country should be carried on *in vacuo*, without reference to the problem of the development of the vast national estate, then it is a sterile and a dangerous doctrine indeed".[1] This is the position which nowadays is generally adopted in economic theory.

[1] *Money*, p. 179.

CHAPTER III

The Determinants of National Income and its Fluctuations

We now have at our disposal the tools necessary to enable us to examine the determinants of national income. These tools comprise the theoretical apparatus developed in the two preceding volumes and the theory of credit developed in the two preceding chapters.

1. Let us recall the way in which we looked at national income in Vol. I. We there presented an *ex post* analysis of national income, i.e. we determined in retrospect how high the level of income had been during the period, and then asked in what different ways this income could be looked at. We showed that national income could be regarded from three different points of view: from the earning side, from the output side and from the expenditure side. The analysis from these three different points of view led to a series of important relationships among the magnitudes which are relevant to the analysis of income. These relationships will play an important part in the examination of the problems to which we now turn. But in Vol. I we merely looked back at the *results* of economic activity in a given period, without asking what factors determined the level of income in that period. Specifically, we did not ask what were the factors which in any given period determined the size of the flow of consumer goods to households, the size of the flow of private investment, the size of the flow of goods and services accruing to the government, and the size of the export surplus (the difference between current exports and current imports). We must now consider the determinants of the level of income.

In contrast to the analysis in Vol. I, our analysis now will be of an *ex-ante* nature. This means that we ask, at the beginning of a year for example, what the year's income will be; and to answer this question we have to know the determinants of income. Similarly, it is impossible to answer questions about the causes of fluctuations in national income without a knowledge of the determinants of income.

2. As was shown in Vols. I and II, the determinants of national income are the dispositions of acting economic units. The dispositions

which are relevant to the determination of income are those which relate to the purchases of goods and services. The level of national income, and by the same token the level of employment, therefore depend upon the purchases of households, of firms and of the government. We thus have to show how the purchases of economic units determine the level of income, given certain economic data.

3. It would be possible to conduct this analysis (which necessarily is a general as opposed to a partial analysis) on a micro-economic basis. In other words, we could conduct the analysis in the same way as we analysed a stationary economy in Vol. II. However, our interest now centres on the determination of the national income, and this is a macro-economic magnitude; and we can simplify our analysis greatly by combining the millions of acting economic units into a small number of large groups. In what follows we shall mostly be dealing with an economy which is divided into three groups: households, private firms and the government. Even this simplified analysis will enable us to obtain important insights into the theory of income determination.

This sort of macro-economic general analysis obviously does not enable us to determine the incomes of individual economic units and other micro-economic variables. But the reader will realise that the reduction of a large number of relationships among micro-economic variables to a small number of relevant relationships among macro-economic variables will enable us to obtain an understanding of the process of income formation which simply could not be got in any other way. At the same time it must never be forgotten that behind the aggregates of total consumption, total investment etc., there are the millions of dispositions which are not considered in a general analysis carried out on a macro-economic basis. At this point the reader should recall the relevant comments made on pp. 58–61 in Vol. I, seventh edition.[1]

4. Our analysis of the determination of income will proceed mainly on the assumption of given productive capacity. At first, therefore (section A, §§ 1–8), we shall assume that the amount of net investment taking place in any period under consideration is very small in relation to the existing stock of capital. The theory of income determination which we are about to develop is therefore a short run theory. We shall present only the bare bones of the theory of long period income formation, i.e. the theory which explains changes in income over decades or longer (section A, § 9).

[1] Macro-economic analysis is as old as economic theory. Quesnay, Malthus and Marx had as good a command of it as any business cycle theorist. Every business cycle theory which we possess is a macro-economic theory.

Section A

THE CASE OF A CLOSED ECONOMY WITHOUT GOVERNMENT ACTIVITY

It was shown in Volume I that in any one period the income accruing to those participating in the productive process is generated (a) by firms, in the course of realizing their production decisions, and (b) by households, through direct purchases of services from non-firms (assuming no economic activity by the government). The factors determining the production decisions of firms (taken as a group), and thus the *ex ante* level of income generated by them, are (a) the level of *household consumption expected by firms* and (b) *intended net investment by firms*. The income generated by households is determined by their planned (intended) purchases from non-firms. Thus the *ex ante* income generated in any period by firms and households together consists of the sum of household consumption expected by firms, the net investment planned by firms, and the planned purchases of households from non-firms. Net investment is planned and realized by firms; it is therefore an action parameter of firms. The purchases by households from firms, however, are expectation parameters from the point of view of firms, whose actual value is determined by households. Similarly, the purchases by households from non-firms are planned and realized by households, and are thus an action parameter of households.[1] Since the actual consumption of households may be different from the level which firms had expected (and on which they based their production decisions), firms may experience surprises which lead them to alter their dispositions. This may be illustrated by a simple arithmetical example. Let us assume that at current prices the planned purchases by households from firms are £150; that firms expect consumption sales of £130 and plan to carry out net investment of £40. In this case, the *ex ante* national income will be £170. The distribution of this income between consumption and net investment, in accordance with the plans of firms, would require that households actually spent £130 on consumption. Only in this case would firms experience no surprises. However, since the actual consumption of households is £150, the actual net investment in the period (assuming unchanged prices) is only £20. The stocks of firms decline by £20, i.e. unintended

[1] In this connection it is important to understand the difference between *planned magnitudes* and *expected magnitudes*. The planned magnitudes of an economic unit are determined and realized by that economic unit, while its expected magnitudes are determined by other economic units.

disinvestment of £20 takes place. These connections will now have to be examined in greater detail. For the sake of simplicity let us first assume that intended investment by firms is positive and constant.

§1. The Case When Intended Net Investment is Positive and Given

1. It was shown in Vol. II[(1)] that, given the tastes of households, the total quantities of goods consumed by them depended on the prices of individual goods $p_1, p_2, \ldots, p_n$ and on the incomes $y_1, y_2, \ldots, y_m$ of the individual households. Thus the amount of consumption in monetary terms, C, is also a function of the prices of goods and of individual incomes:

$$C = C(p_1, p_2, \ldots, p_n; y_1, y_2, \ldots, y_m). \tag{1}$$

Let us now assume that the distribution of income among households depends on the level of national income, Y, in a specified way, and let us replace the series of individual prices of consumption goods by an index P representative of all these prices. If we do this, total consumption appears simply as a function of the "price" of consumption goods and of the national income:

$$C = f(P, Y). \tag{2}$$

Only with given prices can we regard consumption as a function of money income alone.

We must now discuss the properties of this function, i.e. we must ask in what way consumption depends on prices and on national income. The usual assumption is that the amount households wish to spend on consumption depends on the relationship of income to prices, that is on $\frac{Y}{P}$. Moreover, the relationship is assumed to be such that multiplication of Y *and* P by a positive number k will raise consumption k times. In this case equation (2) is of the form:

$$C = P \,.\, f\left(\frac{Y}{P}\right) \tag{3}$$

or

$$\frac{C}{P} = f\left(\frac{Y}{P}\right). \tag{4}$$

Now, $\frac{C}{P}$ is simply an index of real consumption, i.e. of the quantity

[(1)] Ch. I, § 7.

of goods, X, consumed by households (where X is an index which represents household real consumption of all sorts of goods[1]). Similarly $\frac{Y}{P}$ is the real income of households. The assumption which led to the relationship (4) therefore means that *real consumption is a function of real income.* Another way of putting this is to say that, with an equal multiplication of money income and prices, the real amount of consumption would remain unchanged. As we pointed out in Vol. II this sort of behaviour by households may be described by saying that households are *free from money illusion.*[2]

We can also assume that households are not free from money illusion. Households are said to be affected by money illusion in their decisions regarding consumption expenditure if, for example, a doubling of their money incomes and a trebling of all prices leads them to increase their real consumption. In this case real consumption is not written as a function of real income $\left(\frac{Y}{P}\right)$ but as a function of *P and Y*, i.e.:

$$X = \varphi(P, Y) \tag{5}$$

and correspondingly:

$$C = P \,.\, X = P \,.\, \varphi(P, Y). \tag{6}$$

An example may clarify the difference between (3) and (6). In the case of (3)—no money illusion—let:

$$f\left(\frac{Y}{P}\right) = a + b \,.\, \frac{Y}{P}, \tag{7}$$

where a and b are positive and given constants. The consumption function (3) then becomes:

$$C = P \,.\, f\left(\frac{Y}{P}\right) = aP + bY. \tag{8}$$

In case (6)—presence of money illusion—let:

$$\varphi(P, Y) = a \,.\, P + \beta \,.\, Y,$$

where a and b denote positive constants. The consumption function (6) then becomes:

$$C = a \,.\, P^2 + \beta \,.\, Y \,.\, P. \tag{9}$$

[1] These concepts are constantly used in statistics. If the reader should have difficulty with them, let him assume that all consumption goods are produced by a fully integrated firm and, moreover, that the firm produces only one consumer good.

[2] Vol. II, Ch. I, § 2. The term "money illusion" is due to Irving Fisher.

The dependence of consumption on income and prices is therefore entirely different according to whether money illusion is or is not present. Whether or not consumption decisions are affected by money illusion is of great importance in the theory of income determination. Only empirical enquiries can show which of the two assumptions corresponds to reality. So far, economic theory has generally proceeded on the apparently plausible assumption that consumption decisions are free of money illusion. However, the readers' attention should be drawn to the fact that the whole matter of money illusion requires detailed empirical investigation, and that the theory of income determination must also be developed on the assumption that money illusion is present. This is an important field for further research.

2. *In what follows we shall assume that real consumption is an increasing function of real income*, i.e. that the consumption function has the form (4) or (8). With given prices, money consumption can then be regarded as a function of money income, since money income is then directly proportional to real income. Let us denote real income by Y_r, then:

$$(10) \qquad Y_r = \frac{Y}{P},$$

i.e., we obtain money income by multiplying Y_r by prices as expressed by P. If real income is determined, we can find money income only if we know the prices corresponding to that real income, i.e. only if we know the functional relationship between real income and the prices of goods, which can be expressed symbolically as $P = P(Y_r)$.

3. It is important to be quite clear about the content of the consumption function. One possible interpretation is to think of it as showing the relationship between alternative levels of real income and real consumption in the coming period. The consumption function then expresses the households' propensity to consume in the coming period. It shows what would be the level of real consumption in the coming period if real income assumed various alternative values. We call this function the *short period consumption function.*

The long period consumption function is quite different. It shows what level of real consumption corresponds to various alternative levels of real income when real income has remained unchanged over a long period, so that consumption has been fully adjusted to it. Let C_LC_L' in Fig. 16 be the long period consumption function, and assume also that a long period adjustment of consumption to the level of income Y_1 has taken place. The long period consumption corresponding to the level of income Y_1 is C_1. If households expect a short period income of less than Y_1 (e.g. an income of Y_2) they will reduce their consumption in the short period by a smaller amount than they would if they expected income Y_2 to persist permanently. If households regard the fall in income from Y_1 to Y_2 as permanent they will adjust their consumption habits to the lower level of income and will reduce their consumption from Y_2C_2' to Y_2C_2. A corresponding argument applies to a rise in income above Y_1.

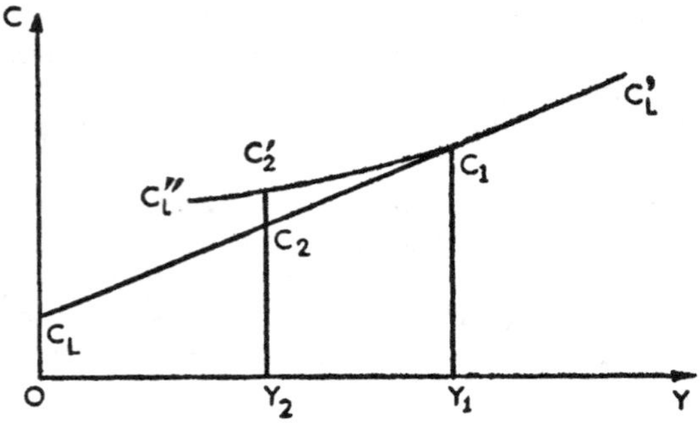

Fig. 16

The short run consumption function alone is relevant to the short run theory of income determination. Formally, however, the considerations set out below apply to the long run also.

4. After these preliminary remarks on the meaning of the consumption function we are in a position to demonstrate the following proposition: *Given the households' propensity to consume, and the net investment of firms, there is one and only one level of income at which there can be equilibrium*, (i.e. at which neither firms nor households experience surprises). For the sake of simplicity we shall at the outset neglect purchases by households fron non-firms.

Let us begin with a simple numerical example. Let the consumption function of households be given by:

$$C = 10 + \tfrac{3}{4} . Y. \tag{11}$$

Unless otherwise specified, C, Y and I are measured in real terms, or—and this amounts to the same—in terms of money at constant prices. This function tells us the level of planned household consumption at various alternative levels of income. We assume intended net investment I_p by firms to be 20:

$$I_p = 20. \tag{12}$$

We know from Vol. I that the income for any period is always equal to the sum of *actual* consumption and *actual* net investment:

$$Y = C + I. \tag{13}$$

If the income in the coming period is to be consistent with the plans of households and firms as expressed in (11) and (12), then C, I and Y must simultaneously fulfil the three conditions (11), (12) and (13). The values of C, I and Y which fulfil this condition can be easily ascertained. Using (11) and (12), we can rewrite (13), as:

$$Y = 10 + \tfrac{3}{4} \,.\, Y + 20. \tag{14}$$

Hence:

$$Y_0 = 120. \tag{15}$$

At this level of income, and only at this level, is the amount households wish to spend on consumption plus the amount firms wish to invest, exactly equal to income. Only if firms, in their production planning, correctly anticipate the level of consumption associated with this level of income (i.e. only if they expect consumption to be 100) will they create an income at which they experience no surprises. Households will then consume the amount which firms have planned to produce and to sell; and the actual net investment of firms will be equal to their intended net investment. We therefore call the level of income $Y_0 = 120$ *the macro-economic equilibrium level of income.*

It is easy to see that any level of income other than $Y_0 = 120$ cannot be a macro-economic equilibrium level of income. Suppose. for example, that the *ex ante* national income was 80 (60 expected consumption and 20 intended net investment). This income cannot be an equilibrium level of income. According to the propensity to consume, the actual consumption of households would be 70, which is greater by 10 than that expected by firms. As a result actual net investment by firms would only be 10. The unexpected higher level of consumption by households would bring about a reduction in the stocks of firms, that is unintended disinvestment, of 10.[(1)] The income of 80 could therefore not persist. Similarly it can be shown that an income of, say, 140 cannot be an equilibrium income. The following table shows the unintended net investment at various levels of income.

[(1)] With flexible prices the higher level of consumption may result in higher prices and thus higher incomes of firms *without* a reduction in their desired stock holdings. In this case the surprises of firms are occasioned by unexpected changes in prices and the firms' money incomes.

Real income	Expected consumption	Intended net investment	Actual consumption	Actual net investment	Unintended net investment
Y	C*	I_p	C	I_r	$I_r - I_p$
80	60	20	70	10	−10
100	80	20	85	15	−5
120	100	20	100	20	0
140	120	20	115	25	+5
160	140	20	130	30	+10

5. These considerations can easily be generalized. For the consumption function

$$C = C(Y)$$

the macro-economic equilibrium level of income is given by the equation:

$$Y = C(Y) + I_0 \tag{16}$$

in which I_0 denotes intended net investment. Only at the level of income Y_0 which fulfils this condition is the sum of intended consumption and intended net investment exactly equal to the income Y_0. Only at this income are the plans of households and firms mutually compatible.

For the special case where $I_0 = 0$, the condition for the equilibrium level of income is given by:

$$Y = C(Y). \tag{16a}$$

6. The relationships discussed so far can be shown geometrically in a simple way. In Fig. 17, *AB* represents the consumption function, which, for the sake of simplicity, we assume to be linear. The ordinates of this curve represent the amounts which households, taken together, actually devote to consumption at various alternative levels of national income. If we add intended net investment by firms to intended consumption at different levels of income (we do this by shifting the line *AB* parallel upwards by an amount equal to I_0), the equilibrium level of income Y_0, as determined in (16), appears simply as the abscissa of the intersection point *S* of the 45° line with the outlay curve *CD*.[1] It can easily be seen that any level of

[1] As far as I know, this useful "45°-line diagram", which is now in general use, was first applied to the theory of income determination in 1935 by the Danish writer Ivar Jantzen in a work entitled "Lidt planøkonomisk Teori" (*Nordisk Tidsskrift for Teknisk Økonomi*, Vol. I, 1935). An English translation of this article can be found in the collection of this writer's main articles which

income different from Y_0 cannot be an equilibrium level. For levels of income smaller (bigger) than Y_0 there will be negative (positive) unintended net investment, which is shown geometrically by the distance *HK*.

7. It must be stressed once again that the equilibrium level of income determined by (16) is a *macro-economic equilibrium*, i.e. an

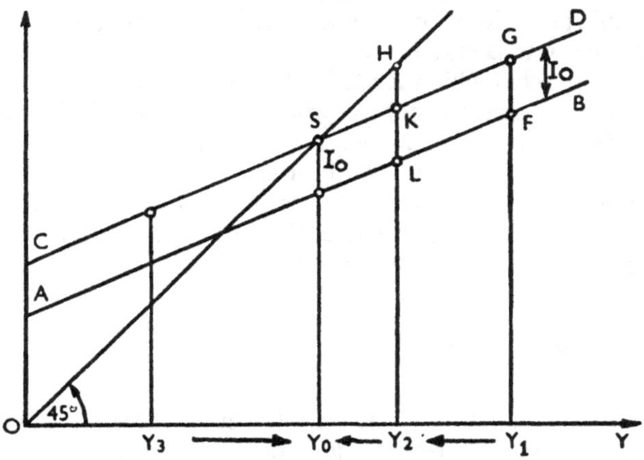

Fig. 17

equilibrium which relates only to the aggregates of consumption and national income. It tells us nothing—absolutely nothing—about the equilibria of the individual economic units contained within these aggregates. This is one of the important limitations of macro-economic analysis. These limitations do not render the analysis valueless, but do limit its range of relevance. Equilibrium in the macro-economic sense is a necessary but not a sufficient condition for total micro-economic equilibrium. In the absence of a macro-economic equilibrium all individual economic units cannot be in micro-economic equilibrium. This is the importance of macro-economic equilibrium from a theoretical and policy point of view. Macro-economic equilibrium, however, is compatible with micro-economic disequilibria, and this is why the presence of macro-economic equilibrium does not rule out tendencies to expansion or

appeared in 1939 entitled *Basic Principles of Business Economics and National Calculation*. This work is of great interest from the point of view of the history of economic theory. To my knowledge it contains the first analysis of the relationship between exports, imports and national income and a clear development of the theory of the foreign trade multiplier.

contraction as far as individual economic units are concerned. This fact must never be neglected in macro-economic analyses.

8. The relationships we have just discussed will be considered further later on. We must now consider the *stability* of the equilibrium situation described by (16).[1] As we know, this problem can be discussed only within the framework of a dynamic analysis.[2] Dynamic analysis attempts to explain how the system develops when a non-equilibrium situation is taken as the starting point. If the equilibrium income is stable, then a non-equilibrium situation must give rise to a process which leads back to equilibrium.

Let us assume that the consumption of households in period t, which we denote by C_t, depends on the income of the preceding period (Y_{t-1}). This means that households expect to receive an income in period t which is the same as that which they received in period $t - 1$. We further assume that firms correctly anticipate household consumption in period t, i.e.[3]

$$C_t^* = C_t \tag{17}$$

where C_t is a function of Y_{t-1}

$$C_t = C_t(Y_{t-1}) \tag{17a}$$

The consumption function *AB* in Fig. 17 must now be reinterpreted as relating the consumption of any period to the income of the preceding period.

On these assumptions the *ex ante* income of period t is equal to:

$$Y_t = C_t + I_0. \tag{18}$$

Since we have assumed that firms correctly anticipate household consumption, the *actual* income of period t, using (17a), is given by:

$$Y_t = C_t(Y_{t-1}) + I_0. \tag{19}$$

Equation (19) links the actual income of period t with the actual income of the preceding period. It is immediately obvious that, on the assumptions of this model, no unintended net investment can occur. Since firms, by assumption, correctly anticipate household consumption expenditure, they cannot experience surprises. Households, however, do experience surprises regarding their expected income; the income they receive in any one period diverges from the expected income. Therefore, starting from any level of income different from Y_0, a sequence of income changes is set up (theoretically

[1] Regarding the problem of the stability of equilibrium see Vol. II, Ch. IV, Section A.

[2] Regarding statics and dynamics see Vol. II, Chapter III.

[3] Starred symbols denote expected magnitudes. Thus C_t^* denotes the amount of consumption firms expect in period t.

an infinite sequence) which leads back to the equilibrium level of income. In Fig. 18, let Y_1 be the income realized in the first period. At this income, household consumption in the following period will be Y_1A_1, an amount correctly anticipated by firms. The output in period 2, based on household consumption and planned net investment, results in the higher level of income Y_2. In period 3 household consumption will be Y_2A_2, which is once again correctly

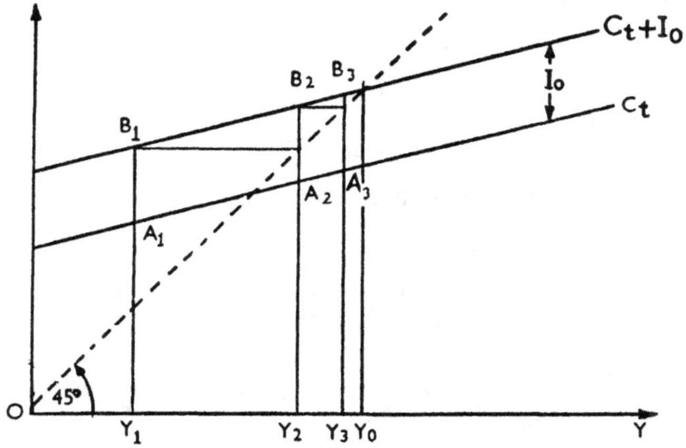

Fig. 18

anticipated by firms. The realized income in period 3 will be Y_3, and so on. As can be seen, an infinite series of rising levels of income is produced which converges to the equilibrium level of income. If the original level of income were larger than Y_0 there would be an infinite series of falling incomes which would converge to Y_0. On the assumptions of our model, the level of income Y_0 in Fig. 18 is a stable equilibrium position. An inspection of Fig. 18 will show that stability is always ensured if the slope of the consumption function, i.e. the *marginal propensity to consume*[(1)] is smaller than 1 in the neighbourhood of Y_0.[(2)]

We move nearer to reality if we assume that firms do not anticipate household consumption correctly, so that unintended investment

(1) Regarding this concept see Vol. II, Ch. I, § 7.

(2) Let b be the marginal propensity to consume in the neighbourhood of Y_0. Then the sequence of incomes can be described by the following equation:

$$Y_t = Y_0 + A \cdot b^t,$$

where A is a constant which depends on the initial level of income. It is immediately apparent that Y_t will converge to Y_0 as t increases if, and only if, $0 < b < 1$.

may take place. We obtain a relevant model if we assume, for example, that firms expect consumption in period t to be the same as that realized in the preceding period:

$$C_t^* = C_{t-1} \tag{20}$$

Retaining the assumption that household consumption depends on the income of the preceding period, the *ex ante* income for period t is obtained from the following equation:

$$\begin{aligned} Y_t &= C_t^* + I_0 \\ &= C_{t-1} + I_0. \end{aligned} \tag{21}$$

Since, however,

$$C_{t-1} = C_{t-1}(Y_{t-2})$$

equation (21) can also be written in the following form:

$$Y_t = C_{t-1}(Y_{t-2}) + I_0. \tag{22}$$

Using the "arrows" suggested by Tinbergen,[1] consumption and income are now linked in the following way:

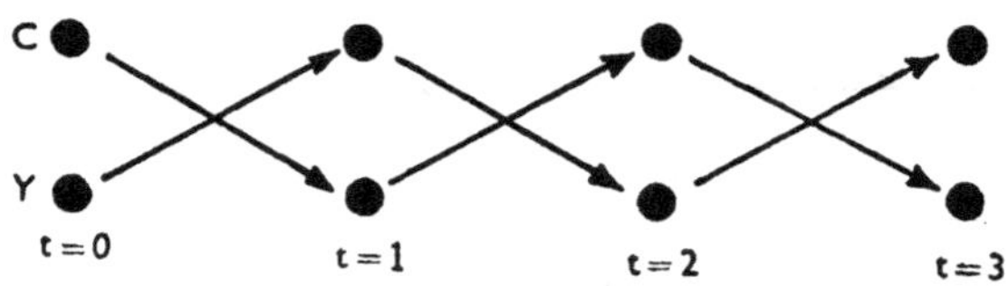

Fig. 19

the income for $t = 0$ determines consumption for $t = 1$, which in turn enters into the determination of the income for $t = 2$. From equation (22) we now derive an expression for income in which the income of any one period is linked to the incomes of *two* preceding periods. It follows that the sequence of incomes through time can be determined only if we know the incomes of two successive periods. The sequence obtained from equation (22) will again converge to the equilibrium level of income Y_0 if the marginal propensity to consume is smaller than 1 in the neighbourhood of the equilibrium income.[2]

[1] See Vol. II, Ch. III.

[2] The solution of the difference equation (22) in the neighbourhood of Y_0 is as follows:

$$Y_t = Y_0 + A(\sqrt{b})^t + B(-\sqrt{b})^t,$$

where A and B are two constants and b denotes the marginal propensity to consume.

At each level of income diverging from the equilibrium level there will be unintended net investment equal to the difference between actual consumption and that anticipated by firms.

The actual net investment in period t (always assuming constant prices) is:

(23) $$I_t = (C_t^* - C_t) + I_0.$$

The difference

(24) $$C_t^* - C_t = C_{t-1} - C_t$$

thus represents unintended net investment, which is equal to zero only in equilibrium, since only then is

$$C_t = C_{t-1} = C_{t-2} = \dots$$

Thus we arrive at the following theorem: *given that the stability conditions are fulfilled, every level of income smaller (greater) than the equilibrium level of income will generate a process of expansion (contraction) which leads back to the equilibrium level of income.* For $Y < Y_0$, firms will experience reductions in their inventories (assuming constant prices), and actual investment will be smaller than intended net investment. Firms will therefore expand production and thus generate a higher level of income. For $Y > Y_0$, firms will experience an increase in their inventories, and actual investment will be greater than intended net investment. Firms will therefore contract output and generate a correspondingly lower level of income.[1]

9. Our results remain unaffected if we include purchases by households from non-firms. Since the level of these purchases also depends on real income, we can simply include this part of consumption in the consumption function. In order to ascertain unintended net investment by firms when income is out of equilibrium, it is only necessary to separate the two components of consumption (i.e. purchases by households from firms and purchases from non-firms). In what follows consumption will always refer to *all* purchases by households.

10. The results established in the preceding paragraphs can be formulated in another way. As we know, the value of output in any one period is equal to the income of those who produced the output. We may say, therefore, that aggregate monetary supply in any one period is equal to the income Y of that period. Total monetary demand

[1] The reader should consider the case where prices are not assumed constant, but where flexibility of prices prevails. He will find that our theorem also holds good in that case.

during any period is given by the sum of intended household consumption plus intended net investment by firms, that is:

$$C(Y) + I_0.$$

In any one period there can be equilibrium only if, at prevailing prices, total demand is equal to total supply i.e. only if

$$Y = C(Y) + I_0.$$

If total demand is larger than total supply, which is the case for all incomes smaller than Y_0 (Fig. 17), national income will expand. Conversely, if total demand is smaller than total supply, which is the case for all incomes larger than Y_0 (Fig. 17), income will contract.

11. Finally, our results can be expressed in yet another way, with which we should become familiar, because it has played an important part in the technical discussion of these problems. We may reformulate our problem simply by using the *savings function*, instead of the consumption. The households' propensity to save is merely the inverse of their propensity to consume. Thus if the propensity to consume is known, the propensity to save is simultaneously given, and *vice versa*. The propensity to consume, expressed by the consumption function, shows how much households wish to spend on consumption at various alternative levels of income, while the propensity to save, expressed by the savings function, shows the amounts which they wish to save at those levels of income. The different amounts, as shown by the savings function, which households may wish to save at various alternative levels of income may also be described as *intended* or *voluntary* savings.

If $C = C(Y)$ is the consumption function which represents the propensity to consume, the *savings function*, which represents the propensity to save, will obviously be:

$$S = Y - C = Y - C(Y), \tag{25}$$

where S indicates voluntary savings at the level of income Y. In Vol. II[(1)] we showed how the savings function, which we may write:

$$S = S(Y), \tag{26}$$

can be derived graphically from the consumption function. The savings function in Fig. 20 shows that at levels of income below $\bar{Y}$ household savings is negative, at the level of income $\bar{Y}$ consumption is exactly equal to income, and at levels of income above $\bar{Y}$ households wish to save positive amounts. A rise (fall) in the propensity

[(1)] Ch. I, § 7.

to save, i.e a fall (rise) in the propensity to consume, means a shift in the savings curve upwards (downwards).[1]

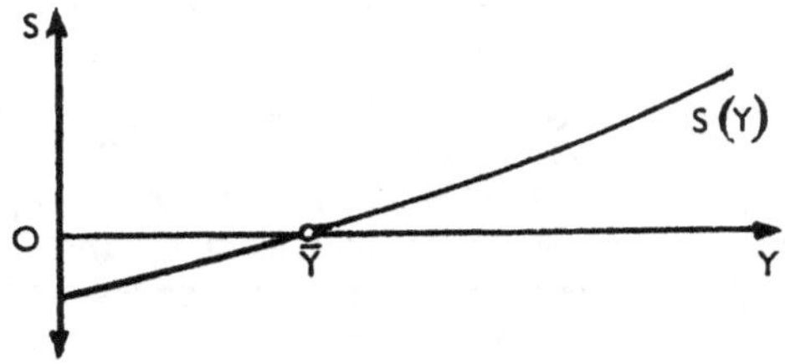

Fig. 20

We have shown above that, given the propensity to consume $C(Y)$ and given the level of net investment I_0, the equilibrium level of income was determined by equation (16):

$$Y = C(Y) + I_0.$$

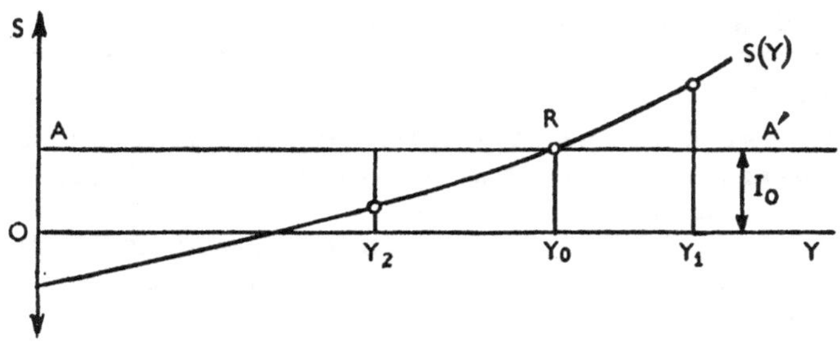

Fig. 21

Now, this equation can also be written in the following form:

(27) $$Y - C(Y) = I_0$$

or

(28) $$S(Y) = I_0.$$

Equation (28), which is obviously only a reformulation of equation (16), now determines the equilibrium level of income. *Equation (28) tells us that, given the savings function and a given amount of net investment, the equilibrium level of income is that at which households wish to save an amount equal to the given net investment.*

The reader should be quite clear about this often misunderstood theorem. In Fig. 21, the curve $S(Y)$ represents the savings function.

[1] Compare Vol. II, Ch. I, § 7.

The line AA' parallel to the Y axis at a distance I_0 represents the amount of given (autonomous) net investment. The equilibrium level of income Y_0, given by equation (28), will now be given by the abscissa of the point R at which the investment line AA' crosses the savings curve $S(Y)$. At this level of income, and only at this level of income, are voluntary savings by households exactly equal to intended net investment by firms. At any level of income other than Y_0 this condition is not fulfilled. At the level of income Y_2 ($<Y_0$) voluntary savings by households would be smaller than I_0, and Y_2 therefore cannot be an equilibrium level of income. At the level of income Y_1 ($>Y_0$) voluntary savings by households would be larger than I_0 and thus Y_1 also could not be an equilibrium level of income.

If the level of income should accidentally be at Y_2, that level could not be maintained if net investment remained at I_0, since at that level of income total demand would exceed total supply, and income would keep rising until voluntary savings were exactly equal to net investment. If the level of income should accidentally be at Y_1, total supply would exceed total demand and income would contract until it reached that level at which voluntary savings were exactly equal to voluntary net investment. We have thus established the following relationships:

If, at a particular level of income, voluntary net savings are smaller than voluntary net investment, a process will ensue which leads to an expansion of income.

If, at a particular level of income, voluntary net savings are larger than voluntary net investment, a process will ensue which leads to a contraction of income.

There will be macro-economic equilibrium only if, at a particular level of income, voluntary net investment is equal to voluntary net savings.

We may express this in yet another way by saying:

If, at a level of income Y, the amount S is voluntarily saved, that level of income can be maintained if, and only if, voluntary investment by firms is equal to the amount saved.

It should be emphasized once again that all these propositions are merely reformulations of the results obtained in sections 1 to 9 of this paragraph. These propositions say no more and no less than the theorems which we derived by using the consumption function, and in principle, therefore, they are redundant for the development of the theory of income determination.[(1)] The fact that this theory

(1) This has been emphasized by B. Ohlin in a discussion with E. Lindahl about methodological problems of dynamic theory:

"The method which regards differences between planned savings and planned

has been developed and taught chiefly with the use of the savings function is doubtless responsible for the occasional misunderstandings of it which still occur. One of these misunderstandings is the false interpretation of the quantitative relationship between savings and investment. It was shown in Vol. I that, in a closed economy without a government, savings and investment are necessarily equal *ex-post*. This theorem in no way contradicts the proposition that *intended* savings in any period may well diverge from *intended* investment in the same period. In a market economy, the decisions about the level of voluntary savings are independent of the decisions regarding the level of intended investment. The transactors who make decisions about savings are, as a rule, different from those who make decisions about the level of intended investment. Thus it would have been pure chance if, say for the year 1952, the planned voluntary savings by households had been exactly equal to planned voluntary investment. As a rule, intended savings will not be equal to intended investment. Similarly, intended investment will not, as a rule, be equal to realized investment, (though for the sake of simplicity we have so far assumed that this is the case). If, in spite of this, *total* savings are equal to *total* investment *ex-post*, i.e. at the end of every period, this is due to the fact that *ex-post* savings and investment include not only intended savings and investment, but also unintended

---

investment as the factor bringing about processes of expansion or contraction is no longer useful for several reasons. It is better and simpler to ask, how do purchases for consumption and business purchases develop from period to period?" (B. Ohlin, "Professor Lindahl om dynamisk Teori," *Ekonomisk Tidsskrift*, 1941, p. 181)

"It has become clear that an excess of planned new investment over planned savings means only that buyers decide to buy more than sellers expect to sell . . . In these circumstances, is there any need to press the analysis of changes in the demand for consumption and for business purposes, as well as the corresponding changes in supply, into the special form of the relationship between savings and investment? Why not analyse directly the expectations of income and the corresponding consumption purchases (or decisions to save, which are the other side of the coin), as well as expected profits and the firms' decisions to buy and sell which are based on them?"

(B. Ohlin, "Metodfrågor inom den dynamiske Teorin," *Ekonomisk Tidsskrift*, 1941, p. 335–336)

See further: E. Schneider, "Saving and Investment in a Closed Economy" *International Economic Papers*, Vol. 1, 1951.

E. Preiser, "Sparen und Investieren." *Jahrbücher für Nationalökonomie und Statistik*. Vol. 159 (1944); and

"Der Kapitalbegriff und die neuere Theorie" (in Festschrift fur Wilhelm Rieger: *Die Unternehmung im Markt*, Stuttgart 1953).

Both papers are now reprinted in E. Preiser, *Bildung und Verteilung des Volkseinkommens*, Göttingen 1957.

(involuntary) savings and unintended (involuntary) investment. The level of unintended savings and unintended investment can be stated only in *ex-post* terms. Thus, for any period it is true that *ex-post*:

$$S_{\text{intended}} + S_{\text{unintended}} = I_{\text{intended}} + I_{\text{unintended}}.$$

Macro-economic equilibrium will prevail only if unintended savings and unintended investment are equal to zero, i.e. only when intended savings are exactly equal to intended investment. The presence of unintended savings and unintended investment always means that individual transactors experience surprises which lead to changes in their dispositions. A situation in which unintended savings or unintended investment occur is always a disequilibrium situation.

In a market economy unintended savings and investment occur as a rule in the case of firms. *Unintended investment occurs in the form of unintended changes in stocks, and unintended savings in the form of differences between the actual and the expected income of firms.*(1) It was shown in Vol. I that the *ex-post* income of firms Y_f for any period is:

$$Y_f = I - S_{nf} + C_f.^{(2)} \tag{29}$$

Let us denote the income which firms expect for the period by Y_f^*, and the difference between the actual and the expected income of firms by ΔY_f; then the above equation can also be rewritten in the following form:

$$Y_f^* + \Delta Y_f = I_{\text{intended}} + I_{\text{unintended}} - S_{nf} + C_f. \tag{29a}$$

Non-firms determine their own consumption (or savings—it comes to the same in this case). Since the income of non-firms is by definition fixed in advance by contract, the determination of consumption implies a simultaneous determination of savings, and vice versa. *Matters are different in the case of firms;* they determine their own

(1) Unintended savings in the case of non-firms could occur only if there were shortages of consumption goods so that the amount of income set aside for consumption was not in fact spent. We neglect this possibility, which can easily be included in equation (29a).

(2) Translator's note:
For those who have not consulted Vol. 1 this can be shown quite simply:

$$Y_f + Y_{nf} = I + C_f + C_{nf}$$

(where the subscripts *f* and *nf* denote magnitudes relating to firms and non-firms respectively), but

$$Y_{nf} = C_{nf} + S_{nf},$$

therefore

$$\begin{aligned} Y_f &= I + C_f + C_{nf} - (C_{nf} + S_{nf}) \\ &= I - S_{nf} + C_f \end{aligned}$$

consumption (C_f), but not their savings. Since their income is always determined residually, and can only be ascertained *ex-post*, firms cannot determine their savings. The level of savings is an expectation parameter for firms, the actual value of which will be determined by the actual level of profits; and actual profits are determined by the actual consumption of households and actual investment by firms.

Thus a situation of disequilibrium is, as a rule, characterized by unexpected profits (= unintended savings by firms) and by unintended changes in stocks.[1] If we make assumptions about the manner in which firms react to surprises, we may describe the path of the system in terms of process analysis; this will be discussed in § 3.[2]

Equilibrium will prevail, if, and only if,

$$\Delta Y_f = 0$$

and

$$I_{\text{unintended}} = 0.$$

The equilibrium condition:

(29b) $$I_{\text{intended}} = S_{\text{intended}}$$

may also be written in the form:

(29c) $$Y_f = I_{\text{intended}} - S_{nf} + C_f = Y_f^*.$$

§2. The Case when Net Investment Depends on National Income

So far we have assumed net investment by firms to be autonomously determined and to be positive and constant. But a casual glance at the facts shows that rising income is usually accompanied by rising investment. It is, therefore, reasonable to regard intended net investment by firms as an increasing function of national income.

(30) $$I = f(Y).$$

This so-called *investment function* indicates the level of net investment which firms carry out at alternative levels of national income. The function describes the firms' propensity to invest in much the same way as the consumption function describes the propensity to consume of households. The case of constant net investment, which we have considered so far, is thus a special case of equation (30).

(1) Compare pp. 128–131.

(2) See E. Lundberg, *Studies in the Theory of Economic Expansion*, London 1937. Also: E. Schneider, "Saving and Investment in a Closed Economy".
E. Preiser, "Multiplikatorprozeß und dynamischer Unternehmergewinn", *Jahrbücher für Nationalökonomie und Statistik*, 1955.

It can easily be seen that the introduction of the investment function (30) in no way modifies the analysis developed in § 1. Instead of equation (16), which there determined the macro-economic equilibrium income, we now simply write the equation:

$$Y = C(Y) + I(Y) \tag{31}$$

or, if we use the savings function $S(Y)$ instead of the consumption function:

$$S(Y) = I(Y). \tag{31a}$$

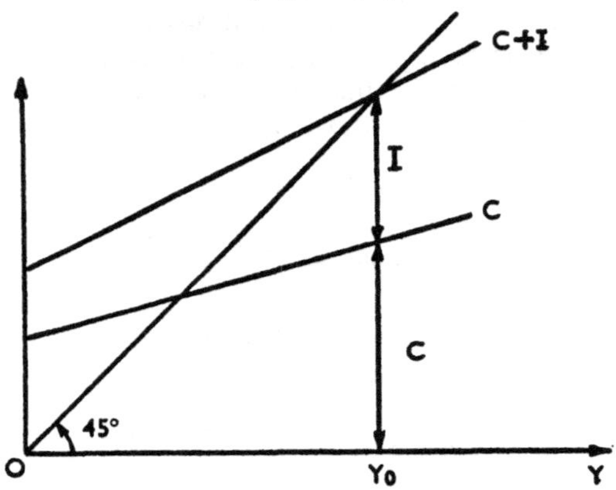

Fig. 22

Fig. 22 shows the geometric solution of equation (31). The righthand side of equation (31) may be described as "*the expenditure function*" or "*monetary demand function*" of the economy, since it indicates the total amount that will be spent on consumption and net investment at any particular level of income. The outlay function indicates the *global propensity to spend.* Using this terminology we may state (31) in the following way:

Given the propensities to spend of households and firms, equilibrium is possible only at that level of income at which total demand is equal to the level of income. The propensity to spend, i.e. effective demand, thus determines the equilibrium level of income.

§3. Changes in National Income Resulting from Changes in the Propensities to Invest and Consume (The Multiplier Problem)

(i) *Comparative-static Analysis*

1. At first, let us once again assume investment to be given and constant. As was shown in § 1, given the propensity to consume the

level of net investment determines the level of income. The equilibrium level of income is given, as we know, by the equation:

$$Y = C(Y) + I. \tag{32}$$

Given the propensity to consume, the level of net investment uniquely determines the level of income. If there is a change in net investment there will also be a change in the level of income (always assuming a given propensity to consume). If we regard net investment as a

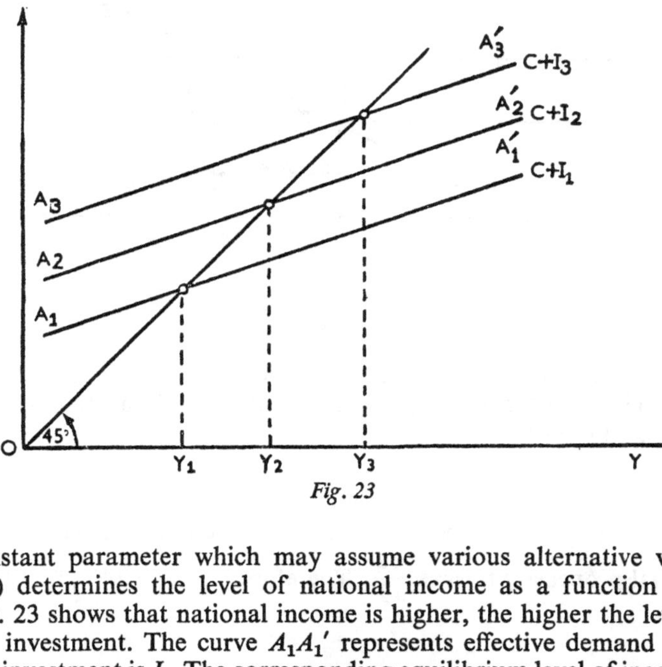

Fig. 23

constant parameter which may assume various alternative values (32) determines the level of national income as a function of I. Fig. 23 shows that national income is higher, the higher the level of net investment. The curve A_1A_1' represents effective demand when net investment is I_1. The corresponding equilibrium level of income is Y_1. If net investment rises to I_2 ($I_2 > I_1$), the curve of effective demand will be shifted upwards by the constant amount $I_2 - I_1$, and assume the position A_2A_2'. The equilibrium level of income will rise to Y_2, and so on.

2. We now wish to ask by how much the equilibrium level of income rises when, given the propensity to consume, net investment rises by the amount ΔI. This is a problem in comparative statics. We compare the equilibrium level of income corresponding to the level if investment I with that corresponding to the level of investment $I + \Delta I$.

It is easier to handle our problem by using the savings function instead of the consumption function. As we know, the equilibrium level of income corresponding to a given level of net investment is that level of income at which total voluntary household savings are exactly equal to net investment. In Fig. 24, Y represents the equilibrium level of income corresponding to the level of investment I. As can be seen from the figure, when net investment rises by ΔI the corresponding equilibrium level of income rises by ΔY. What

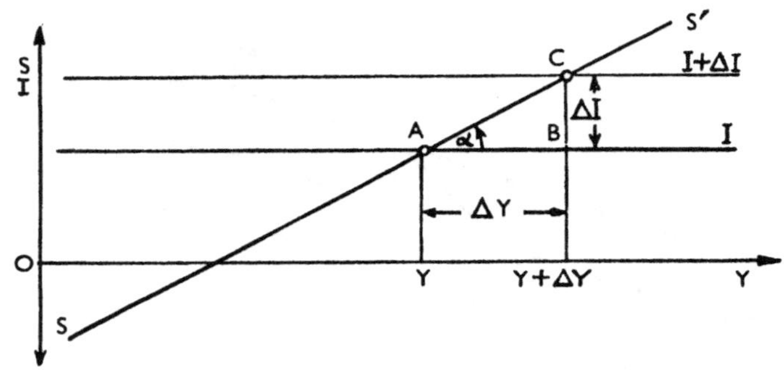

Fig. 24

can we say about the size of ΔY? Let us first assume that the savings function is linear (as in Fig. 24). The triangle ABC immediately gives the following relationship:

$$\Delta Y = \frac{1}{\tan \alpha} \cdot \Delta I. \tag{33}$$

Now, tan α, i.e. the slope of the savings function, is of course the marginal propensity to save $\frac{dS}{dY}$. Therefore:

$$\Delta Y = \frac{1}{\frac{dS}{dY}} \cdot \Delta I. \tag{33a}$$

Since the sum of the marginal propensity to consume and the marginal propensity to save is equal to 1, (33a) may also be written in the form:

$$\Delta Y = \frac{1}{1 - \frac{dC}{dY}} \cdot \Delta I. \tag{33b}$$

It can be easily shown that the relationship (33a) or (33b) holds good generally, i.e. also for non-linear savings functions. At a small interval around point A any curve may be replaced by the tangent at that point (Fig. 25), so that the relationship (33a) or (33b) is at any rate approximately valid for non-linear savings functions. The deviation between the precise and the approximate value of ΔY as calculated according to (33) is smaller, the smaller ΔI. For relatively small (rigorously: for infinitesimally small) changes in I, (33*a*) or (33b) indicates the precise value of ΔY.

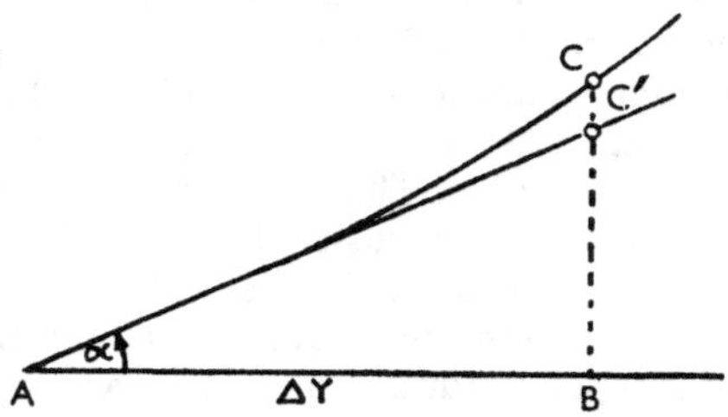

Fig. 25

The exact proof is as follows: equation (32) determines the equilibrium income as a function of I. (32) thus implicitly states the relationship between Y and I. If we differentiate both sides of (32) with respect to I we have:

$$\frac{dY}{dI} = \frac{dC}{dY} \cdot \frac{dY}{dI} + 1$$

or:

$$\frac{dY}{dI} \cdot \left(1 - \frac{dC}{dY}\right) = 1$$

or:

(33c) $$dY = \frac{1}{1 - \frac{dC}{dY}} \cdot dI.$$

Now, $\frac{dC}{dY}$ is the marginal propensity to consume, and thus $1 - \frac{dC}{dY}$ is the marginal propensity to save. Therefore:

(34) $$dY = \frac{1}{\text{marginal propensity to save}} \cdot dI$$

We have thus established the following theorem, which is generally valid: given the propensity to consume, a small rise (fall) in autonomous investment (ΔI) *leads to a rise (fall) in the equilibrium level of income by an amount equal to the product of the change in investment and the reciprocal of the marginal propensity to save.*

3. Let us now consider the interpretation of this important theorem. As we saw in Vol. II, the value of the marginal propensity to consume will generally not exceed 1.[(1)] As a rule, the marginal propensity to consume, and therefore the marginal propensity to save, will lie between 0 and 1. The reciprocal of the marginal propensity to save, therefore, will generally be greater than 1. A rise in net investment by the amount ΔI thus leads to a change in the equilibrium level of income equal to a multiple of the change in investment. Hence the reciprocal of the marginal propensity to save is called the *investment multiplier.* The investment multiplier is bigger, the smaller the marginal propensity to save. With a marginal propensity to save of $\frac{1}{2}$ the multiplier is equal to 2. A rise in net investment of 100 per annum then leads to a rise in the equilibrium level of income of 200 per annum. If the marginal propensity to save is only $\frac{1}{4}$, a rise in net investment of 100 per annum leads to a rise in the equilibrium level of income of 400 per annum. An increase in net investment will have no multiplier effect only when the marginal propensity to save $= 1$. In this case a rise in net investment of 100 per annum leads to a rise in the equilibrium level of income by the same amount.

4. The multiplier relationship remains valid whether a rise in money income comes about through (a) a rise in prices only, or (b) a rise in real income and employment, prices remaining constant, or (c) a rise in real income *and* prices. As will be shown in Appendix I, these three cases differ only as regards the marginal propensity to consume and hence the size of the multiplier. Which of the three cases occurs depends upon the initial position of the economy.

5. So far we have assumed intended net investment to be constant. Our results, however, can easily be extended to the case when net investment depends on the level of income (or, more generally, to the case in which the propensity to *spend*, i.e. the sum of the propensity to consume and the propensity to invest, depends on the level of national income). A rise (fall) in the propensity to spend $[C(Y) + I(Y)]$ will entail a correspondingly higher (lower) equilibrium level of income (Fig. 26). The size of the change in the equilibrium level of income will now be determined by the *marginal propensity to spend*, which is the sum of the marginal propensity to consume and the marginal propensity to invest.

If the total outlay function is $A(Y, \alpha)$, where α is a variable

(1) The reader should consider what happens when the marginal propensity to consume is greater than 1.

parameter indicating the position of the function, the equilibrium level of income will be given by the condition:

$$Y = A(Y, \alpha). \tag{35}$$

This equation determines the equilibrium level of income as a function of α. Differentiating with respect to α we have:

$$\frac{dY}{d\alpha} = \frac{\dfrac{\partial A}{\partial \alpha}}{1 - \dfrac{\partial A}{\partial Y}}. \tag{36}$$

The value of the right-hand side of (36) represents the "*expenditure*

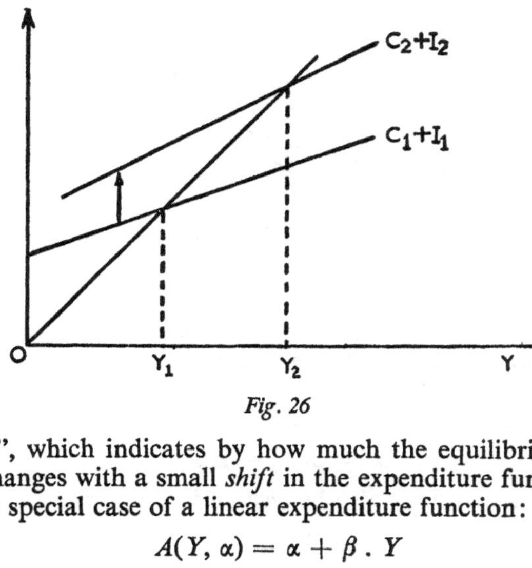

Fig. 26

multiplier", which indicates by how much the equilibrium level of income changes with a small *shift* in the expenditure function.

For the special case of a linear expenditure function:

$$A(Y, \alpha) = \alpha + \beta \,.\, Y \tag{37}$$

we have:

$$\frac{dA}{d\alpha} = 1 \quad \text{and} \quad \frac{dA}{dY} = \beta.$$

The expenditure multiplier now becomes:

$$\frac{dY}{d\alpha} = \frac{1}{1 - \beta}. \tag{38}$$

From (36) and (38) it follows that a rise in the propensity to spend leads to a new equilibrium only if the marginal propensity to spend is less than one.

It is immaterial whether the rise in the equilibrium level of income comes about through a rise in the propensity to consume or a rise in the propensity to invest. A rise (fall) in the propensity to consume always leads to an expansion (contraction) in the equilibrium level of income, as does a rise (fall) in the propensity to invest. *The equilibrium level of income always depends on the combined effect of both influences.* For example, if a rise in the propensity to invest is accompanied by a fall in the propensity to consume, or a rise in the

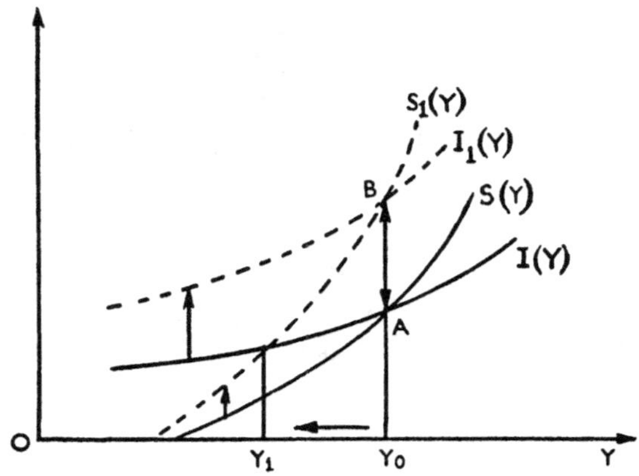

Fig. 27

propensity to consume is accompanied by a fall in the propensity to invest, there may be no change in the equilibrium level of income, as can easily be seen. Since this is of particular importance we shall explain it in yet another way. Let us recall the familiar equation:

$$Y = C(Y) + I(Y) \tag{39}$$

which, as we know, may also be written in the form:

$$S(Y) = I(Y), \tag{40}$$

where $S(Y)$ denotes the savings function. Fig. 27 shows how the savings and investment functions determine the equilibrium level of income. This figure describes the same relationships as those described in Fig. 21, except that intended net investment is now assumed to be a rising function of income.

We now assume that there is a rise in the savings function (a fall in the consumption function). The new savings function is $S_1(Y)$ (Fig. 27). At the level of income Y_0, AB more will be saved than before. If the propensity to invest remains unchanged, this leads to a contraction in income; national income falls to Y_1. Depending on the initial situation, such a fall in money income may take the form of a fall in prices only, or a fall in real income and prices, or a fall in real income only. This contraction in income is called a *deflationary process;* and the distance *BD* in Fig. 28, or *AB* in Fig. 27, which is the difference between the actual expenditure at the level of income Y_0 and that expenditure which would be necessary for the maintenance of the level of income at Y_0, is called a *deflationary gap* (Fig. 28). If the decline in income due to the rise in the propensity

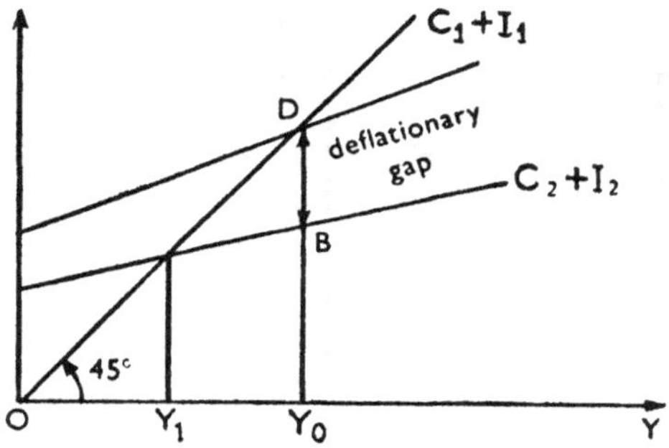

Fig. 28

to save is to be avoided, the propensity to invest must rise *pari passu* with the rise in the propensity to save; in terms of Fig. 27, intended net investment at the level of income Y_0 must rise by the amount *AB*. The fall in consumption must be precisely compensated by a rise in investment, so that there is no diminution in effective demand.

Fig. 29 describes an inflationary situation, i.e. a situation where output can no longer be expanded, given productive capacity, while effective demand (for consumption and net investment) exceeds the income corresponding to that situation. At the level of income *OA*, *AD* is intended expenditure for consumption and investment; effective demand thus exceeds supply by the amount *BD*. Through the multiplier this will lead to an expansionary process, which in this case results only in rising prices, since production cannot be expanded. On certain assumptions this process of rising prices can lead to a cumulative (inflationary) process, and the distance BD is therefore called an *inflationary gap.*

6. Our analysis enables us to clarify a question about which there is still much needless misunderstanding. *The question is whether the carrying out of additional voluntary investment requires a previous or simultaneous increase in voluntary savings of the same amount.* Let the initial situation be the level of income Y_1 in Fig. 27. We now assume a rise in the propensity to invest, so that at the level of income Y_1 more will be invested than previously. We wish to know whether

this additional investment requires a previous or simultaneous rise in voluntary savings of the same amount out of the income Y_1, i.e. whether it requires an appropriate upward shift in the propensity to save. Behind this question there is usually the supposition that the "means" required for the new investment can be made available only through savings. If by "means" we understand the money necessary for the carrying out of the investment, such a supposition is false, as

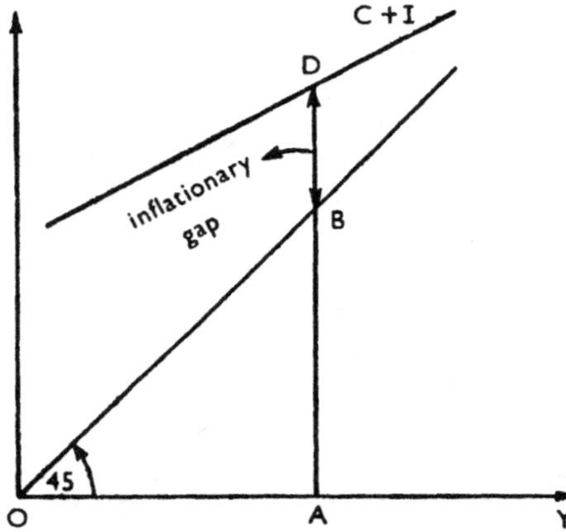

Fig. 29

the reader saw in Chapter II. The required money can be made available to an investor through a bank loan; and the granting of such a loan does not depend on the savings of any other transactor. But how do matters stand if by "means" we understand the labour and other means of production, for whose remuneration the investor requires the money he borrows? We have shown that a rise in the propensity to save leads to a fall in national income, a contraction in production and thus to a release of labour and other means of production. If, at the time when the additional investment is to be carried out, the economy is in a *state of underemployment, with unused capacity at all stages of production*, it is clear that neither labour nor other means of production need to be released in order to make the new investment possible. Unused labour and capacity are already available; the available labour only needs to be employed within the framework of the existing productive capacity. This clearly does not require a rise in the propensity to save. We have also shown that a rise in the propensity to invest which is accompanied by an equal rise in the propensity to save leaves national income unchanged (Fig. 27); in this case the new investment would have no expansionary effect. Matters are different if, at the time when the new investment takes place, the economy is in a *state of full employment*. Even in this situation the provision of credit for investment, which is *always* needed, does not depend on the savings of any transactors. However, a rise in the propensity to save is necessary if effective demand and thus national income are to remain unchanged. Now the investment can be carried out only if labour and other means of production are released; in the absence of price increases this release is possible only if transactors voluntarily save more. *An inflationary gap can be avoided only if the rise in effective demand, due to the new investment, is offset by an equal fall in effective demand through a rise in voluntary savings.* This, *and this alone*, is the significance of a rise in the propensity to save when there is an increase in intended investment in a fully employed economy. If the additional investment is not compensated by a rise in the propensity to save, ". . . the increased monetary demand principally takes the form of rivalry between employers for labour, raw materials and natural facilities, etc. which consequently leads to an increase in their price, and indirectly, owing to the increased money income of labour and landlords and the increased demand for commodities, to a rise in the price of all consumption goods . . . ."[1] This rise in prices, extending over the whole economy, contains the germ of further cumulative price rises. Competition for workers and means of production would lead to a cumulative, i.e. inflationary, process of price increases.[2]

(ii) *Dynamic Analysis*

1. So far we have analysed the multiplier problem in terms of comparative statics. That is, we started with a macro-economic equilibrium situation and asked what would be the new equilibrium

[1] K. Wicksell, *Lectures on Political Economy* Vol. II, p. 195.

[2] In Wicksell's classic book the reader will find a detailed description of this process, which is also known as "the Wicksellian cumulative process". Wicksell, incidentally, clearly saw the need to distinguish sharply between an under-employed and a fully employed economy when dealing with the problems considered in this section.

Regarding these questions, see especially: E. Preiser, "Sparen und Investieren" (*Jahrbücher für Nationalökonomie und Statistik*, Vol. 159, 1944) and "Geldschöpfung oder Sparen?" (Vol. 162, 1950). E. Preiser, "Der Kapitalbegriff und die neuere Theorie", in *Festschrift fur W. Rieger* (Stuttgart 1952); C. Föhl, *Geldschöpfung und Wirtschaftskreislauf*, Munich and Leipzig *1937* (2nd edin. Berlin 1955);

H. Gestrich, *Kredit und Sparen*, 3rd edit., Düsseldorf and Munich 1957; E. Lukas, *Aufgaben des Geldes*, Stuttgart 1937.

On the theory of inflation, see especially: B. Hansen, *The Theory of Inflation*,

corresponding to a change in net investment of a given amount, and how the new equilibrium would differ from the original one. We have not, so far, analysed the process of movement from equilibrium situation 1 to equilibrium situation 2. Such an analysis would be superfluous if the speed of adjustment of the economy to changes in data (in our case to a change in the autonomous net investment) were infinite. If this were the case, an analysis in terms of comparative statics would be sufficient. In the real world, however, adjustment to a change in net investment requires time. In order to gain a more

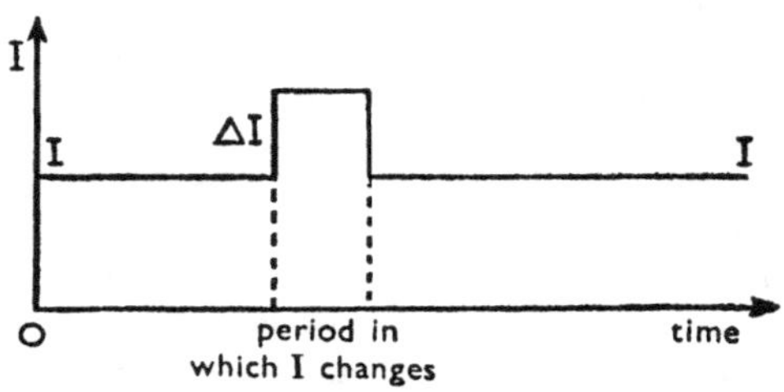

Fig. 30

complete picture of the events connected with a change in net investment, we have to follow the process of movement from equilibrium situation 1 to equilibrium situation 2. These considerations were explained in Vol. II,[1] where it was shown that an enquiry into the process of movement requires dynamic analysis. We shall now treat the multiplier problem in terms of dynamic analysis.

2. We begin with a situation of macro-economic equilibrium, and assume that this equilibrium is disturbed by a *temporary* increase in net investment of £100, but that investment subsequently falls back to its original level. Let net investment rise during *one* period *only* (say a year); from the second period onwards investment falls back to the original level (Fig. 30). We may express this by saying that our system is exposed to an *investment shock*. This investment shock does not have an immediate effect on the economy. It is clear

---

Oxford 1953. J. Pedersen, "The Theory of Inflation." *Weltwirtschaftliches Archiv*, Vol. 73, 1954.

It should be noted that *three* conditions must be fulfilled if an inflationary, i.e. cumulative process is to develop: (a) effective demand must exceed supply at ruling prices; (b) there must be full employment of the economy's resources; (c) there must be complete flexibility of prices and incomes. If the cause of the inflationary gap is a spontaneous rise in effective demand, one speaks of a *demand induced inflation*. If the cause of the inflationary gap is an autonomous rise in money wage rates, one speaks of a *wage induced inflation*.

[1] Vol. II, Chapters III and IV.

that, in the period in which the investment shock occurs, national income rises simultaneously with the increase in investment and by an equal amount. If, during a year (but only during that year) additional houses are built to the value of £100,000,000, national income during that year rises immediately by £100,000,000; the increase in income accrues to all those participating in the building of houses. In the next period the building of houses falls back to the original level, so that the additional income of those engaged in the building industry also falls off. The economic effects of the rise in national income in period 1 are not exhausted in the second and in the following periods. For purposes of illustration let us assume that the recipients of the additional income of £100,000,000 have a marginal propensity to consume of ½ and respond to a change in income in any one period by changing their consumption expenditure only in the following period. *For the sake of simplicity we shall assume that firms correctly anticipate the rise in consumption and hence that no unintended investment occurs in the course of the process of adjustment.*[1] In period 2 £50,000,000 will be spent on consumption, so that national income in period 2 will be £50,000,000 higher than in the original equilibrium. Transactors who receive the increase in income of £50,000,000 in period 2 increase their consumption expenditure correspondingly in period 3. Let us assume that these transactors also have a marginal propensity to consume of ½, so that national income in period 3 will be £25,000,000 higher than in the original situation. The recipients of this additional income increase their consumption expenditure by £12·5 mill. in period 4 (always assuming that all transactors have the same marginal propensity to consume). The subsequent course of this process can easily be seen. The following table shows the effect over time of an investment shock of 100 (in mill. £s).

Period	Change in investment	Change in consumption	Change in income during the period
1	100	—	100
2	—	50	50
3	—	25	25
4	—	12·5	12·5
5	—	6·25	6·25
.	.	.	.
.	.	.	.
.	.	.	.
n	—	$100(\frac{1}{2})^{n-1}$	$100(\frac{1}{2})^{n-1}$

[1] Firms thus experience surprises only with respect to their incomes; the actual income of firms diverges from their expected income. This divergence determines the subsequent movement of the system.

Fig. 31 shows the time sequence of the deviations of income (measured from the original level of income) in each individual period. It can easily be seen that the rise in income in the *n*th period (compared with the original income) is $100 \times (\frac{1}{2})^{n-1}$; the increase in income converges towards zero as *n* increases. Thus the investment shock loses its income-raising effect, theoretically after an infinite

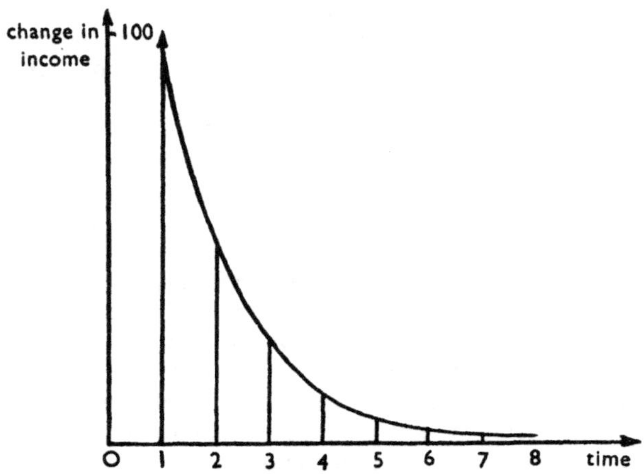

Fig. 31

number of periods, in practice after a relatively small number of periods. The level of income falls back to the original level after a few periods. Thus, with a marginal propensity to consume between 0 and 1, a single investment shock does not lead to a permanent rise in the level of income.

If the marginal propensity to consume is greater than 1, the change in income in any period is larger than in the preceding period, and the system will expand indefinitely.

3. The analysis of a single investment shock can be easily extended to cover the analysis of the effects over time of *a permanent change in net investment.* A permanent increase in net investment may be looked upon as a continuous series of investment shocks of equal size. Let the original equilibrium be disturbed by a permanent increase in net investment of 100 per period of time (Fig. 32). The level of investment now exceeds the original level by 100, not only in period 1 but in all the following periods. In each period an investment shock of 100 now occurs. We simply add the effects over time of the individual investment shocks to obtain the total effect

of the rise in the level of net investment. For the sake of simplicity let us again assume that all transactors have a marginal propensity to consume of ½, and that they react to a change in income in any one period by changing consumption expenditure only in the following period. On these assumptions, the process resulting from a permanent increase in net investment of 100 per period is as follows: in period 1 national income rises by 100. In period 2 this rise in income leads to a rise in consumption of 50 and thus to a rise in

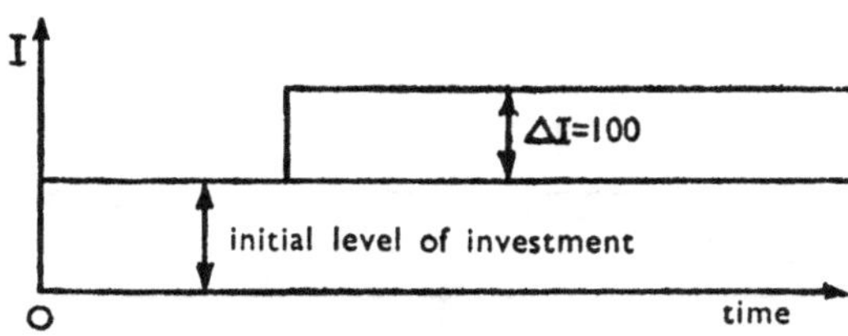

Fig. 32

income (above the original level) of 50. But in period 2 there is again additional net investment of 100, and thus a further increase in income of 100, so that the total increase in income (over the original level) in period 2 is 150. In period 3 the rise in income is 175, consisting of the additional investment of 100 in period 3, of 50 increased consumption expenditure (resulting from the increase in income due to the increase in investment in period 2) and of 25 increased consumption expenditure (resulting from the increase in income due to the increase in consumption expenditure in period 2). The process can be represented by the following table:

Period	Change in investment	Induced change in consumption				Change in in income
1	100 ↘					100
2	100 ↘	50 ↘				150
3	100 ↘	50 ↘	25 ↘			175
4	100 ↘	50 ↘	25 ↘	12·5 ↘		187·5
5	100	50	25	12·5	6·25	193·75
.	.					.
.	.					.
.	.					.
↓	↓					↓
∞						200

The arrow pointing from the investment of one period shows the effect of a single investment shock. The horizontal line for any one period contains the components of the increase in income during that period, and shows from which investment shock the individual components derive. With a marginal propensity to consume of $\frac{1}{2}$, the increases in income in the individual periods are given by the following expressions:

1st period: 100
2nd period: $100 + \frac{1}{2} \cdot 100$
3rd period: $100 + \frac{1}{2} \cdot 100 + (\frac{1}{2})^2 \cdot 100$
....
nth period: $100 + \frac{1}{2} \cdot 100 + (\frac{1}{2})^2 \cdot 100 + \ldots + (\frac{1}{2})^{n-1} \cdot 100.$

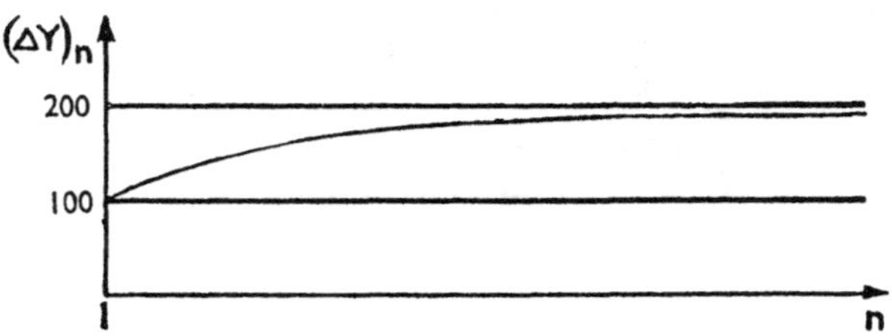

Fig. 33

The increase in income in the nth period represents a geometric series of n terms with a ratio $\frac{1}{2}$. According to the formula for the sum of a finite geometric series the increase in income $(\Delta Y)_n$ is given by

$$(41) \qquad (\Delta Y)_n = \frac{100}{1 - \frac{1}{2}} \cdot [1 - (\tfrac{1}{2})^n] = 200 \, . \; [1 - (\tfrac{1}{2})^n].$$

Since $(\frac{1}{2})^n$ tends towards zero as n increases, (ΔY_n) increases with n and asymptotically approaches 200. Thus we have

$$(42) \qquad \lim_{n \to \infty} (\Delta Y)_n = \Delta Y = 100 \, . \frac{1}{1 - \frac{1}{2}} = 200.$$

Fig. 33 shows the increase in $(\Delta Y)_n$ as n increases. With a marginal propensity to consume of $\frac{1}{2}$ the final effect of a permanent increase in net investment of 100 is a permanent rise in national income of 200. The curve in Fig. 33 shows the path by which this increase is finally reached. As can be seen, the final effect of the multiplier process is achieved only after an infinite number of periods; in practice, however, the new higher equilibrium level of income is reached after a few periods (in our example after five periods).

The relationships which we have illustrated numerically can easily be generalized. For any change in investment ΔI and any marginal propensity to consume $\frac{dC}{dY}$ (41) becomes:

$$(\Delta Y)_n = I \,.\, \frac{1}{1 - \frac{dC}{dY}} \cdot \left[1 - \left(\frac{dC}{dY}\right)^n\right]. \qquad (43)$$

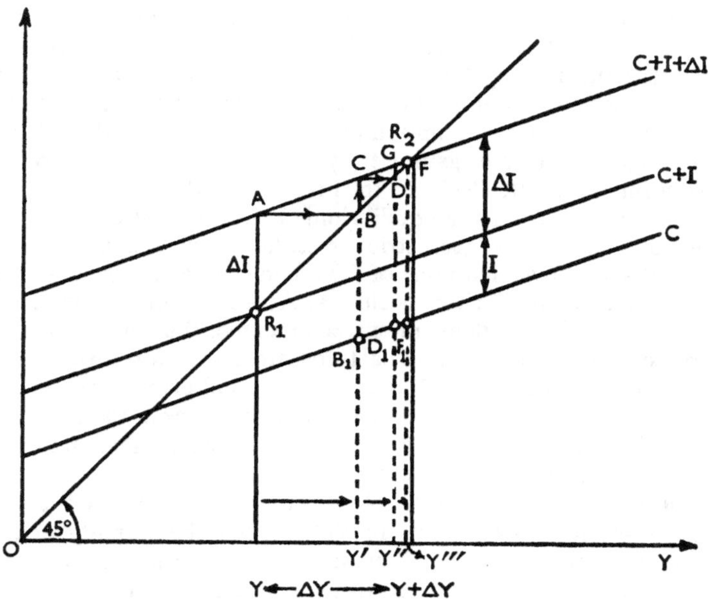

Fig. 34

If $0 < \frac{dC}{dY} < 1$, then as n rises $(\Delta Y)_n$ tends towards:

$$\Delta Y = \Delta I \,.\, \frac{1}{1 - \frac{dC}{dY}}, \qquad (44)$$

that is, to the expression which we already derived in connection with our comparative static analysis (equation 33b).

If the marginal propensity to consume is greater than 1, income increases indefinitely.

4. The effect of a permanent change in net investment can easily be followed on a diagram. In Fig. 34 the curve $C + I$ represents

effective demand (as a function of income), and R_1 or Y the corresponding equilibrium level of income. If net investment now increases permanently by the amount ΔI, this means a parallel upward shift of the curve of effective demand by the amount ΔI, and the new equilibrium income is $Y + \Delta Y$. The diagram shows the path through which the system approaches the new equilibrium. In the first period income rises by ΔI ($= AB$) to the level Y'. In the second period the amount spent on consumption—as given by the consumption function—will be $Y'B_1$ and total effective demand for consumption and net investment will be $Y'C$. Thus in the second period income rises further—by CD—to the level Y''. In the same way, the amount spent on consumption is $Y''D_1$ in the third period, and total effective demand for consumption and net investment will be $Y''G$, which means that income again rises by GF to the level Y''', and so on. The step function $ABCDGF$ . . . thus represents the path by which the system moves from the equilibrium Y to the new equilibrium income $Y + \Delta Y$. This geometric presentation of the process of movement also shows that none of the incomes lying between Y and $Y + \Delta Y$ can be equilibrium positions. At all incomes between Y and $Y + \Delta Y$, effective demand exceeds income, thus giving rise to an expansionary process; individual transactors, therefore, experience surprises. Only when point R_2, i.e. the new equilibrium position, is reached, is effective demand equal to income, and there is no tendency for the level of income $Y + \Delta Y$ to change. Then, and only then, is the system in equilibrium.

Our argument also demonstrates the stability of the new equilibrium position. It was shown in Vol. II that the stability of an equilibrium position can be discussed only in terms of dynamic analysis. We have just considered this sort of analysis; it has shown that whenever the system deviates from point R_2 changes in income result which bring the system back to R_2.

5. The propositions we have demonstrated for the case of a permanent rise in net investment apply similarly to the case of a permanent fall in net investment. A permanent fall in net investment of ΔI will ultimately lead to a fall in income which is larger than ΔI, the extent of the fall in income depending on the investment multiplier, i.e. on the size of the marginal propensity to consume.

6. We can similarly analyse the process of contraction resulting from a *fall in the propensity to consume*. In the following example we suppose that *firms do not foresee the fall in the propensity to consume.*

Let us assume that the economy consists of two vertically integrated firms, each producing one consumer good. Each firm has at its disposal all the raw materials needed for production. For the sake of simplicity let us also assume that buildings and machines never wear out. In the initial position the economy is in a stationary equilibrium in which all workers are employed eight hours per day. The stationary circular flow is given by the following numerical table:

	Firm I	Firm II
Number of workers	150	400
Number of hours worked per day	1200	3200
Hourly wage in £'s	1	1
Total daily wage-bill in £'s	1200	3200
Amount of consumption goods produced and sold per day (in number of units)	1200	3200
Price (in £'s) per unit of consumption goods	1·50	1·25
Daily turnover in £'s	1800	4000
Profit per day in £'s	600	800

The distribution of sales is as follows:

	Firm I		Firm II	
	£'s per day	units per day	£'s per day	units per day
Households of workers employed by Firm I	600	400	600	480
Households of workers employed by Firm II	450	300	2750	2200
Households of Firm I	450	300	150	120
Households of Firm II	300	200	500	400
Totals	1800	1200	4000	3200

The effective demand of workers' households H_{nf} is £4400 per day, and that of firms' households H_f is £1400 per day. The national income of the stationary economy is thus £5800 per day.

The circular flow of the creation and use of income in this stationary economy may be depicted as follows (Fig. 35):

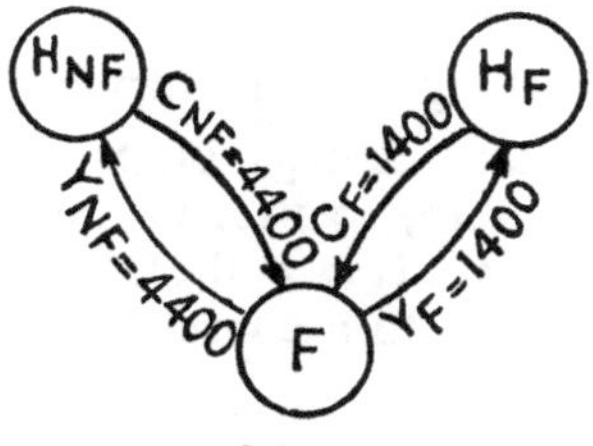

Fig. 35

Let us now assume that workers' households reduce their consumption by £1100 per day from a certain day onwards; this reduction is brought about by the workers of firm I reducing their consumption by £600 per day, and those of firm II by £500 per day. What effect does this voluntary reduction in workers' consumption have at the end of the first day? Firms will obviously experience surprises; they will be unable to sell part of their daily production, which previously had been entirely sold. Firm I will have an unsold stock of 400 units, as will firm II. For both firms these unsold stocks represent unintended investment. The original cost of this unintended net investment is £800, which is equal to the wages paid for producing the unsold stocks. Moreover, at the end of the first day on which the additional savings take place, firms will have received a smaller income than hitherto. Their income will have fallen by £300, that is by an amount equal to the profits formerly obtained on the stocks now unsold. On the first day the *ex-post* income of firms will be £1100,[(1)] and this implies that their savings are negative; the consumption of firms has exceeded their income by £300. On the first day firms will have had to increase their debts by £300 in order to maintain their consumption at the previous level. They will have had to increase their debts by a further £800 in order to finance the unintended net investment. At the end of the first day the result is that firms will have been forced to incur debts to an amount exactly equal to the voluntary savings of workers. Figure 36 shows the *ex-post* circular flow of the first day. The Keynesian equation applies at the end of the first day. In our example, $S = 1100 - 300 = 800$, and $I = 800$. *Ex-post* S and I are always and necessarily equal, since for the economy as a whole net investment in any period is the same thing as net savings in the same period, and vice-versa. *There cannot be positive net savings for the economy as a whole unless there is an equal amount of net investment.* The equation $I = S$ is fulfilled at every moment of time, since it represents a necessary *ex-post* identity. But it would be a serious error to confuse this identity with the equilibrium condition

$$\text{voluntary savings} = \text{voluntary investment}.$$

In our example, voluntary savings on the first day are £1100; voluntary investment is zero, so that voluntary savings are larger than voluntary investment. Hence there is disequilibrium which (as was shown above) leads to a contraction in income as long as

(1) This follows immediately from the macro-economic equation for the profits of firms in a closed economy (see Vol. I, 7th edn., p. 55). According to this equation, the following always holds *ex-post*:

$$\begin{aligned} Y_f &= I - S_{nf} + C_f \\ &= 800 - 1100 + 1400 \\ &= 1100 \end{aligned}$$

voluntary savings exceed voluntary net investment. *Our example clearly shows how this process of contraction comes about. Unintended net investment and the negative savings of firms induce firms to curtail production.* Workers become unemployed only as a result of this curtailment of production during the second day. The savings of workers thus do not *automatically* lead to unemployment. If, from the second day on, firms were willing to undertake net investment of £800 per day and to consume £300 per day in excess of their

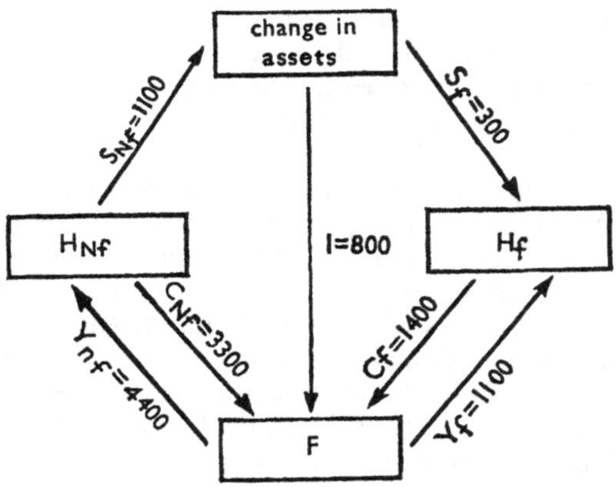

Fig. 36

income (i.e. if firms were willing to incur debts equal to the voluntary savings by workers) the circular flow of income from day to day would be maintained as above. Such behaviour on the part of firms is, however, unlikely; it would mean a continual accumulation of unsold stocks and a continual rise in debts to finance the consumption of firms. It is more likely that firms will react by curtailing production further on the third day; and the contraction will continue until national income has fallen so low that voluntary savings are once more equal to zero.

§4. The History and Development of Multiplier Theory (The Multi-Sector Multiplier)

1. The idea that a change in effective demand has multiplier effects on income and employment already appears in economic theory around the turn of the century. The theory of inflation developed by Wicksell in his book *Interest and Prices* is a multiplier theory, even if it is not explicitly couched in such terms. N. Johannsen

developed the multiplier theorem clearly—using the same term—for the deflationary case in his theory of economic depressions, first published in 1903, and reformulated in his book *Die Steuer der Zukunft* (Berlin 1913). In two sections of this book, "The Multiplying Principle" and "The Importance of the Multiplying Principle" (pp. 232 ff and 259 ff), Johannsen gives a lucid account of the multiplier process. A few quotations should demonstrate his achievement: "This principle (the multiplier principle [*E.S.*]) rests on the fact that those individuals whose incomes are reduced through the savings process (in its disturbing form) in turn reduce their expenditure and thus further reduce total demand.

The expert will say that in reality the principle can never operate in the simple manner assumed above, that numerous economic factors intervene which substantially modify the result, e.g. reductions in prices, the opening up of foreign markets, and so on. Quite so. But this is not the point. The purpose of the above analysis is to demonstrate the effect of the principle alone, excluding all other modifying factors. Only in this way can one get a clear picture of the inherent value of the principle and of its importance.

In any case it is not difficult to observe the multiplier principle and its effects in the real world. Let us assume that there is a reduction in capital accumulation, e.g. as a result of a crisis, which leads to depression. This will have the following effects: there will be an immediate reduction in the employment of workers, businessmen and traders, who so far participated in the expansion. Let us denote this unemployment by K. As long as this group was employed and earning, and spent its income on the necessities of life, it created income and employment for another group L which produced these necessities. Group L in turn spent its income on the necessities of life, and thus provided income and employment for a group M. In this way, as in an endless chain, one group provides income and employment for another. If group K now becomes unemployed the whole chain is affected. Group K has lost its income, and must reduce its consumption to a minimum, thus reducing the income of group L. Group L cannot spend as much as before, which leads to a reduction in the income of group M, and so on. The damaging effect levels off as the process continues, but at each round it is distributed over a larger number of individuals. The damaging effect takes place inexorably and in its entirety amounts to much more than the original loss to group K—due to the multiplier principle" (pp. 234, 235).

Later, Johannsen attempts to provide a quantitative estimate of the multiplier effect: "If the primary damage is 2 billion, i.e. if this is the amount which group K, so far engaged in the expansion, loses in income through being unemployed, is there anything to tell us how far the multiplier principle will spread the damaging effect over the groups L, M, N and so on (p. 235)?

"In the absence of any statistics we can only conjecture as to the probable effects.

"If group K loses 2 billion in the course of a year, it will reduce its consumption, but not by the same amount. Even the worker who is completely unemployed does not remain without food, shelter and clothing. If he cannot fall back on savings, he will borrow money from friends, fail to pay his rent, sell anything he can do without, perhaps receive financial support from his trade union or become a burden on public charity. It is probably realistic to assume that he reduces his consumption to a third of what it was, thus reducing his previous consumption by two-thirds. Analogously with this individual example we may reasonably assume that the members of group K reduce their consumption on the average by two-thirds of the loss in income. Accordingly, a completely unemployed worker would reduce his consumption from the previous 1,500 M to 500 M per annum. The worker whose wages are halved (who now earns 750 M) reduces his consumption from 1,500 M to 1,000 M; the businessman who previously spent 3,000 M a year and who suffers a reduction in his income of 900 M will reduce his expenditure by 600 M—to 2,400 M. That is to say, on our assumption, the entire group K on the average reduces its consumption by two-thirds of its loss of income" (pp. 262/63).

Johannsen thus estimates a marginal propensity to consume of $\frac{2}{3}$ and calculates the multiplier effect on this basis. Even though Johannsen is primarily concerned with the downward multiplier effect, he obviously realizes that the same effect can work in an upward direction: "If in practice the multiplier principle has a powerful influence in increasing the damaging effect of any fall in demand, so too the principle will work in a desirable direction if something happens to stimulate total demand. If a new market were found, at a time when business was quiet, where an additional million's worth of goods could be sold, this would raise total sales and total production not only by 1 million, but by at least 5 million" (pp. 266/67).

More recently a detailed analysis of the multiplier process was given by R. F. Kahn in an article "The Relation of Home Investment to Unemployment", *Economic Journal*, 1931. In this article Kahn gave a precise exposition of the same concepts but applied them to an expansionary process. However, the theory of the multiplier became one of the focal points of discussion only when J. M. Keynes made it an integral part of his *General Theory of Employment, Interest and Money* (London 1936). This discussion still continues. On the one hand there were, and still are, some points which require clarification. On the other hand, the highly simplified models of Johannsen and Kahn require extension in certain directions. We shall mention two of the many questions with which current research is concerned, so as to indicate to the reader where further work still remains to be done.

2. The first question relates to the time it takes for the multiplier process to work itself out. In our dynamic analysis we spoke of the multiplier effect in the first, second etc. period, and saw that already after a small number of periods the size of the effect was very near the final equilibrium value. However, we still have to know how long these periods are, whether they last a week, a month or a year. This is especially important from the point of view of economic policy. Johannsen was of the opinion that "in the processes analysed here the interval between cause and effect is not long; for example, it is not the case that during one year the effect of the disturbing savings (that is, savings without investment [E.S.]) prevails and in the next year the multiplication of the disturbance ensues. Rather, cause and effect proceed together hand in hand" (loc. cit., p. 267). It is possible, indeed probable, that Johannsen's conjecture is correct. Yet, to answer our question, we require detailed empirical investigations of the reactions of firms and households to changes in demand and income, and of the technical possibilities regarding the speed of adjustment in production. Attempts to answer these questions were made by F. Machlup[1] and more recently by G. Ackley.[2]

3. The second question arises in connection with the assumption which is usually made—and which we too have made—that all economic units have the same marginal propensity to consume. This assumption is permissible when demonstrating the fundamental relationships. However, the theory must also be developed on the assumption that the individual groups (e.g. firms' households and workers' households) have different marginal propensities to consume, and that the marginal propensities to consume change in the course of time. The development of the theory on the basis of this more general assumption requires the disaggregation of the large aggregates of consumption and net investment into smaller aggregates

(1) F. Machlup, "Period Analysis and Multiplier Theory"; reprinted in *Readings in Business Cycle Theory* (Allen & Unwin 1944), p. 203 ff.

(2) G. Ackley, "The Multiplier Time Period: Money, Inventories, and Flexibility". *American Economic Review*, Vol. 41, 1951, p. 350 ff.

relating to the individual sub-groups. We must do this, however, without basing the analysis on the ultimate individual decision-making units. An important part of current research is concerned with this problem, but only recently has this necessary extension of the theory of the multiplier been attempted (R. Goodwin, "The Multiplier as Matrix").[1]

4. An important development of multiplier theory in this direction has been achieved by the attempt to ascertain quantitatively the repercussions of changes in demand on the various sectors of an economy. Because of its importance we shall illustrate the multi-sector multiplier on the simplest assumptions, using the so-called input-output analysis developed by W. Leontief.[2] Assume an economy which produces two goods, 1 and 2, say coal and electricity; good 1 is produced in sector 1 (mining) and good 2 in sector 2 (electricity production). Both electricity and coal are required in the production of coal. Sector 1 thus purchases electricity from sector 2, and coal from itself. Both electricity and coal are required in the production of electricity. Sector 2 thus purchases coal from sector 1, and electricity from itself. The aggregate production of coal must meet the demand for coal in both the mining and electricity sectors, and the demand for coal for consumption and investment. The total output of electricity must meet the corresponding requirements. Let us call the demand for goods 1 and 2 for purposes of consumption and investment *autonomous demand*, and the demand for those goods arising in sector 1 and 2 *derived demand.*

Let us denote the sales (at ruling prices) of sector 1 to sector 1 and 2 by x_{11} and x_{12} respectively. We similarly denote the sales of sector 2 to sector 1 and 2 by x_{21} and x_{22} respectively. The first subscript thus denotes the *supplying* sector, and the second subscript the *receiving* sector.

Let x_{1a} and x_{2a} represent the amounts supplied by sectors 1 and 2 respectively to meet the autonomous demand (for consumption and investment).[3] If we denote the total output (measured in units of

(1) *Economic Journal*, Vol. 59, 1949, pp. 537 ff. A discussion of further controversial issues connected with the theory of the multiplier is to be found in the article by G. L. S. Shackle "Twenty Years on: A Survey of the Multiplier", *Economic Journal*, Vol. 61, 1951.

(2) See especially: W. Leontief, *The Structure of the American Economy* 1919–1939, 2nd edn. New York 1951; and *Studies in the Structure of the American Economy*, New York 1953; O. Morgenstern, *Economic Activity Analysis*, New York 1955; W. Leontief, "Die Methode der Input-Output-Analyse". *Allgemeines Statistisches Archiv*, Vol. 36, 1952; R. Dorfman, "The Nature and Significance of Input-Output". *The Review of Economics and Statistics*, Vol. 36, 1954, p. 121 ff.

(3) Leonteif designates x_{1a} and x_{2a} as "the final bill of goods".

money) of sectors 1 and 2 in any one period by X_1 and X_2 respectively, then by definition:

$$X_1 = x_{11} + x_{12} + x_{1a} \tag{45}$$
$$X_2 = x_{21} + x_{22} + x_{1a}$$

The following table, which is simply an *input-output table* familiar to readers of Vol. I,[1] shows how the sectors are linked to one another.

Sales \ Purchases	1 Coal	2 Electricity	Autonomous demand (a)	Total
1 Coal	x_{11}	x_{12}	x_{1a}	X_1
2 Electricity	x_{21}	x_{22}	x_{2a}	X_2

This sort of table merely represents the truistic information contained in the identities (45); yet, it can be used for analytic purposes if we know what determines the purchases of one sector from another. It is reasonable to assume that, given productive equipment and prices,[2] the purchases of one sector from another are a function of the sector's total output,[3] i.e. that:

$$x_{ik} = f_{ik}(X_k) \qquad (i, k = 1, 2) \tag{46}$$

For the sake of simplicity we assume that the function is linear and has the following form:

$$x_{ik} = a_{ik} \,.\, X_k \qquad (0 \leqq a_{ik} < 1) \tag{47}$$

where a_{ik} is a constant. The sales of sector i to sector k are thus assumed to be proportional to the total output of sector k. If we write equation (47) in the form:

$$a_{ik} = \frac{x_{ik}}{X_k}, \qquad (i, k = 1, 2) \tag{48}$$

we see that a_{ik} represents the amount of good i necessary for the production of one unit of good k, and is thus identical with the technical coefficients of production, explained in Vol. II.[4] In our

(1) See Vol. I, 7th edn., 1958, pp. 125–126.

(2) This assumption enables us to neglect the possibilities of substitution.

(3) This assumption takes us into the field of input-output *analysis*, which conceptually must be distinguished from the input-output *table*.

(4) The numerical value of these coefficients may be ascertained either directly from the production function or from an input-output table.

example we have four technical coefficients which are given by the following relationships:

(49)
$$x_{11} = a_{11} \cdot X_1 \qquad x_{21} = a_{21} \cdot X_1$$
$$x_{12} = a_{12} \cdot X_2 \qquad x_{22} = a_{22} \cdot X_2.$$

Using these equations (45) becomes:

(50)
$$X_1 = a_{11} \cdot X_1 + a_{12} \cdot X_2 + x_{1a}$$
$$X_2 = a_{21} \cdot X_1 + a_{22} \cdot X_2 + x_{2a}.$$

In these two equations the coefficients a_{ik} are given constants which are technically determined. X_1 and X_2 denote the total output of sectors 1 and 2 respectively. Let us now assume that the autonomous demand for the two goods for consumption and investment (i.e. the values of x_{1a} and x_{2a}) is given exogenously. The system of equations (50) then enables us to calculate the necessary output of the two goods, by solving for X_1 and X_2. We then have:

(51)
$$X_1 = \frac{1 - a_{22}}{D} \cdot x_{1a} + \frac{a_{12}}{D} \cdot x_{2a}$$
$$X_2 = \frac{a_{21}}{D} \cdot x_{1a} + \frac{1 - a_{11}}{D} \cdot x_{2a},$$

where
$$D = 1 - a_{11} - a_{22} + a_{11} \cdot a_{22} - a_{21} \cdot a_{12}$$

If we abbreviate:
$$A_{11} = \frac{1 - a_{22}}{D}; \qquad A_{21} = \frac{a_{21}}{D}$$
$$A_{12} = \frac{a_{12}}{D}; \qquad A_{22} = \frac{1 - a_{11}}{D},$$

the solution of the system of equations (50) is of the following form:

(52)
$$X_1 = A_{11} \cdot x_{1a} + A_{12} \cdot x_{2a}$$
$$X_2 = A_{21} \cdot x_{1a} + A_{22} \cdot x_{2a}.$$

The total output of the individual sectors is thus solely determined by the size of the autonomous demand and the technical conditions of production. This is so since the coefficients A_{11}, A_{12}, A_{21}, A_{22}, are determined uniquely by the technical production coefficients a_{ik}.(1)

Now let us ask how the size of the total output of both sectors varies with the level of autonomous demand, i.e. in what way X_1 and X_2 change when there is a change in x_{1a} or x_{2a}. Equation (52) immediately gives an answer to this question. If x_{1a} is to change by the amount dx_{1a}, then X_1 must change by an amount dX_1, which is obtained by multiplying dx_{1a} by the coefficient of x_{1a} in equation (52), i.e. by A_{11}. Therefore:

$$dX_1 = \frac{1 - a_{22}}{D} \cdot dx_{1a}.$$

Similarly X_2 must increase by an amount dX_2:

$$dX_2 = \frac{a_{21}}{D} \cdot dx_{1a}$$

The increase in the autonomous demand for good 1 thus has an effect on *both* sectors; and the size of this effect is given by the two coefficients of x_{1a} in the system of equations (52). These two coefficients are therefore called *sector multipliers* for good 1. Similarly

(1) Consider a numerical example. Let

$$a_{11} = 0{\cdot}4; \qquad a_{12} = 0{\cdot}3$$
$$a_{21} = 0{\cdot}1; \qquad a_{22} = 0{\cdot}6.$$

Then

$$X_1 = \tfrac{40}{21} \cdot x_{1a} + \tfrac{30}{21} \cdot x_{2a}$$
$$X_2 = \tfrac{10}{21} \cdot x_{1a} + \tfrac{60}{21} \cdot x_{2a}.$$

The total output of both goods thus depends on the level of autonomous demand for consumption and investment. For example, if

$$x_{1a} = 21 \qquad \text{and} \qquad x_{2a} = 42,$$

then it must be the case that

$$X_1 = 100 \qquad \text{and} \qquad X_2 = 130.$$

Total output will be divided between the individual sectors in the following way:

Sales \ Purchases	1	2	*a* Autonomous demand	*X* Total
1	40	39	21	100
2	10	78	42	130

The production of 21 units of good 1 and of 42 units of good 2 for consumption and investment thus requires an output of 100 units of good 1 and of 130 units of good 2; and of this output 79 units of good 1 and 88 units of good 2 are absorbed by sectors 1 and 2 in the course of production.

the coefficients of x_{2a} in (52) represent the sector multipliers for good 2.[1] Although we have used a two-sector model in our example the analysis can be applied directly to a model of more than two sectors. If there are m ($m \geqq 2$) non-autonomous sectors and goods we have the following system instead of the system of equations (50):

$$
\begin{aligned}
X_1 &= a_{11} \cdot X_1 + a_{12} \cdot X_2 + \ldots + a_{1m} \cdot X_m + x_{1a} \\
X_2 &= a_{21} \cdot X_1 + a_{22} \cdot X_2 + \ldots + a_{2m} \cdot X_m + x_{2a} \\
&\ldots\ldots\ldots\ldots\ldots\ldots\ldots\ldots\ldots\ldots \\
X_m &= a_{m1} \cdot X_1 + a_{m2} \cdot X_2 + \ldots + a_{mm} \cdot X_m + x_{ma},
\end{aligned}
\tag{53}
$$

where the coefficients a_{ik} ($0 \leqq a_{ik} < 1$) denote the technical coefficients of production and the variables x_{ia} ($i = 1, 2, \ldots, m$) the autonomous demand for the m goods. If we solve this system for $X_1, X_2, \ldots, X_m$, we obtain the value of the total output of the individual sectors as a function of the technical coefficients of production and of autonomous demand. It can be shown that the solution of (53) may be written in the same way as that for the two-sector case (52):

$$
\begin{aligned}
X_1 &= A_{11} \cdot x_{1a} + A_{12} \cdot x_{2a} + \ldots + A_{1m} \cdot x_{ma} \\
X_2 &= A_{21} \cdot x_{1a} + A_{22} \cdot x_{2a} + \ldots + A_{2m} \cdot x_{ma} \\
&\ldots\ldots\ldots\ldots\ldots\ldots\ldots\ldots\ldots\ldots \\
X_m &= A_{m1} \cdot x_{1a} + A_{m2} \cdot x_{2a} + \ldots + A_{mm} \cdot x_{ma}.
\end{aligned}
\tag{54}
$$

In this system the coefficients A_{ik} of x_{ia} ($i = 1, 2, \ldots, m$) denote the sector multipliers. They show by how much the total output of all sectors must be increased when there is a change in the autonomous demand for one good. The system of equations (53) and (54) shows

[1] In our numerical example the sector multipliers for good 1 are:

$$\frac{\partial X_1}{\partial x_{1a}} = \frac{40}{21}; \qquad \frac{\partial X_2}{\partial x_{1a}} = \frac{10}{21}$$

and those for good 2:

$$\frac{\partial X_1}{\partial x_{2a}} = \frac{30}{21}; \qquad \frac{\partial X_2}{\partial x_{2a}} = \frac{60}{21}.$$

If, for example, the autonomous demand for good 1 increases from 21 to 42, total production of sector 2 must be increased by 10:

Sales \ Purchases	1	2	*a* Autonomous demand	*X* Total
1	56	42	42	140
2	14	84	42	140

the interdependence of all sectors. It also shows the direct and indirect effects on the whole system of a change in autonomous demand for consumption and investment.[1]

§5. The Case When Net Investment Depends on the Rate of Interest

1. We must now extent and supplement the first, simple, model of income determination developed in § 1 and § 3 by changing the assumptions at some important points. Until now we assumed that net investment was either constant or depended solely on the level of income. But our analysis of investment planning in Vol. II[2] showed that the decisive factors in the investment decisions of firms are expected receipts, expected outlays and the internal rate of interest. We must now consider how our analysis is modified when we assume that, with given expectations, intended investment by firms is a function of the rate of interest. On this assumption the rate of interest appears as a new variable in our analysis. We have to introduce the rate of interest to gain a real understanding of the process of income formation in a market economy.

2. It was shown in Vol. II that an investment is profitable to a firm if its capital value, discounted to the time immediately before the beginning of the project, is not negative. The relevant discount rate is the internal discount rate used by the firm for planning purposes. It was shown further that of several profitable investment opportunities, the most profitable is that whose capital value is greatest. Given expectations regarding the series of receipts and outlays, the decision to carry out an investment project thus depends solely on the internal rate of interest at which these are discounted. It was also shown in detail in Vol. II that this rate of interest is subjectively determined: it depends on the long term rate of interest, the desired profit and the risks of the investment. This rate will never be lower than the long-term market rate, but will be above it to an extent dependent on the level of desired profits and the risks involved. However, economic policy can have a direct influence only on the market rate of interest. In the context of the theory of income determination, therefore, we must ask the following question: given expectations regarding the series of receipts and outlays, what is the relationship between the long-term market rate of interest and the level of intended investment, or, how does a change in the rate of interest

(1) The reader who is interested in input-output analysis should consult the literature listed on p. 135. Also: P. Nørregaard-Rasmussen, *Studies in Inter-Sectoral Relations*, Copenhagen 1956.

(2) Vol. II, Ch. II, Section F.

affect the investment decisions of firms? This question, too, was discussed in detail in Vol. II, where we showed that (always assuming given expectations) the decisions regarding *certain* investment projects are hardly affected by the market rate of interest and perhaps not at all. To this group belong those investment projects which the firm discounts by an internal rate of interest which is considerably above the market rate. But decisions to carry out certain other investment projects depend to a considerable extent on the market rate of

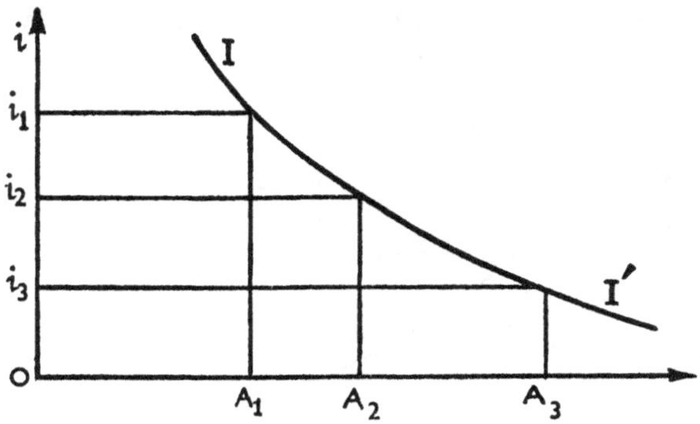

Fig. 37

interest. To this group belong the relatively safe investments and especially investments of long duration, where even a small change in the rate of interest will bring about a considerable increase in investment. All these considerations must be borne in mind during the analysis which follows, where we shall regard the level of investment in any one period (measured by the total amount firms devote to net investment, given current and expected prices) as a function of the market rate of interest. In Fig. 37 the rate of interest is measured along the vertical axis and the level of net investment along the horizontal axis. The curve *II'* indicates the dependence of the level of net investment on the rate of interest, given expectations regarding the stream of future receipts and outlays. This curve describes the *firms' propensity to invest* at alternative rates of interest. A fall (rise) in the propensity to invest means that firms (taken as a group) will wish to invest less (more) at each possible rate of interest, which will be expressed by a shift of the investment curve to the left (right). This is shown in Fig. 38. A change in the propensity to invest must be distinguished sharply from the dependence of net investment on the rate of interest, *given* the propensity to invest. The latter is expressed by the elasticity of net investment with respect to the rate of interest. Let the investment function be:

$$I = I(i), \tag{55}$$

then the elasticity $\eta_{I,i}$ will be given by:

$$\eta_{I,i} = \frac{dI}{I} \div \frac{di}{i} \cdot \frac{dI}{di}. \tag{56}$$

The elasticity of I with respect to i thus refers to a small change along a given investment curve, while a change in the propensity to invest

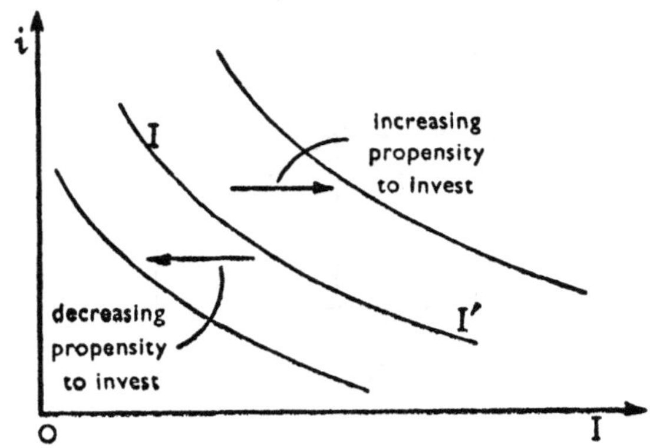

Fig. 38

refers to a shift in the investment curve. As will be seen later, the elasticity of I with respect to i is as important in the analysis of this and the following paragraphs as a shift in the propensity to invest. Given the propensity to invest, the numerical value of the elasticity of investment depends on the rate of interest. Depending on the shape of the investment function, the elasticity of investment at any given rate of interest might be zero, smaller than 1, equal to 1, or greater than 1. Indeed it is possible that net investment might be completely inelastic with respect to the rate of interest, so that $\eta_{I,i}$ is equal to zero at *each* value of i. In this case no matter how large the change in the rate of interest, there will be no change in net investment. Given expectations regarding receipts and outlays, investment decisions are determined by the internal rate of discount of individual firms, and this rate might not be affected by a fall in the market rate of interest. But even if the propensity to invest is not completely interest inelastic a fall in the market rate of interest need not lead to a rise in the level of investment. The rise in investment which would then occur, if the propensity to invest remained unchanged, might in fact not take place because of a simultaneous fall in the propensity to invest. Similarly, there might be an increase in the level of investment, because of a rise in the propensity to invest, even though the rate of interest remained unchanged. In an atmosphere of optimism it might be unnecessary to manipulate the rate of interest in order to bring about an expansion in investment; and in a period of depression and deep pessimism neither reductions in the rate of interest nor other measures might stimulate the desire of firms to undertake new investment projects.

3. We can now indicate how national income is determined if both the investment and consumption functions are known. Since we are assuming that net investment is a function of the rate of interest (assuming given expectations regarding receipts and outlays) we have the following equations to determine income:

(57a) $$Y = C + I$$

(57b) $$C = C(Y)$$

(57c) $$I = I(i).$$

Equation (57a) describes the equilibrium condition; equations (57b) and (57c) are behaviour equations, which express the propensity to consume of households and the propensity to invest of firms. Using (57b) and (57c), (57a) becomes:

(58) $$Y = C(Y) + I(i).$$

Equation (58) contains two variables—Y and i, so that we can determine income only if i is given. As we know from Vol. II, we express this by saying that our system has one degree of freedom, which means that the numerical value of one variable may be chosen arbitrarily. *If the value of i is determined autonomously by the central bank*, this determines the level of investment via the propensity to invest. Equation (58) then yields the level of income corresponding to this level of net investment. The relationship between the rate of interest and the level of income can be seen more easily if we use the savings function $S(Y)$ instead of the consumption function $C(Y)$. Equation (58) is then replaced by:

(58a) $$S(Y) = I(i).$$

Fig. 39 comprises two sets of co-ordinates with a common vertical axis. The savings function is represented on the right-hand side of the diagram (with S and Y on the axes), and the investment function on the left-hand side of the diagram (with I and i on the axes). Let us assume that the rate of interest is autonomously determined at i_1. At this rate of interest firms will carry out investments at the level A_1B_1. As we know, the equilibrium level of income corresponding to this level of investment is that at which total voluntary savings by households are equal to planned investment. To find this level of income, we need only draw a line parallel to the horizontal axis at a distance A_1B_1. The equilibrium level of income Y_1 corresponding to the level of net investment A_1B_1 is given by the value on the horizontal axis immediately below the intersection of this parallel

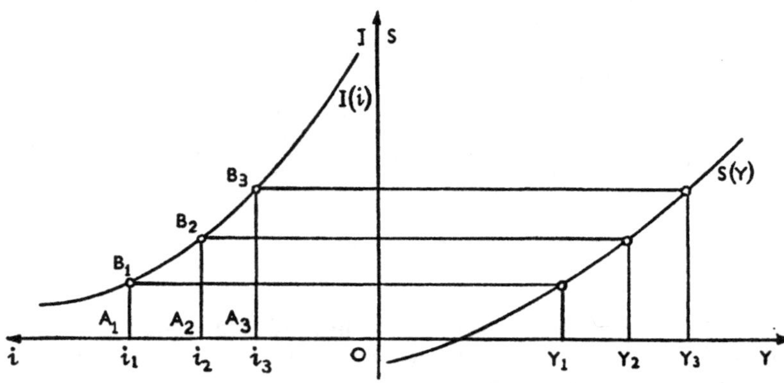

Fig. 39

line with the savings curve $S(Y)$. If, instead, the rate of interest were i_2 ($i_2 < i_1$) firms would carry out the higher level of investment A_2B_2, as indicated by the propensity to invest. The corresponding equilibrium level of income would be Y_2. A yet higher level of income Y_3 would correspond to the lower rate of interest i_3. Given the propensities to invest and to consume, the lower the rate of interest the higher the equilibrium level of income. Equations (58a) or (58) determine a unique level of income for each rate of interest. *This establishes the following theorem: given the propensities to invest and to save, the rate of interest determines the equilibrium level of income.*

The extent to which a small fall in the rate of interest raises the equilibrium level of income depends on two factors: (a) the elasticity of net investment with respect to the rate of interest and (b) the elasticity of savings with respect to income. If net investment is completely interest inelastic, a change in the rate of interest will not lead to a change in income.

Fig. 39 also shows (in terms of comparative statics) how the relationship between the rate of interest and income, as indicated by equation (58a), changes when there is an upward shift in the propensity to invest, the propensity to save remaining the same. A rise in the propensity to invest means a shift upward in the investment curve, i.e. at each rate of interest more is invested than before. At the rate of interest i_1 net investment is now greater than A_1B_1 and thus the equilibrium level of income is higher than Y_1; at the rate of interest i_2 net investment is now greater than A_2B_2 and thus the equilibrium level of income is higher than Y_2, and so on.

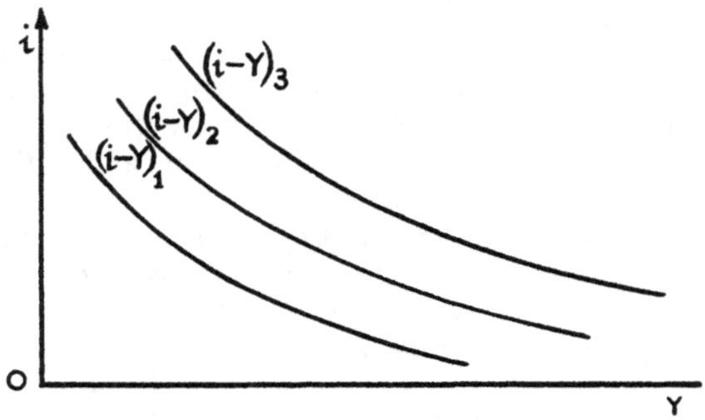

Fig. 40

In Fig. 40 the curve $(i - Y)_1$ represents the relationship between i and Y at a given propensity to invest, and the curves $(i - Y)_2$, $(i - Y)_3$ represent the same relationship at higher propensities to invest.

4. We may add to the relation (58a) the demand function for central bank money:

$$L(Y, i) = M \tag{59}$$

which was explained in Chapter II, §4,(ii). This merely supplements the analysis just developed. The introduction of equation (59), which describes the demand for central bank money for transactions and speculative purposes, does not alter the number of degrees of freedom in our system. We have added one variable (M) but have at the same time added a new equation, the demand-function for central bank money. Thus the system of equations (58a) and (59) also possesses only one degree of freedom, i.e. one variable may be chosen arbitrarily.

If the central bank fixes the rate of interest, equation (58a) determines the equilibrium level of income through the savings and investment functions. Equation (59) then indicates the quantity of money demanded for transactions and speculative purposes at this rate of interest and at this level of income. The level of income given by (58a), which corresponds to the fixed rate of interest, can only be attained if the central bank makes available the appropriate quantity of money. Instead of asking which level of income and what quantity of money correspond to an autonomously fixed rate of interest, we may ask what the rate of interest and the quantity of money must be if a certain level of income is to be reached, say a level corresponding to full employment. This second way of putting the question is a simple example of the kind of problem that arises in *decision models* with which so much current research is concerned.[1] One of the variables, income, now becomes a goal variable, while the rate of interest is an instrument of policy, and the quantity of money a passive variable. The rate of interest is an instrument of an economic policy which aims at a given level of income; the quantity of money will adjust passively to the desired level of income and to the rate of interest corresponding to that income.

5. *If the central bank fixes the quantity of money*, equations (58a) and (59) determine the rate of interest and national income.

Given the propensity to consume (or to save), the propensity to invest, liquidity preference and the quantity of money, the equilibrium level of income and the rate of interest must be such that (a) voluntary savings at that level of income are equal to voluntary net investment at that rate of interest, and (b) the demand for money for transactions and speculative purposes is equal to the quantity of money available in the economy.

The equilibrium values can be ascertained easily using the following diagram. Let us draw the curves representing the two equations (58a) and (59) in one set of co-ordinates (Fig. 41.). The form of the function given by equation (58a) is represented in Fig. 40. The relationship between Y and i, given M, which is derived from the liquidity preference function, was explained in Chapter II, pp. 77–80. The co-ordinates of the point T where the two curves intersect give the values i_0 and Y_0 of the rate of interest and income respectively, which are the equilibrium values satisfying equations (58a) and (59). This method of determining the equilibrium values of Y and i was suggested by J. R. Hicks.[2] A second method of ascertaining the equilibrium values of Y and i was developed by T. Palander.[3] We now add a third set of co-ordinates (axes i and Y, Fig. 42) to

(1) See J. Tinbergen, *On the Theory of Economic Policy*, Amsterdam, 1952, and the same author's, *Economic Policy; Principles and Design*, Amsterdam 1956.

(2) J. R. Hicks, "Mr. Keynes and the Classics; a Suggested Interpretation", *Econometrica*, Vol. V, 1937, pp. 152–153.

(3) T. Palander, "Keynes' almänna teori och dess tillämpning inom ränte-, multplikator- och pristeorien". *Ekonomisk Tidsskrift*, Vol. 44, 1942; p. 233 ff, especially pages 239–240.

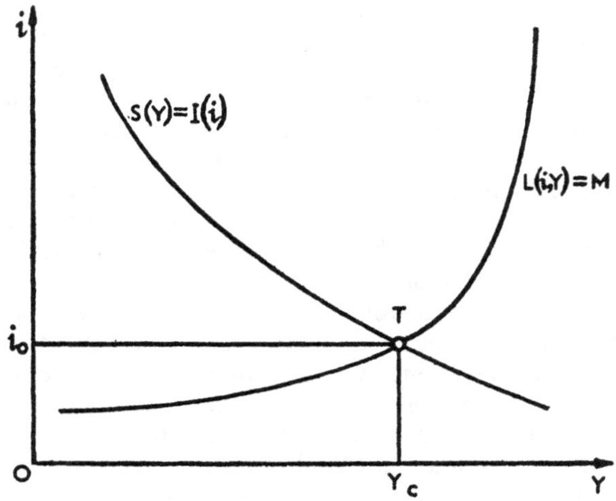
i
S(Y)=I(i)
L(i,Y)=M
T
i_0
O
Y_c
Y

Fig. 41

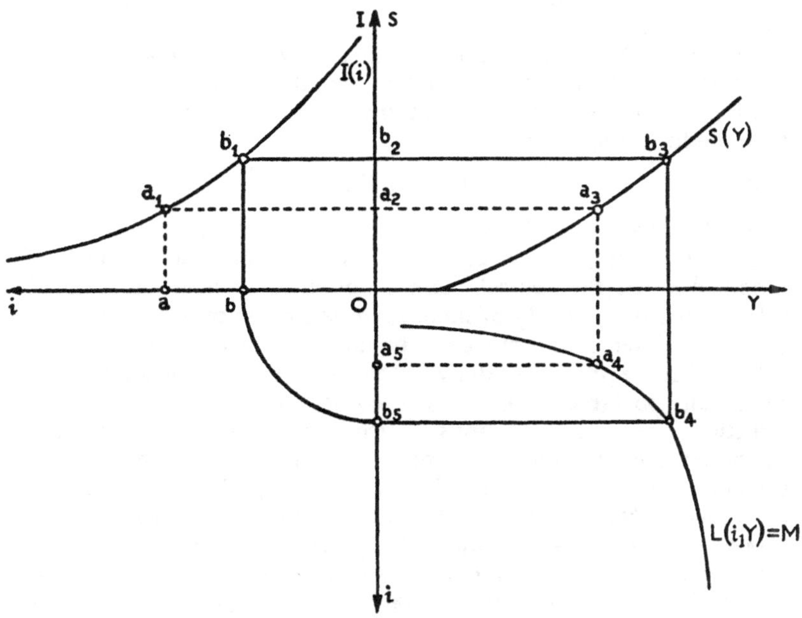
I
S
I(i)
b_1
b_2
b_3
S(Y)
a_1
a_2
a_3
i
a
b
O
Y
a_5
a_4
b_5
b_4
L(i,Y)=M
i

Fig. 42

the two sets representing the savings and investment functions shown in Fig. 39. In the third set we represent the relationship between Y and i given by equation (59), i.e. the function $L(i, Y)$. We must now look for those values of i and Y and of S and I which *simultaneously* satisfy the three functions represented by the curves. Let us begin by assuming that the rate of interest is at point a on the horizontal i-axis. Given the propensity to invest, the net investment corresponding to that rate of interest is aa_1. Given the propensity to save, the income corresponding to that level of investment is a_2a_3. But with the given liquidity preference and the given quantity of money, the level of income $a_2a_3 = a_4a_5$ would require a rate of interest a_5, which is smaller than the assumed initial rate of interest a. Thus the rate of interest a and the level of income a_2a_3 cannot represent equilibrium values. The equilibrium rate of interest must be smaller than a. By trial and error one finds that there will be equilibrium when the rate of interest is at point b on the horizontal axis. As can be seen, the level of income corresponding to the rate of interest b is b_2b_3, and at this level of income voluntary savings and net investment are equal. Moreover the values of i and Y also fulfill the condition $L(i, Y) = M$.

6. Our results would not be fundamentally altered if we assumed net investment to depend not only on the rate of interest but also on the level of national income. The investment function would then take the following form:

$$I = I(i, Y). \tag{60}$$

The detailed analysis of this case is left to the reader.

The reader might also consider how our conclusions must be modified when the central bank autonomously fixes the rate of interest *and* the quantity of money, i.e. when the central bank fixes the rate of interest and pursues a policy of credit rationing.

7. Before we proceed to draw further conclusions let us summarize the results so far established. The corner-stones of our analytical structure are three functions which express certain behaviour relations: the consumption function, or its inverse, the savings function, the investment function, and the liquidity function. *The behaviour relations expressed by these functions, together with the rate of interest (or the quantity of money) fixed by the banking system, simultaneously determine the level of national income as well as the levels of consumption, net investment and the quantity of money (or the rate of interest).* This proposition contains the core of the analysis presented by J. M. Keynes in his *General Theory of Employment, Interest and Money*. The importance of the insight contained

in this proposition has never been better expressed than by A. C. Pigou—once an ardent opponent of Keynes: "Whatever imperfections there may be in his working out of the fundamental conceptions embodied there, the conception itself is an extremely fruitful germinal idea. In my original review-article on the *General Theory* I failed to grasp its significance and did not assign to Keynes the credit due for it. Nobody before him, so far as I know, had brought all the relevant factors, real and monetary at once, together in a single formal scheme, through which their interplay could be coherently investigated."(1)

Much as one recognizes and admires Keynes' contribution, one can hardly call it a revolution in economic theory. Like all scientific achievements, Keynes' contribution was developed from existing knowledge. Almost each single element in Keynes' structure can be found in the works of earlier writers,(2) such as Malthus, Marx, Wicksell, Aftalion, Irving Fisher, N. Johannsen and others. At the turn of the century Wicksell and Johannsen already had a clear conception of the effects of a discrepancy between voluntary savings and voluntary investment. Wicksell and Fisher gave a detailed analysis of the investment function. In Walras can be found the rudiments of the concept of the liquidity function (encaisse désirée).(3)

The Keynesian analysis is not a revolutionary break with the past. It is, however, a most important development in the reformulation of relevant questions. ". . . in setting out and developing his fundamental conception, Keynes made a very important, original and valuable addition to the armoury of economic analysis."(4)

The theoretical apparatus and the concepts forged by Keynes have proved extraordinarily fruitful, as the more recent development of the theory has shown. Almost all modern theoretical discussion

(1) A. C. Pigou, *Keynes' General Theory: A Retrospective View*, London 1950, p. 65.

(2) This is generally accepted in recent literature. A. Hansen, for instance, writes: "Keynes' theory of money and prices . . . runs nonetheless in a stream of thinking that has its sources far back in the history of monetary ideas." (*Monetary Theory and Fiscal Policy*, New York, 1949, p. 83). L. Klein devotes a whole chapter of his book the *Keynesian Revolution* (New York, 1947) to anticipations of the *General Theory*. See also: G. Haberler, "The Place of the General Theory of Employment, Interest and Money in the History of Economic Thought" (*Review of Economics and Statistics*, Vol. 28, 1946, pp. 187 ff.).

(3) See: O. Lange, "The Rate of Interest and the Optimum Propensity to Consume" (*Economica*, Vol. V, New Series, 1938, pp. 12 ff.).

(4) A. C. Pigou, Loc. cit. p. 66. Regarding the significance of the Keynesian contribution, see especially P. A. Samuelson, "Lord Keynes and the General Theory," *Econometrica*, Vol. 14, 1946, p. 87 ff. and further: *The New Economics: Keynes' Influence on Theory and Public Policy* (ed. S. E.

of money, fluctuations, and the theory of fiscal policy is conducted within the Keynesian analytical framework. It is, therefore, important for the reader to become familiar with this analytical framework, since otherwise he will not be in a position to follow the development of the theory. This development has meanwhile led to important extensions of the original Keynesian construction.[1] It soon became obvious that this construction rested on assumptions which were in part very restrictive, and therefore required extension and generalization:[2]

(a) The construction contained in equations (58a) and (59) refers to a closed economy without economic activity by the government. It remains to be shown how the system is changed when we allow for economic activity on the part of the government, and when we drop the assumption of a closed economy. Research during the past fifteen years has shed considerable light on these questions, and we shall discuss them in Sections B and C below.

(b) The Keynesian construction is a theory of the *short run* determination of income and employment. Technology and productive capacity are assumed to be constant; i.e. it is assumed, as was pointed out earlier, that the net investment taking place in any period under consideration has negligible effects on the stock of capital and the techniques of production. The theory thus needs to be developed into a theory of long-run income determination (see below, § 9).

(c) These attempts are closely linked with the endeavour to break through the static nature of the Keynesian system. In equations (58a) and (59) all the variables refer to the same period of time, which means that the analysis is static. As we know, such an analysis enables us only to describe the properties of the equilibrium position; and to compare two different equilibrium positions corresponding to two different constellations of the data. It is true that this sort of comparative-static analysis enables us to make important statements

---

Harris), New York 1947; J. M. Clark, *Alternative to Serfdom*, New York 1948 (ch. IV, Revolution in Economics: after Keynes what?); R. F. Harrod, *The Life of John Maynard Keynes*, London 1951; A. Smithies, "Reflections on the Work and Influence of John Maynard Keynes", *Quarterly Journal of Economics*, Vol. 65, 1951, p. 578 ff.; E. Scheider, "Der Streit um Keynes; Dichtung und Wahrheit in der neueren deutschen Keynes-Diskussion," *Jahrbücher für National-ökonomie und Statistik*, 1953, Vol. 165, p. 89 ff.

(1) See: K. E. Kurihara, *Post-Keynesian Economics*, London 1955.

(2) As Pigou rightly points out, this observation does not imply a belittling of the importance of Keynes' achievement: "When a man has devised a new way of tackling an unclimbed mountain, we may, indeed, regret that this way has not led him to the top. But for the effort which has advanced him *towards* the top nothing is due but praise" (*loc. cit.* pp. 64–65).

regarding the direction in which the system tends to move as a result of a change in the data; but it cannot tell us anything about the path of movement to the new equilibrium situation—assuming a new equilibrium exists. Any discussion of the path of movement requires dynamic analysis; and hence the need to dynamize the Keynesian system. This range of problems is also of central interest in current research.

(d) Finally, there is the attempt to extend the simple system described by equations (58a) and (59) by splitting up the large aggregates C, I and Y into smaller sub-groups. Here, too, notable progress had been achieved. It must be stressed that the issue is not whether to use aggregation or not; but rather the extent to which the process of aggregation should be carried. It is impossible to decide *a priori* how far the process of disaggregation is to be carried; this must be decided with reference to the questions that are being asked and the possibilities of computation. One has to try to find a compromise between an analysis which uses the large aggregates and one which proceeds without any aggregation, e.g. the Walras-type of analysis; and the nature of the compromise must depend on the questions being asked. An example of an analysis using smaller aggregates is the input-output analysis discussed in §4 of this section.

In an introductory book it is impossible to present these recent developments in detail. We must restrict ourselves to a few major questions which we shall discuss in §§ 6 ff. of this section, and in the second and third sections of this chapter. Before turning to these questions, however, we still have to show what conclusions can be drawn from static equilibrium analysis, as it is presented above.

8. We have seen that, given the quantity of money, the system (58a) and (59) simultaneously determines income, consumption, investment and the rate of interest. Previously we stated[(1)] that, given the level of income, the rate of interest was determined by liquidity preference and the quantity of money. It can now be seen that this theorem is valid only for a partial analysis restricted solely to the credit market. The liquidity theory of interest was presented in these terms in Vol. II. The knowledge we have obtained meanwhile enables us to see that liquidity preference and the quantity of money are only two of the determinants of the rate of interest. *In terms of a general macro-economic analysis it is clear that the propensity to consume (or save) and the propensity to invest are as important in determining the rate of interest (and the level of income) as is liquidity preference and the quantity of money. This in turn means that, while the rate of interest is a monetary phenomenon, its level is affected by*

[(1)] See Vol. II, Ch. IV, Section B, § 5, and p. 74 of this volume.

such non-monetary factors as the propensities to consume and to invest. A change in the propensity to consume (save), or (and) the propensity to invest affects the rate of interest and the level of income as does a change in liquidity preference, and (or) the quantity of money. Thus it is clear that those interest theories which seek to explain the rate of interest either by the propensity to save (abstinence theories), or by the propensity to invest (marginal productivity theories of interest), shed light on only *one*, albeit important, aspect of the phenomenon of interest. This also applies to the liquidity theory of interest. *All these theories are one-sided. It cannot be emphasized too strongly that it is the propensity to save, the propensity to invest, and the liquidity preference of economic units, which, together with the quantity of money, simultaneously determine the rate of interest and the level of income.*

9. The nature of these relationships emerges clearly from a comparative static analysis. Let us consider the results which can be obtained from a comparative static analysis of the system (58a) and (59). For this purpose it is best to use the Hicksian method of ascertaining the equilibrium values of Y and i (Fig. 41). For our purposes it is important to note that the curve expressing the relation $L(i, Y) = M$ is infinitely elastic (or almost infinitely elastic) at a certain low rate of interest, has a finite elasticity at higher rates of interest, and becomes completely interest-inelastic above a certain rate of interest. Where the curve is completely interest-inelastic a certain level of money income cannot be exceeded, given the quantity of money, simply because of liquidity preference. A higher level of income is possible only with a larger quantity of money.

Let us now consider how the equilibrium values of Y and i change when there is a change in one of their determinants.

CASE 1: *A rise in the propensity to invest.* As was shown above, this means that the SI curve also shifts upwards, and the extent of the shift, given the rise in the propensity to invest, depends on the elasticity of S with respect to Y and the elasticity of I with respect to i. In Fig. 43, SI_1 refers to a low propensity to invest, SI_2 to a higher propensity to invest, SI_3 to a yet higher one, and so on. The intersection points $T_1, T_2, \ldots$ of the SI curves with the LL curve denote the alternative equilibrium positions of Y and i. It can be seen from Fig. 43 that if we start with T as the original position, a continuous rise in the propensity to invest leads first to a rise in income, with a completely or almost completely unchanged rate of interest; subsequently to a rise in income and a simultaneously rising rate of interest, and finally to a rising rate of interest with the level of income rising very little or remaining constant. Yet, it is quite possible that, even though the propensity to invest rises continually and conditions of full employment are approached, the equilibrium income remains on the horizontal part of the LL-curve, provided the quantity of money is sufficiently large. Conversely, the rising part of the LL-curve could be reached long before conditions of full employment prevail, if the available quantity of money is very small. In this

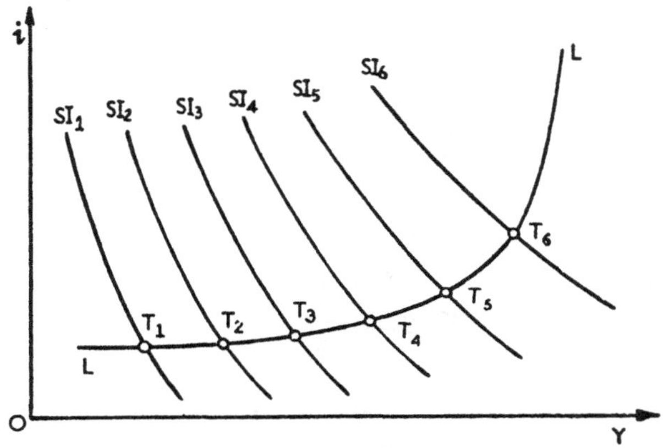

Fig. 43

case the small stock of money prevents the attainment of full employment.

CASE 2: *A rise in the propensity to consume.* This means a shift in the savings curve to the right, which in turn means a shift of the *SI* curve (Fig. 41) to the right. The effects of a rise in the propensity to consume are thus the same as those of a rise in the propensity to invest.

CASE 3: *The banking system increases the quantity of money.* As was shown in Chapter II, pp. 80–82, an increase in the quantity of money leads to a shift in the *LL* curve to the right, in the way indicated in Fig. 44. The horizontal portions of the *LL* curve almost coincide. This entails the following important results (which Fig. 44 shows):

(a) If the propensities to invest and to save are such that the *IS* curve intersects the *LL* curve in its horizontal section (as shown by position *a* of the *IS* curve in Fig. 44) an increase in the quantity of money will not lead to a change in the rate of interest, the level of income, or the level of employment. Thus, if the initial position corresponds to conditions of slump, an expansionary open market policy will not succeed in bringing about recovery.

(b) If the propensities to invest and to save are such that the *IS* curve cuts the *LL* curve in its rising portion (position *b* of the *IS* curve in Fig. 44) an increase in the quantity of money leads to a fall in the rate of interest, and to a rise in the level of income. In this case it is possible to raise the level of income and employment by monetary means alone.

(c) If the propensity to invest is completely interest-inelastic the *IS* curve will be parallel to the *i* axis. In this case an increase in the

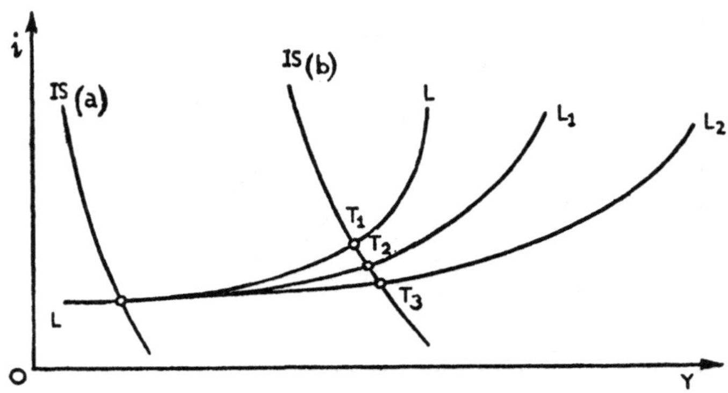

Fig. 44

quantity of money cannot bring about a rise in the level of income, no matter what the position of the *IS* curve. The level if income can be raised only by a rise in the propensity to invest or (and) the propensity to consume.

CASE 4: *A fall in liquidity preference.* It is easy to see that in this case the *LL* curve shifts to the right in the same way as when, *ceteris paribus*, there is an increase in the quantity if money. The results obtained in this case are the same as those in case 3.

10. We now wish to show what happens to the multiplier relation when investment depends on the rate of interest and there is a change in the propensity to invest. The theory of the multiplier explained in §3 assumed investment to be independent of the rate of interest. We started with a given level of net investment, *I*, and, given the savings function, ascertained the corresponding equilibrium level of income. We then asked how a change in investment by the amount ΔI would affect the equilibrium level of income (Fig. 45). If we now assume that the propensity to invest depends on the rate of interest, the corresponding question must be put as follows: what is the change in the equilibrium level of income when

there is a parallel shift in the investment curve by the amount *da*, i.e. when at each rate of interest voluntary net investment exceeds the previous level by the amount *da*? Let the investment curve in Fig. 39 shift parallel by the amount *da*. In order to be able to state the resulting changes in the equilibrium level of income we must

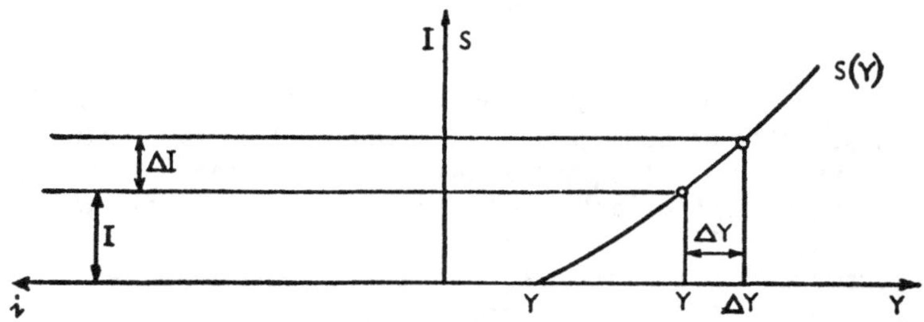

Fig. 45

once more consider the system of equations (58a) and (59). But now we write (58a) in the form

$$S(Y) = I(i) + a$$

in which the constant *a* indicates the position of the investment curve. From (58a) and (59) it is clear that the equilibrium values of Y and i depend on the value of *a*. We can therefore ascertain how Y changes when *a* varies by the amount *da*. The calculation, (which we do not give here), leads to the following result:

(61) $$dY = \frac{1}{\dfrac{dS}{dY} + \dfrac{\dfrac{dI}{di} \cdot \dfrac{\partial L}{\partial Y}}{\dfrac{\partial L}{\partial i}}} \, . \, da.$$

In this equation the fraction which is multiplied by *da* represents the *generalized multiplier*. It is now clear that the multiplier derived in § 3—the Keynesian multiplier—is merely a special case of the more general case described by the system (58a) and (59). The special Keynesian multiplier is equal to the reciprocal of the marginal propensity to save:

(62) $$dY = \frac{1}{\dfrac{dS}{dY}} \, . \, da.$$

It can be seen from (61) that the generalized multiplier coincides with the special multiplier if either

$$\frac{dI}{di} = 0 \tag{63}$$

or

$$\frac{\partial L}{\partial i} = \infty. \tag{64}$$

(63) states that the propensity to invest is completely interest inelastic; (64) states that liquidity preference is infinitely interest-elastic. In both cases the second expression disappears from the denominator of the generalized multiplier. *The special multiplier relation (62) is valid and applicable only in the cases of a completely interest-inelastic propensity to invest and (or) an infinitely elastic liquidity preference, i.e. in the cases to which Keynes primarily devoted his attention.*

11. In the model described by equations (58a) and (59), we assumed that the propensity to invest depends on the rate of interest, given expectations about the future series of receipts and outlays, or, and this amounts to the same, given profit expectations. Profit expectations, however, were not introduced explicitly as one of the variables determining the level of investment. Now, empirical research has demonstrated convincingly that realized and expected profits are more relevant to the investment decisions of firms than all other factors.(1) It therefore seems appropriate to introduce the level of profits expected by firms, taken as a group, as an explicit variable among the determinants of the level of income and employment. A model of this kind was constructed by C. Föhl.(2) The model of Föhl, slightly altered, but essentially unchanged, consists of the following building blocks. We denote the income of non-firms by Y_{nf}, the income of firms (the profits of firms) by Q. The aggregate propensity to save of firms and non-firms is thus a function of the income Y_{nf} of non-firms and the income Q of firms:

$$S = S(Y_{nf}, Q). \tag{65}$$

(1) See: J. Tinbergen, *Statistical Testing of Business-Cycle Theories*, I. *A Method and its Application to Investment Activity*. League of Nations, Geneva 1939.

(2) C. Föhl, *Geldschöpfung und Wirtschaftskreislauf*, Munich and Leipzig 1937 (2nd edition, Berlin 1955). This work represents one of the most important German achievements in the field of the modern theory of the circular flow of income.

A brief presentation of the construction of Föhl will be found in two articles by the present author, "Kinematik und Dynamik des Wirtschaftskreislaufs," and "Die Erhaltung der Vollbeschäftigung" which appeared in the *Nordisk Tidsskrift for Teknisk Økonomi* 1941, p. 121 ff. and 237 ff.

The income of non-firms, which results from the decisions of firms, is assumed to depend on the profits of firms Q, and on the rate of interest i:

(66) $$Y_{nf} = Y_{nf}(Q, i).$$

Planned investment by firms is viewed as a function of the profits of firms Q, and of the rate of interest i:

(67) $$I = I(Q, i).$$

To these three equations, which describe the behaviour of firms and households, we add as a fourth equation the equilibrium condition:

(68) $$I = S$$

We may note that, given wage-rates, the decisions of firms to create non-firm income of Y_{nf} in the planning period simultaneously determine the level of employment (measured in terms of work hours per year). This means that we can add a further equation, which represents the level of employment, N, offered by firms as a function of Y_{nf}, or, because of (66), as a function of Q and i:

(69) $$N = N(Q, i)$$

This system consists of five equations and contains six variables: S, Y_{nf}, Q, I, i and N. It therefore possesses one degree of freedom, which means that the value of one variable may be chosen arbitrarily (autonomously). If the value of one variable is fixed the system (65)–(69) determines all the remaining variables. Föhl chooses the rate of interest as the autonomously fixed variable, in which case the equations (65)–(69) determine all the remaining variables as a function of the rate of interest. At a given rate of interest, there will be a certain level of profits of firms at which a certain level of non-firm income is created, such that voluntary savings by firms and non-firms are exactly equal to voluntary net investment. Fig. 46 shows the graphical method Föhl used to ascertain this equilibrium position. The relation (66) is represented in the upper right-hand corner of the diagram. The function (66) has the property (*a*) that with given profit expectations the non-firm income created by firms rises with a falling rate of interest, and (b) that with a given rate of interest non-firm income increases with rising profit expectations ($Q_1 < Q_2 < Q_3 < Q_4$).

The function (67), which represents the propensity to invest of firms, is shown graphically in the upper left-hand corner. This function has the following properties: given Q, investment rises with a falling rate of interest, and also rises with increasing profit expectations, given the rate of interest.

The function (65) is represented in the bottom right-hand corner. The curves show the amounts which firms and non-firms together save voluntarily at alternative levels of Y_{nf} and Q. As in the other

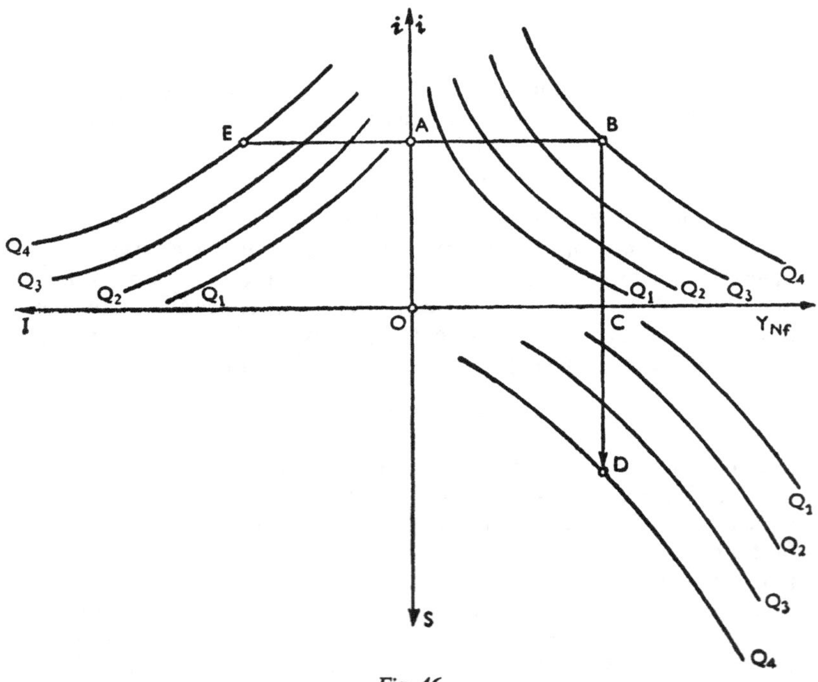

Fig. 46

two co-ordinate systems, each curve refers to a given value of Q. In the case represented in Fig. 46 equilibrium prevails when the rate of interest is at OA and profits of firms at Q_4, since only then is income such that voluntary savings CD is equal to voluntary investment AE. The level of employment corresponding to these equilibrium values of Q and i is given by equation (69). As was pointed out, in this model the rate of interest may be fixed arbitrarily. By inserting the liquidity preference equation,

$$L(Y, i) = M \tag{70}$$

we can determine the required quantity of money (given ruling prices and wage rates).

The construction of Föhl represents a considerable advance over the models discussed so far. This is so because it introduces the incomes of firms and non-firms as separate variables and thus takes a step towards the splitting up of at least *one* of the variables which so far has been treated as an aggregate. Furthermore, it introduces explicitly the profits of firms as a determinant of investment decisions, and of the level of employment offered by firms.

12. Before turning to new problems we have yet to answer an important question. Our models enable us to state, in terms of static equilibrium analysis, what determines the level of money income and the level of employment, *given prices and wage rates*. The analysis has shown that various equilibrium positions are possible, depending on the prevailing behaviour relations with respect to consumption, investment, and liquidity-preference. It is thus quite possible that the resulting equilibrium might be an under-employment equilibrium. Moreover, it is clear that this unemployment persists, and that this equilibrium is a stable one if, the propensities to save and invest, and liquidity preference remaining unchanged, prices and wage rates also remain constant. But does the unemployment still persist if we drop the assumption of constant prices and wage rates? In other words, can we say that a situation of under-employment is a stable equilibrium position, if prices and wage rates are assumed to be completely flexible? To answer this question we should have to insert prices and wage rates as explicit variables in our models, which can be done quite easily.(1) Here however, we shall merely give a verbal exposition of the main lines of reasoning involved.

Let us begin with a situation of full employment, i.e. a situation in which there is no involuntary unemployment. This in turn means that, at prevailing prices and wage rates, firms demand that quantity of labour-services which workers offer willingly. The older theory maintained that, if all prices and wages are completely flexible, and there is perfect competition in all markets, a permanent downward deviation from this situation of full employment is impossible. For example, suppose that a rise in the propensity to save leads to an excess of voluntary savings over voluntary investment. This would immediately lead to a fall in the rate of interest, which in turn would lead to a reduction in voluntary savings and an increase in voluntary investment. These changes in savings and investment would be just

(1) The reader interested in this question may consult the mathematical appendix in L. Klein, *The Keynesian Revolution*, New York, 1947.

sufficient to restore equilibrium between savings and investment at full employment. This argument rests on the following assumptions: (a) that voluntary savings at a given level of income increase with a rise in the rate of interest; (b) that at a given level of income net investment diminishes with a rising rate of interest, and (c) that there always exists a positive rate of interest, at which voluntary savings and investment are equal. If we denote the full-employment level of

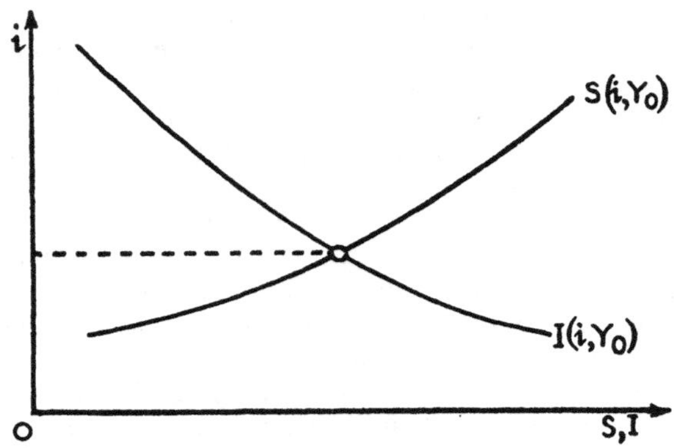

Fig. 47

income by Y_0, the above argument assumes that the solution of the equation

$$S_{\text{volunt.}}(i, Y_0) = I_{\text{volunt.}}(i, Y_0)$$

will always yield a positive i (Fig. 47). This argument, however, is untenable. As was explained earlier, voluntary savings depend primarily on the level of income, and they are completely, or almost completely, interest-inelastic. Again, decisions to invest are made independently of decisions to save (excepting the case in which the same individual both saves and invests). It is by no means certain that a fall in the rate of interest will always sufficiently stimulate investment, or that a rise in the rate of interest will always sufficiently reduce it. Thus, if voluntary savings should exceed voluntary investment at the full-employment income, it is *possible* that the interest rate mechanism assumed in the older theory might not work.

This important theorem can also be demonstrated in the following way, by using the relations represented in Fig. 39. We start with the equilibrium situation corresponding to the rate of interest i_0, (Y_0 and M_0 in Figs. 48a and 48b respectively). Now let the propensity to save rise from S_1 to S_2, so that at the existing level of income Y_0 more is saved than before. With the rate of interest fixed at i_0, and the propensity to invest unchanged, income falls to $\overline{Y}_0$. The public, however, will wish to hold the existing quantity of money OM_0 only

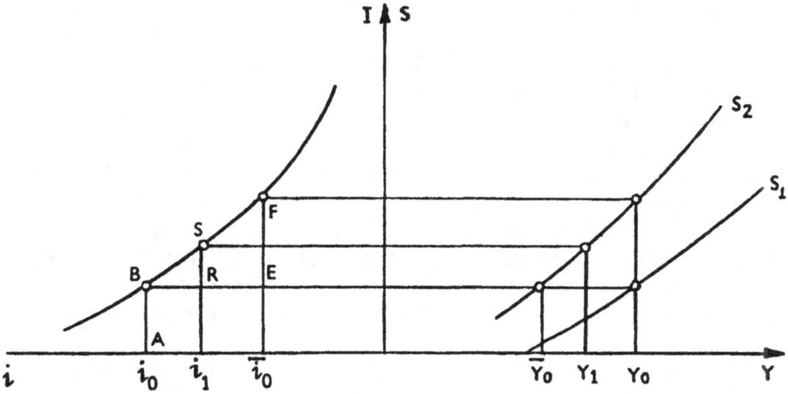

Fig. 48a

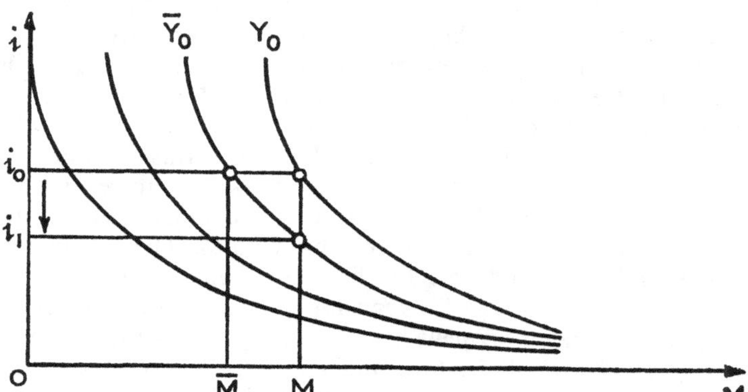

Fig. 48b

at the lower rate of interest i_1 (Fig. 48*b*), and the rate of interest will fall from i_0 to i_1 (assuming the central bank remains passive, i.e. allows the market to establish that rate of interest at which the public is just willing to hold the existing quantity of money). The fall in the rate of interest leads to a rise in investment by the amount *RS* (Fig. 48a), so that income rises to Y_1. The rise in the level of income to Y_1 in turn leads to a rise in the rate of interest to a level between i_1 and i_0, assuming the quantity of money remains at M_0. This, in turn, results in a fall in the level of investment and a reduction in the level of income to between Y_1 and $\bar{Y}_0$, and so on. The new equilibrium level of income, and the new equilibrium rate of interest, corresponding to the new constellation of the data, will lie between Y_1 and $\bar{Y}_0$ and between i_0 and i_1 respectively. The original level of income Y_0 is not restored. Thus, the assertion of the older theory, that the original level of income Y_0 would *always* be restored via falls in the rate of interest and increases in investment, is false. The extent of the change in income resulting from the rise in the propensity to save depends on the elasticity of the savings function (with respect to Y), the elasticity of the investment function (with respect to i), and the elasticity of the liquidity-preference function (with respect to i). Income cannot fall below $\bar{Y}_0$. It will reach this limit if the demand for money is completely elastic at the prevailing rate of interest, and (or) the propensity to invest is completely interest-inelastic.

It follows from what has been said that there is no guarantee that a situation of under-employment could be overcome by a reduction in the rate of interest. However, we have assumed not only a flexible rate of interest, but completely flexible prices and wage rates. In these circumstances, will the involuntarily unemployed not try to get employment by accepting lower wage rates, and might not these reductions in wage rates restore full employment? According to the older theory the answer to this question was also unequivocally in the affirmative. The basis for this answer was roughly as follows: competition among workers reduces money wage rates, which as a rule results in a fall in money wage rates relative to prices, i.e. in a fall in real wage rates. The fall in real wage rates makes it profitable for firms to demand more labour services. Thus, a process of expansion ensues which continues until involuntary unemployment has disappeared.[1] Now, it is true, as was explained in Vol. II, that under perfect competition a fall in real wage rates increases an individual firm's demand for labour. *Yet it is by no means certain that a proposition which is valid for an individual firm is also true for the economy as a whole.* Theorems concerning individual economic units cannot just simply be applied to the economy as a whole. From the point of view of the economy as a whole wage rates are not only an element in costs, but are also an element in income. It cannot be assumed that, when wage rates

[1] See A. C. Pigou, *Employment and Equilibrium*, London, 1941, Chapter 4, "The Classical View."

fall everywhere, the demand for the products of firms, and thus the derived demand for labour, will remain unchanged. Some firms may increase their demand for labour, others may reduce it. The effect of a reduction in wages depends on the net changes in the demand for labour. The decisive question regarding the effect of a reduction in wage rates on the level of employment, in an under-employed system, is in what way this reduction affects total effective demand for consumption and investment.[1] The question is, how does a reduction in wage-rates affect the three main determinants of the level of income and employment, i.e. how does it affect the propensity to consume, the propensity to invest, and liquidity-preference?[2] The answer, in terms of comparative static analysis, is that a reduction in wage rates *may* have an expansionary effect on income and employment. A reduction in wage rates may lead to a fall in the transactions demand for money; and, given an unchanged quantity of money, part of the cash balances so far used for transactions purposes become available for speculative purposes. If liquidity preference is elastic with respect to the rate of interest, this will lead to a fall in the rate of interest. If the fall in the rate of interest leads to a rise in investment (which depends on the interest-elasticity of the propensity to invest) there will be an expansion in income and employment. However, if the propensity to invest is completely interest-inelastic there will be no change in income and employment along this route. Even if the propensity to invest is not completely interest-inelastic, no change can occur if liquidity preference is completely interest-elastic. In this case the money released from transactions holdings is not used to purchase securities, but is added to speculative balances.

Haberler and Pigou, however, have pointed out that the situation of under-employment cannot be an equilibrium position, even if the propensity to invest is completely interest-inelastic and (or) liquidity preference is completely interest-elastic. When wages and prices are flexible, unemployment leads to falling wages and prices,

(1) "Whilst no one would wish to deny the proposition, that a reduction in money wages accompanied by the same aggregate effective demand as before will be associated with an increase in employment, the precise question at issue is whether the reduction in money wages will or will not be accompanied by the same aggregate effective demand as before measured in money, or, at any rate, by an aggregative effective demand which is not reduced in full proportion to the reduction in money wages." (Keynes, *General Theory*, pp. 259–60).

(2) "Does a reduction in money wages have a certain or probable tendency to affect employment in a particular direction through its certain or probable repercussions on these three factors?" (Keynes, *General Theory*, p. 260).

as a result of which there is a rise in the real value of cash balances and savings accounts. According to their argument, this will lead, sooner or later, to a fall in the propensity to save (a rise in the propensity to consume),[1] and will thus have an expansionary effect. The argument also holds if prices do not fall in proportion to wage rates. This so-called *Pigou effect* is operative as long as there is unemployment, and it ensures the automatic restoration of full employment. Here full employment is attained by means of a deflationary process, i.e. a downward wage-price spiral. If one accepts the Haberler-Pigou argument, the proposition of the older theory (i.e. that there is an automatic tendency to full employment, given perfect competition and complete flexibility of all prices) remains intact. Yet, it must be emphasized that the Pigou effect is a completely untested hypothesis. Moreover, Pigou's attempt to rescue the older conception is of little realistic significance, since his argument is valid only in terms of static or comparative static analysis. It would be rash, to say the least, to draw policy conclusions from the results of comparative static analysis; for example, policy conclusions to the effect that a system in a state of under-employment may be left to itself, because the resulting deflationary process of continuous wage-price reductions would automatically restore full employment. The reader by now knows that the results of comparative static analysis could be applied directly to reality only if the economy adjusted instantaneously to changes in data. In reality, of course, adjustments to changes in, for example, wage rates, prices, the rate of interest, the propensity to save etc., do not take place instantaneously and for this reason a realistic theory of income and employment determination must necessarily be dynamic. This is stressed in current theory, and has been stated in the following way by Don Patinkin: "Whether or not an under-employment equilibrium exists; whether or not full employment equilibrium always will be generated in a static system—all this is irrelevant. The fundamental issue raised by Keynesian economics is the *stability of the dynamic system*."[2]

[1] This argument assumes that consumption depends not only on the level of real income, but also on the real value of accumulated savings.

[2] D. Patinkin, "Price Flexibility and Full Employment," *American Economic Review*, 1948, pp. 562–63.
See also:
J. M. Keynes, *General Theory*, Chapter 19.
A. C. Pigou, *Employment and Equilibrium*, London, 1941.
A. C. Pigou, *Lapses from Full Employment*, London, 1945.
O. Lange, *Price Flexibility and Employment*, Bloomington, 1944.
F. Modigliani, "Liquidity Preference and the Theory of Interest and Money," *Econometrica*, Vol. 13, 1944.

From this point of view the distinction between the older conception and the newer one, which derives from Keynes, emerges clearly.

According to the older conception the speed of adjustment of economic units to price and interest rate changes is so swift that a deviation from full-employment equilibrium is always automatically and quickly corrected. Modern theory denies that households and firms in a free market economy react so quickly; rather, it maintains that there are no automatic market forces which would quickly remove under-employment once it had appeared. In a market economy left to its own devices, under-employment, or more generally, any state of disequilibrium, might persist for a long time.

The decisive question to be asked is: *how sensitive are the reactions of a market economy, in the absence of government intervention, to changes in wage rates, prices, interest rates, the quantity of money, the propensity to consume, the propensity to invest*, etc.?

Although this question can only be answered exhaustively in terms of process analysis[1] this certainly does not mean that the static and comparative-static treatment of income and employment determination gives no important insights. It is most important to know the tendencies of change and the properties of equilibrium situations which static theory reveals, but one must be conscious of the limitations of this analysis.

A complete treatment of this question is outside the scope of an introductory book. Here we shall merely give a brief indication of the kind of argument involved. Moreover, the reader should be aware that several aspects of it still require detailed research. The

---

J. Tobin, "Money Wage Rates and Employment," in: *The New Economics* (ed. S. Harris), New York 1947, p. 572 ff.

L. Klein, *The Keynesian Revolution*, New York, 1947.

G. Haberler, *Prosperity and Depression*, (4th edn., London, 1958).

A. H. Hansen, "The Pigouvian Effect," *Journal of Political Economy*, Vol. 59, 1951.

G. Haberler, "The Pigou Effect once More," *Journal of Political Economy*, Vol. 60, 1952.

H. Haller and W. Krelle, *Lohnhöhe und Beschäftigung* (Schriften des Vereins für Sozialpolitik; Theoretischer Ausschuss, ed. E. Schneider), Berlin, 1955.

(1) This is also the view of Haberler: "In order to arrive at a definite conclusion on this question, it would be necessary to work out a whole theory of employment and output in dynamic terms." (*Prosperity and Depression*, 3rd edn., p. 495).

An important step in this direction was taken in a work of B. Ohlin, *Penningpolitik, offentliga Arbeten, Subventioner och Tullar som Medel mot Arbetslöshet*, Stockholm 1934, which appeared as early as 1934, and in E. Lundberg, *Studies in the Theory of Economic Expansion*, London, 1937.

crux of the analysis always lies in the attempt to answer the question, whether and how quickly effective demand expands when the economy is in a state of under-employment.

Let us assume that wage rates and prices can move freely, and that a fall in wages takes place. If this is soon followed by price reductions which induce expectations of further price falls, there will be a further shrinkage in effective demand, so that income and employment are reduced yet more. The result may be a deflationary process lasting a long time, which only makes the slump worse. The process of contraction may come to an end when prices have fallen so low that the Pigou effect becomes operative. However, there is no assurance that this effect will become operative within a reasonably short period of time.

Quite possibly events may take a completely different course. If prices initially remain unchanged, the reduction in wages may well lead to a contraction in the demand for consumer goods, but may at the same time raise the demand for investment goods, because of expectations of higher profits. It is possible, but by no means certain, that this may result in a net expansion of effective demand.

The reader may contemplate any number of possible effects of a fall in wage rates, yet he will always be forced back to the conclusion which J. M. Clark has stated in the U.N. Report *National and International Measures for Full Employment* (1949):[1] neither rising nor falling wage rates, with or without corresponding price adjustments, are *a priori* reliable cures for unemployment; nor can one rely on the effectiveness of an expansionary open-market policy in conditions of under-employment. As we saw, open-market policy *may* not reduce the rate of interest, and *even* if it did, there may be no effect on investment. For this reason, Keynes came to the following conclusion as early as 1936: "There is, therefore, no ground for the belief that a flexible wage policy is capable of maintaining a state of continuous full employment;—any more than for the belief that an open-market monetary policy is capable, *unaided*, of achieving this result. The economic system cannot be made self-adjusting along these lines" (our italics).[2]

Thus, it is necessary to look for measures which, together with appropriate monetary, wage, and price policies, effectively raise or stabilize the level of employment. In other words, it is necessary to find measures which aim directly at shifting the propensities to consume and to invest. This will be discussed in the next section.

[1] Loc. cit. p. 101.
[2] J. M. Keynes, *General Theory*, p. 267.

§ 6. The Quantity Theory of Money

The preceding discussion enables us to assess a theory which for a long time was the core of monetary economics, and is regarded as such by some people even to-day. For this reason we interrupt our exposition at this point, in order to discuss the content and validity of the so-called *quantity theory of money*.

1. *The quantity theory of money postulates a causal relationship between a change in the quantity of money and a change in the prices of goods.* If we denote the quantity of money by M, the level of prices (measured by an index) by P, there is, according to the quantity theory, a functional relationship between M and P:

$$P = f(M)$$

such that P rises when M rises. An increase (decrease) in the quantity of money is regarded as the *cause* of the rise (fall) in P. *The naive form* of the theory asserts that prices vary in direct proportion with the quantity of money:

$$P = k \cdot M.$$

The less rigid form of the quantity theory only maintains that P is a rising function of M. In careful formulations of the theory it has been added that the causal relationship holds good only "*ceteris paribus.*" Yet, K. Wicksell pointed out as early as 1898 that "... among the 'things' that have to be supposed to remain 'equal' are some of the flimsiest and most intangible factors in the whole of economics—in particular the velocity of circulation of money.... It is consequently impossible to decide *a priori* whether the quantity theory is *in actual fact* true—in other words, whether prices and the quantity of money move together in practice."[1]

The assertion of the quantity theory must, of course, be understood in a comparative-static sense. The theory states that if, given an initial equilibrium position, there is a change in the quantity of money, other things being equal, prices in the new equilibrium situation will be correspondingly higher or lower.

2. The reader familiar with the theory of price (as explained in Vol. II) will find the assertion of the quantity theory completely at variance with the previously given explanation of the level of prices. It was shown in Vol. II that the market price of a good depends on the dispositions of buyers and sellers; and we also explained what determines these dispositions. The market price of a good can

[1] *Interest and Prices*, p. 42, London, 1936.

change only when there is a change in demand and (or) supply; what is true of the market for an individual good is also true of a system of interdependent markets. In a market economy price-changes are always the result of changes in dispositions with regard to demand and supply. Now we are suddenly told that the quantity of money, and changes in it, are somehow decisive in the formation of prices! A general rise in prices is possible only if, at ruling prices, there is an excess of demand over supply *in all markets.* Since the quantity theory postulates a causal relationship between the quantity of money and prices, it must show that an increase in the quantity of money necessarily leads to excess demand in all markets. It must explain the process through which a change in the quantity of money influences effective demand and thus leads to a general change in prices. If there is any causal connection between changes in the quantity of money and changes in prices, it can only be an indirect one.

K. Wicksell stated clearly that the problem must be viewed in this way: "*A general rise in prices is therefore only conceivable on the supposition that the general demand has for some reason become, or is expected to become, greater than the supply. . . . Any theory of money worthy of the name must be able to show how and why the monetary or pecuniary demand for goods exceeds or falls short of the supply of goods in given conditions.*"(1)

It is important to note that an excess of demand over supply in all markets is only a *necessary* condition for a general rise in prices; it is not a *sufficient* condition. Whether, and to what extent, prices rise in response to excess demand clearly depends on the price-elasticity of the supply of goods. The possibilities are:

(a) an increase in supply with constant prices (perfectly elastic supply of goods);

(b) an increase in supply with rising prices (more or less elastic supply of goods);

(c) unchanged supply with rising prices (completely inelastic supply of goods).

Case (c) applies when productive capacity is fully employed, and a rise in effective demand in these circumstances leads solely to price changes. Case (a) applies when there is unused capacity at all stages of production, and firms operate in the region of constant marginal costs. In this case a rise in effective demand leads to an increase in production and supply at unchanged prices.(1) Case (b) occurs when the economy approaches conditions of full utilization of capacity, i.e. when firms operate in the region of rising marginal

(1) *Lectures on Political Economy*, Vol. II, 159–60.

costs.[1] In this case a rise in effective demand leads to a rise in output and a simultaneous increase in prices. *Thus, the effect of an increase in effective demand on prices depends entirely on the initial position of the economy.* This is all that needs to be said about the connection between changes in the quantity of money and changes in prices; the critical point is that any possible effects of changes in the quantity of money on the level of prices can operate only via effective demand.[2]

3. *Next, we have to consider whether a change in the quantity of money leads to a change in effective demand. The second question is whether a change in effective demand brings about a change in prices.*

As we know, only the central bank has the power to change the quantity of money in the economy *arbitrarily or autonomously*, i.e. independently of the buying decisions of economic units. This the central bank can do by means of open market operations. By buying or selling fixed-interest securities, the central bank can directly increase or decrease the quantity of money. Let us assume that the central bank deliberately increases the quantity of money by buying securities. The sellers of the securities—commercial banks and the public—now have larger cash balances, and this may, but does not necessarily, result in an increase in effective demand. The effect will depend on the form of the equations contained in the fundamental system (58) and (59) which we discussed in 5:

$$C(Y) + I(i) = Y \tag{58}$$

$$L(Y, i) = M \tag{59}$$

We showed that, given the propensity to consume, the propensity to invest and liquidity preference, a rise in M does not lead to a rise in effective demand and income if

(a) the propensities to invest and consume are such that the IS curve cuts the LL curve in its horizontal portion, i.e. if the demand for money is perfectly elastic at the ruling rate of interest; or

(b) the propensity to invest is completely interest-inelastic.

It follows that effective demand need not necessarily rise when the central bank deliberately increases the quantity of money.

Whether or not a change in the quantity of money will influence effective demand depends simply on the propensities to consume and

[1] Strictly speaking, these relationships between price and marginal cost only hold good on the (realistic) assumption that firms do not assume an increasing elasticity of demand when demand shifts.

[2] In this connection see especially J. M. Keynes, *General Theory*, Chapter 21 ("The Theory of Prices").

invest, and on liquidity preference; whether or not an increase in effective demand will raise prices depends mainly, as was just explained, on the conditions of employment prevailing when the increase in demand takes place. The sale of securities to the central bank, in the course of open market operations, leads in the first instance merely to a change in the assets structure of sellers (they acquire cash in place of securities). Under certain circumstances, depending on the shape of the liquidity function, this sale also leads to a fall in the rate of interest. Whether or not the additional cash balances, and the possible reduction in the rate of interest, will lead to a rise in effective demand depends solely on the decisions of the relevant economic units. O. von Zwiedineck-Südenhorst remarked as early as 1909[(1)] that "It is a mistake to attribute any objective force to the quantity of money; what is decisive are the subjectively determined decisions regarding the use of assets."[(2)] Any expansion or contraction in economic activity always depends on an expansion or contraction in effective demand. *Only in certain cases do changes in the quantity of money influence effective demand, and through it, under certain circumstances, prices.*[(3)]

4. The causal relationship considered by the quantity theory of money is this: a change in the quantity of money causes a rise in effective demand and hence a rise in prices. The theory does not allow for the possibility of a reverse connection, namely that a change in effective demand may induce a change in the quantity of money. This is a rather important omission. Consider the system of equations (58) and (59). This system contains two relations between the three variables Y, i and M, and thus possesses one degree of freedom. In keeping with the causal relation considered by the quantity theory, we chose M arbitrarily and asked what were the equilibrium values

(1) O. von Zwiedineck-Südenhorst, "Die Einkommensgestaltung als Geldwertbestimmungsgrund," *Schmöllers Jahrbuch für Gesetzgebung, Verwaltung und Volkswirtschaft im Deutschen Reich*, 33rd year, 1909, p. 160.

We strongly recommend this classic work, since it contains important principles of modern monetary theory, which are developed there with great clarity.

Further reference may be made to a work which appeared in the same year (1909): F. von Wieser, "Der Geldwert und seine Veränderungen," *Schriften des Vereins fur Sozialpolitik* Vol. 132, Munich 1909.

(2) H. Höpker-Aschoff expresses the same idea in the following way: "Demand does not derive from money, but from people who use money for purchases." (*Geld und Gold*, Jena, 1939 (p. 132)).

(3) "Households' expectations of income and firms' expectations of profits, which primarily determine buying decisions, are not affected *directly* by changes in the quantity of money." (B. Ohlin, "Stockholmskolan contra Kvantitetsteorien," *Ekonomisk Tidsskrift*, 1943, pp. 42–43; —our italics).

of Y and i at various alternative values of M. Now let us choose i arbitrarily, i.e. let us assume that the banking system fixes a certain rate of interest, and is prepared to supply the quantity of money which economic units demand at that rate of interest. The rate of interest is now a given constant, and equations (58) and (59) determine Y and M. Let there be an autonomous rise in the propensity to invest, i.e. a shift to the right of the I curve, and thus a rise in effective demand (which is given by the left-hand side of equation (58)). Equation (58) now gives a new, higher equilibrium level of income; and equation (59) indicates that, at the prevailing fixed rate of interest, the higher equilibrium level of income requires a larger quantity of money. In other words, the higher level of income can be financed only if the banking system makes available a larger quantity of money for transactions purposes. *In this case the role of the banking system is passive.* The reason for the increase in the quantity of money is the rise in effective demand; the banking system merely adjusts the quantity of money to what is required at the higher level of income (and at the prevailing, fixed, rate of interest). Here the causal relationship is exactly the reverse of that envisaged by the quantity theory.

Effective demand and income can of course rise while the quantity of money remains unchanged, but this may require a rise in the rate of interest (as was shown in § 5).

5. The quantity theory must not be confused or identified with the *quantity equation* or the *equation of exchange*, which is introduced in Vol. II.[1] If we denote by M the quantity of money which households and firms hold at a moment of time, the national income by Y, then the fraction $\frac{Y}{M}$ represents the income velocity of circulation of money v.[2] The equation

$$\frac{Y}{M} = v \tag{71}$$

thus *defines* the income velocity of circulation of money. The value of v can be ascertained only if Y and M are known. Since the money income of any period is, by definition, equal to the product of the real income Y_r of the period and the price of the components of the real income, as measured by a price index P, i.e.

$$Y = Y_r \, . \, P, \tag{72}$$

[1] Vol. II, Ch. IV, Section C, § 2b.
[2] Vol. I, seventh edn., p. 68.

we may rewrite the definitional equation (71):

$$(73) \qquad \frac{Y_r \, . \, P}{M} = v$$

or

$$(73a) \qquad Y_r \, . \, P = M \, . \, v.$$

This relation, known as the *quantity equation* or the *equation of exchange*, represents an identity which is always fulfilled, and is simply the definitional equation for the income velocity of circulation of money. The quantity *theory*, however, asserts a *causal* relationship between a change in M and a change in P. But a definitional equation such as (73a) clearly does not contain any assertions about a possible causal relation between M and P. The argument, for example, that: "If M doubles, v and Y_r remaining unchanged, P must also double", overlooks the fact that v can remain constant only if Y doubles as a result of a doubling of M. *Whether or not this happens depends on the system of equations* (58) *and* (59); *and this system shows clearly that changes in Y are determined by the propensity to consume, the propensity to invest and liquidity-preference.*[1] The income velocity of circulation of money is not an institutionally determined constant.[2]

The equation of exchange is thus completely useless for the analysis of the relationship between M, Y and P; also the concept of income velocity of circulation is superfluous for this analysis. v is a magnitude derived from Y and M; all statements about changes in v are simply statements about changes in Y in relation to changes in M. Instead of saying v has risen, it is sufficient to say Y has risen more than M. *Changes in Y and M are the causal factors, whereas changes in v are not.*

§ 7. The Acceleration Principle

1. After this digression we return to the problem of the determination of national income. The analysis presented in §§ 1–5 still requires important extensions. Let us once more consider our first, simplest, model in which private net investment is assumed to be autonomously given. With a given level of net investment I_1 and a given propensity to consume $C(Y)$ the national income is determined by the condition:

$$C(Y) + I_1 = Y$$

(1) The reader should consult the lucid exposition of these matters in Joan Robinson, *Introduction to the Theory of Employment* (London, 1937, p. 93 ff.).

(2) See the calculations in E. M. Doblin, "The Ratio of Income to Money Supply; an International Survey." (*The Review of Economics and Statistics*, Vol. 33. 1951, p. 201 ff.)

We showed that, the propensity to consume remaining unchanged, a higher level of investment I_2 ($I_2 > I_1$) is associated with a higher level of income Y_2, and that the change in income is determined by the multiplier. The dynamic analysis of this multiplier process showed that the rise in income brought about by the increase in autonomous investment consists solely of further induced increases in consumption. The multiplier analysis thus rested on the assumption that the primary increase in income brought about by the rise in investment leads solely to an increase in consumption, which leads to a secondary increase in income, and the secondary increase in income once again leads solely to an increase in consumption, and so on. That is, it was assumed that the successive changes in income, between the initial and the final equilibrium situation, induce only expansions in consumption, but do not induce new investment. In other words, the multiplier theory assumes that the investment decisions of firms are not affected by the expansionary process resulting from the autonomous increase in investment. Such an assumption is permissible and even necessary as a first approximation, so as to illustrate the pure multiplier process. A more realistic theory of the determination of income, however, must take into account the fact that the primary, secondary, etc., increases in income, brought about by the rise in autonomous investment, may in turn induce new investment. *We therefore have to ask whether and in what way such induced investment takes place, and what part it plays in the process of income formation.*

2. Let us for a moment consider a stationary economy. As we know, in such an economy net income is equal to the value of consumption; gross investment is equal to depreciation and net investment is equal to zero. Now let us assume a rise in the propensity to consume (Fig. 49). When all adjustments have taken place, the new stationary equilibrium position will be one with a higher level of income, a higher level of consumption, and, given unchanged technology, a correspondingly higher level of replacement investment, since the stock of capital used in the production of income is greater in situation 2 than in situation 1. We can say, therefore, that with given technology re-investment in a stationary economy depends solely on the level of consumption; and the dependence is one of direct proportionality to the level of consumption. If we denote replacement investment by I_r then:

$$I_r = \alpha \, . \, C. \tag{74}$$

In a progressive economy the available capital stock must not merely be maintained by replacement, but must expand. Clearly, the "progress" from situation 1 to situation 2 (Fig. 49) is only possible if there is an appropriate expansion of the capital stock. This expansion of the capital stock (which represents net investment) is induced by the increase in consumption; and the amount of this *induced net investment* is larger, the larger the *change* in consumption.[1] If we denote the course of consumption through time by the function $C(t)$,

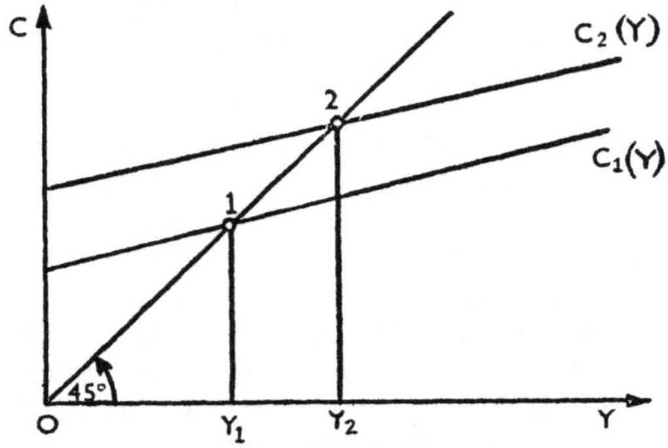

Fig. 49

the change in consumption at a point of time t (i.e. during an infinitely small interval of time $t \rightarrow t + dt$) will be given by the first derivative of C with respect to t: $\left(\frac{dC}{dt}\right)$, so that net investment I is a rising function of $\frac{dC}{dt}$ when $\frac{dC}{dt}$ is positive. The simplest assumption of direct proportionality between changes in consumption and the net investment, I_{ind}, induced by them probably corresponds to reality in many cases:

$$(75) \qquad I_{\text{ind}} = \beta \, . \, \frac{dC}{dt} \, .$$

Gross investment at any point of time thus consists of (a) re-investment, which depends solely on the absolute level of consumption, (b) induced net investment, which depends solely on the *change* of consumption through time and (c) autonomous (spontaneous) net investment. Since we are interested only in that part of gross investment which is related to consumption we may neglect autonomous net investment. We are thus concerned only with the sum:

$$(76) \qquad I_r + I_{\text{ind}} = \alpha \, . \, C + \beta \, . \, \frac{dC}{dt} \, .$$

[1] We assume that the induced net investment can be financed.

If we wish to consider discontinuous changes in consumption (75) will be replaced by a relationship such as:

$$(75a) \qquad I_t^{\text{ind}} = \beta \, . \, (C_t - C_{t-1})$$

or also:

$$(75b) \qquad I_t^{\text{ind}} = \beta \, . \, (C_{t-1} - C_{t-2}).$$

Equation (75a) states that net investment induced during any period is proportional to the difference between consumption in the same period and consumption in the preceding period. Equation (75b) is to be interpreted similarly.

Since investment decisions are made by firms, the equations (75) describe a particular *behaviour pattern of firms*: a given change in consumption causes firms to undertake net investment of a given amount. This assumption need not contradict the assumptions previously made, that the investment decisions of firms depend mainly on profit expectations. After all, it is quite possible, indeed probable, that a positive change in consumption (sales) is associated with the expectation of rising profits.

If we remember that induced net investment is the addition to the capital stock brought about by a change in consumption, we can see clearly that equation (75) simply states that, at each point of time, *firms seek to adjust their capital stock precisely to the level of consumption (i.e. to the level of demand).*[1]

The relations (75) and (75a)–(75b) state the *acceleration principle,*[2] and the constant β in (75) is called the *accelerator.*

The relations (75), (75a), (75b) and (76) are dynamic, from which it follows that the acceleration principle cannot be stated in terms of static analysis.

(1) This, of course, does not apply to autonomous investment.

(2) T. N. Carver recognized this relationship as early as 1903, but it was analysed in detail only in 1909 by A. Aftalion. The term "acceleration principle" was introduced by J. M. Clark (1917) to whom we owe detailed studies of the relationships described by this principle.

Further reference may be made to the bibliography given in G. Haberler, *Prosperity and Depression*, 4th edn., London, 1958. The following are the basic works:

J. M. Clark, "Business Acceleration and the Law of Demand: a Technical Factor in Economic Cycles" (1917) reprinted in: *Readings in Business Cycle Theory*, London, 1944. S. Kuznets, "Relation between Capital Goods and Finished Products in the Business Cycle", in: *Economic Essays in Honor of Wesley Clair Mitchell*, New York, 1935. J. Tinbergen, "Statistical Evidence on the Acceleration Principle", *Economica*, Vol. 5, 1938.

The Effect of the Acceleration Principle
(numerical example)

Period	Sales (= Consumption) (in £'s)	Depreciation (in £'s)	Reinvestment (in £'s)	Gross investment (in £'s)	Net investment (in £'s)	Capital-stock (in £'s)	Number of Machines: Available	Number of Machines: Required	Changes: in Sales (in £'s)	Changes: in Gross investment (in £'s)
1	200	120	120	120	—	1200	40	40	—	—
2	200	120	120	120	—	1200	40	40	—	—
3	210	120	120	180	+ 60	1260	42	42	+10	+ 60
4	240	120	120	300	+180	1440	48	48	+30	+120
5	300	120	120	480	+360	1800	60	60	+60	+180
6	350	120	120	420	+300	2100	70	70	+50	−60
7	370	120	120	240	+120	2220	74	74	+20	−180
8	370	120	120	120	—	2220	74	74	—	−120
9	365	120	90	90	− 30	2190	73	73	− 5	− 30
10	360	120	90	90	− 30	2160	72	72	− 5	—
11	350	120	60	60	− 60	2100	70	70	−10	− 30
12	320	120	—	—	−120	1980	66	64	−30	− 60
13	260	180	—	—	−180	1800	60	52	−60	—
14	220	300	—	—	−300	1500	50	44	−40	—
15	220	480	300	300	−180	1320	44	44	—	+300
16	230	420	420	480	+ 60	1380	46	46	+10	+180

3. Let us consider what conclusions can be drawn from equation (75). *Equation (75) shows the course of induced net investment when the course of consumption is given.* In the top part of Fig. 50 it is assumed that the stationary equilibrium of an economy is disturbed by a rise in real consumption. Until the point of time t_1 consumption grows at an increasing rate; from t_1 onwards consumption continues to grow absolutely but at a decreasing rate, and from t_2 onwards

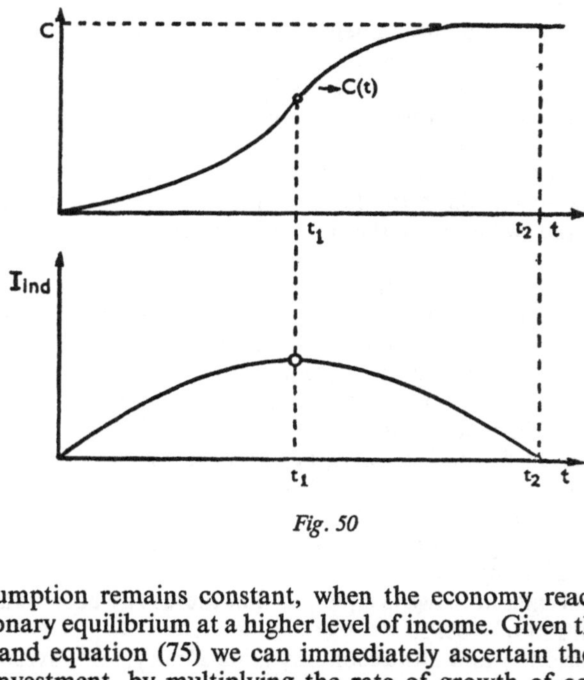

Fig. 50

consumption remains constant, when the economy reaches a new stationary equilibrium at a higher level of income. Given the function $C(t)$ and equation (75) we can immediately ascertain the course of net investment, by multiplying the rate of growth of consumption (mathematically: the first derivative of consumption with respect to time) by the accelerator. Given the form of $C(t)$ which we have assumed, the rate of growth $\frac{dC}{dt}$ rises with rising t until the point of inflection t_1; between t_1 and t_2 the rate of growth declines with rising t. From t_2 onwards the rate of growth is zero. The resulting time path of induced net investment thus has the form indicated in the bottom part of Fig. 50. The figure gives the following results:

(a) *rising consumption leads to rising induced net investment as long as consumption grows at an increasing rate*;

(b) *when consumption rises at a decreasing rate induced net investment declines.*

As soon as the rate of growth of consumption—not the absolute level of consumption—declines, a fall in induced net investment occurs. Investment activity declines in spite of a continuing rise in the level of consumption.

The maintenance of induced net investment at the level reached at point t_1 is possible only if consumption continues to grow at its rate of growth at t_1.

Proposition (b) is of fundamental importance in the analysis of fluctuations in investment activity.

If consumption declined after t_2, its negative rate of growth would induce negative net investment. As long as the absolute value of this negative induced net investment is smaller than replacement investment (depreciation) the acceleration principle remains operative. Depreciation sets a limit to the actual volume of dis-investment only when the value of induced dis-investment is greater than depreciation.

Let us attempt to clarify these relationships once more with the help of the numerical examples in the adjoining table (p. 176). At the same time we may draw attention to several other points. The table is drawn up on the following assumptions:

The capital stock in period 1 consists of 40 machines, each valued at £30, so that the value of the capital stock is £1200.

In each period 4 machines wear out and are written off. In other words, we assume depreciation is 10% of the capital stock, i.e. that machines have a life of 10 years.

The capacity output of consumption goods of each machine is £5 per machine at going prices.

Output and sales are always equal, so that there is no accumulation or decumulation of stocks.

During periods 1 and 2 the economy is stationary, and investment limited to replacement.

Consumption begins to rise in period 3, at first at an increasing rate (until period 5), then at a decreasing rate (until period 7). From period 8 onwards consumption begins to decline. What happens to the course of gross investment, net investment, and the capital stock? Since consumption rises by £10 in period 3, two new machines must be procured. Gross investment and net investment thus rise by £60. In period 4 consumption rises by a further £30, so that six more machines are required. Net investment rises by £120, gross investment by £120, and so on. The table confirms our conclusion, namely that net investment rises as long as consumption rises at an increasing rate (periods 3–5), and that net investment declines as soon as the rate of growth of consumption declines (periods 6–8).

In period 9 consumption declines by £5, which leads to dis-investment of £30. This means a decline in re-investment of £30, i.e. one worn out machine is not replaced, and the capital stock declines from £2220 to £2190. This reduction in the capital stock continues until period 12.

In periods 13 and 14 the acceleration principle is not operative; the stock of machines can only be reduced by a complete cessation of replacement investment.

A further interesting fact emerges from our numerical example. From period 2 to 3 consumption rises by 5%, while gross investment rises by 50%. From period 4 to 5 consumption rises by 25%, while gross investment rises by 60%. The percentage rise in gross investment is thus substantially larger than the corresponding percentage increase in consumption. In our example, the same applies to the decrease in consumption in periods 9 to 12. Although this phenomenon can be observed in the course of fluctuations, it is by no means generally valid. It is quite possible that gross investment remains constant in the face of increasing consumption, as can be seen from the following numerical example.[1]

Period	Consumption	Rate of Change of Consumption	Induced Net Investment	Re-investment	Gross Investment	Capital Stock at the End of the Period
	C	$C_t - C_{t-1}$	$1000 \,.\, (C_t - C_{t-1})$	$I_r = 0{\cdot}1 \,.\, K_{t-1}$		K_t
$t = 1$	100	—	—	—	—	100,000
2	110	10	10,000	10,000	20,000	110,000
3	119	9	9,000	11,000	20,000	119,000
4	127·1	8·1	8,100	11,900	20,000	127,100
5	134·39	7·29	7,290	12,710	20,000	134,390
.	.	.	.	.	.	.
.	.	.	.	.	.	.
.	.	.	.	.	.	.
∞	0	0	0	20,000	20,000	200,000

It is also possible that the course of gross investment should show damped fluctuations. Gross investment is given by equation (76); and this equation shows that the level of gross investment is affected by re-investment, which depends on C, as well as by induced net

[1] From: R. Frisch, "The Inter-relation Between Capital Production and Consumer Taking" (*Journal of Political Economy*, Vol. 34, 1931, p. 650). The reader should consult this important work.

investment, which depends on $\frac{dC}{dt}$. When consumption grows at a decreasing rate, re-investment increases with rising consumption, while induced net investment declines. The course of gross investment depends on which of these two components predominates; and this in turn depends on the decline in the rate of growth of consumption, and on the rate of depreciation (= wear-and-tear). When depreciation is very small, the course of induced net investment is decisive; but if the rate of depreciation is very high, the latter is decisive for the course of gross investment.

Equation (76) enables us to state both the necessary and sufficient condition for an increase or decrease in gross investment. Gross investment increases (decreases) when

$$\frac{d(I_r + I_{\text{ind}})}{dt} = \alpha \, . \frac{dC}{dt} + \beta \, . \frac{d^2C}{dt^2}$$

is positive (negative). The acceleration principle asserts that induced net investment falls even though consumption increases, provided consumption increases at a decreasing rate. It should be noted that this applies *only to induced net investment*; it is quite possible for gross investment (reinvestment + induced net investment) to increase in spite of decreasing net investment.

4. The validity of the acceleration principle in the form expressed in equation (75) rests on the assumption that the capital stock is directly proportional to the level of real consumption, i.e. that

$$K = \beta \, . \, C \tag{77}$$

where K is the capital stock and C consumption. It follows that the rate of growth of the capital stock $\left(\frac{dK}{dt}\right)$, i.e. net investment, is also proportional to the rate of growth of consumption $\left(\frac{dC}{dt}\right)$. β in equation (77) is the accelerator.

It follows from equation (77) that the validity of the acceleration principle is limited, since the assumptions underlying (77) hold only under certain circumstances.

The assumption that the capital stock varies in direct proportion to consumption requires (a) no change, or no substantial change, in the techniques of production and (*b*) full utilization of the capital stock, or that excess capacity is a constant percentage of total capacity. Given these assumptions, the acceleration principle is valid only if the decline in consumption is within the limits within which the resulting dis-investment does not exceed depreciation.

It follows that the acceleration principle is not operative with respect to fixed durable capital when there is unused capacity, so that an increase in consumption does not require an increase in the capital stock. The acceleration principle is certainly not operative with respect to durable capital in times of general depression, when there is unused capacity at all stages of the productive process.

The situation is different as regards inventories (stocks of raw materials, half-finished and finished goods). Experience shows that firms adjust the level of their inventories to the level of sales, and as a rule vary inventories in proportion to the level of sales. The fundamental relation (77), which is the basis of the acceleration principle, here applies precisely or almost precisely, so that the course of induced net investment in inventories can be explained with the help of the acceleration principle. This explanation is now generally accepted.(1)

§ 8. The Acceleration Principle and The Determination of Income

1. We are now in a position to answer the question which led us to examine the acceleration principle: what form does the process of income formation take when an increase in consumption, brought about by a rise in income, in turn induces net investment? Consider again our simplest model of income determination, which was developed in § 1. We showed that, given the propensity to consume $C(Y)$ and autonomous net investment I_0, the level of income Y is determined by the equation:

$$C(Y) + I_0 = Y \tag{78}$$

In this simple model an increase in autonomous net investment of ΔI_0, leads to a new higher equilibrium level of income which is given by the equation:

$$C(Y) + (I_0 + \Delta I_0) = Y \tag{79}$$

This analysis, however, even if carried out dynamically, overlooks the fact that the process which raises income to a higher level may induce net investment. It is possible that this induced investment may affect the process of income formation and lead to a different

(1) See especially: J. Tinbergen, "An Acceleration Principle for Commodity Stock Holding and a Short Cycle resulting from it" (in: *Studies in Mathematical Economics and Econometrics*, in Memory of Henry Schultz, Chicago, 1942). Further: J. Meyer and E. Kuh, "Acceleration and Related Theories of Investment: an Empirical Enquiry", *The Review of Economics and Statistics*, Vol. 37, 1955 pp. 217 ff. J. Meyer–E. Kuh, *The Investment Decision: An Empirical Study*, Cambridge, Mass., 1957.

equilibrium level of income from the one which is obtained when induced net investment is neglected, i.e. when the possible operation of the acceleration principle is neglected. We must now examine this problem more closely.

2. We begin with a simple numerical example to illustrate the nature of the problem. Let us assume a closed economy, a marginal propensity to consume of $\frac{1}{2}$, and an accelerator of 2. Let us assume further that a rise in income in one period affects consumption only in the following period. Let net investment rise by £100 per period. We wish to know the process by which income changes under these circumstances.

In period 1 income rises by £100. This rise in income leads to a rise in consumption of £50 in period 2. This rise in consumption in period 2 simultaneously induces net investment of £100, so that total net investment is £200 and thus the rise in income in period 2 is £250. This rise in income leads to a further increase in consumption of £125 in period 3, and induced investment in the same period is £150, and so on. The course of the individual variables is given in the following table, where all figures indicate the changes from the initial situation in period 0.

Period	Autonomous Investment	Induced Consumption	Induced Investment	Income
1	100	—	—	100
2	100	50	100	250
3	100	125	150	375
4	100	187·50	125	412·50
5	100	206·25	37·50	343·75
6	100	171·88	−68·74	203·14
7	100	101·57	−140·62	60·95
8	100	30·48	−142·18	−11·70
9	100	−5·85	−72·66	21·49
10	100	10·75	33·20	143·95
11	100	71·98	122·46	294·44
12	100	147·22	150·48	397·70

For other values of the marginal propensity to consume and the accelerator the resulting time sequences of income are different. We can only state the course of income over time for various alternative values of the marginal propensity to consume and the accelerator by treating the problem generally, i.e. without using specific numerical values.

The income of any period t is given by the definitional equation

$$Y_t = C_t + I_t$$

For our purposes we have to split up net investment I_t into autonomous net investment I^a and induced net investment I_t^i. We therefore write the income equation in the form:

$$Y_t = C_t + I_t^i + I^a, \tag{80}$$

in which the values of all the variables give the deviations from the values prevailing in the initial position.

Let the initial position be disturbed by a permanent increase in autonomous investment by the constant amount I^a. We wish to know how this rise in autonomous investment influences the course of income.

Let us assume that consumption during any period depends on the income of the preceding period:

$$C_t = \alpha \,.\, Y_{t-1} \qquad (0 < \alpha \leqq 1) \tag{81}$$

and that induced investment in period t depends on the difference between consumption in period t and consumption in period $t - 1$ (the acceleration principle):

$$I_t^i = \beta \,.\, (C_t - C_{t-1}), \qquad (\beta > 0) \tag{82}$$

The three equations (80)–(82) enable us to indicate the course of income through time for all possible combinations of the marginal propensity to consume (α) and the accelerator (β).

Using (81) and (82), (80) becomes:

$$\begin{aligned} Y_t &= \alpha \,.\, Y_{t-1} + \beta(\alpha \,.\, Y_{t-1} - \alpha \,.\, Y_{t-2}) + I^a \\ &= \alpha \,.\, (1 + \beta) \,.\, Y_{t-1} - \alpha \,.\, \beta \,.\, Y_{t-2} + I^a \end{aligned} \tag{83}$$

Equation (83) now contains only income as a variable, and it contains the values of income in three successive periods. If we know income for January and February, (83) enables us to compute income for March, and so on. The entire course of income through time is determined by the values of income in the first two periods. In our numerical example we had $\alpha = \frac{1}{2}$ and $\beta = 2$, in which case (83) takes the form:

$$Y_t = \frac{3}{2} \cdot Y_{t-1} - Y_{t-2} + 100. \tag{83a}$$

We also assumed $Y_1 = 100$ and $Y_2 = 250$. From (83a) $Y_3 = 375$, $Y_4 = 412{\cdot}5$, and so on.

The solution of equation (82) shows how the path of income through time depends on the values of the marginal propensity to consume (α) and the accelerator (β). We do not give the mathematical process of solving the so-called difference equation (83). A statement of the results must suffice.(1) As Samuelson has shown, the change of income over time may follow one of four alternative paths, depending on the position of the point α,β in Fig. 51.

Combinations α, β in segment A are marked by a low value of the accelerator. In this case income rises continuously and asymptotically approaches the value:

$$\frac{1}{1-\alpha} \cdot I^a. \tag{84}$$

Here the final result is determined solely by the multiplier effect.

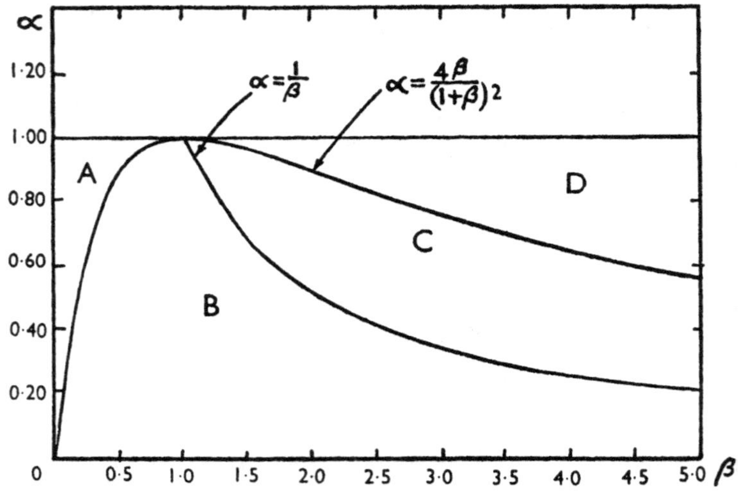

Fig. 51

If the numerical values of α and β are those indicated in segment B, income is subject to damped fluctuations, and gradually approaches the value given by equation (84).

For combinations α, β lying in segment C, income fluctuates

(1) Here we rely on the fundamental work of P. A. Samuelson, "Interactions between the Multiplier Analysis and the Principle of Acceleration" (*Review of Economic Statistics*, Vol. 21, 1939) where these relationships were analysed for the first time. See also: P. A. Samuelson, "A Synthesis of the Principle of Acceleration and the Multiplier" (*The Journal of Political Economy*, Vol. 47, 1939, pp. 786 ff.)
Further: A. Hansen, *Fiscal Policy and Business Cycles*, London 1941, pp. 276ff).

around the value given by (84) with oscillations of ever growing amplitude.

Finally, if the combinations α, β are those in segment D, i.e. if α and β have large values, income expands continuously. Theoretically, the result is a never ending cumulative expansionary process.

It can be seen that for a wide range of values of α and β (segments A and B) induced net investment has no effect on the new equilibrium level of income.

It should be noted that the theoretical model from which these results have been deduced rests on highly simplified assumptions. The marginal propensity to consume and the accelerator are assumed to remain constant throughout the whole process. Yet, even this simple model shows how complicated is the economic process which results from a change in autonomous net investment.(1)

§ 9. The Basic Principles of The Theory of Long-Run Growth(2)

1. The theory of income determination presented so far is a short-run theory. It was assumed that the net investment taking place in the period under consideration is small in relation to the stock of capital existing at the beginning of the period. In other words, it was assumed that the *capacity-increasing effect of investment* could be neglected. In a short-run theory one may restrict the analysis to the *income-generating effect of investment*, i.e. to the effect of investment on the level of income, since short-run theory tries to elucidate the determinants of national income, *given productive capacity, technology and population*. However, when we consider longer periods of time we cannot overlook the dual effects of investment, i.e. its effects on income *and* productive capacity. Positive net investment raises the stock of capital and hence, as a rule, productive capacity.(3) Additions to the capital stock of only 3% per annum result in a doubling of the capital stock within 23 years. This is why,

(1) It is, of course, possible to analyse these relationships on the assumption that α and β vary with the level of income. But we cannot stay to do this.

(2) See: E. D. Domar, "Capital Expansion, Rate of Growth and Employment", *Econometrica*, Vol. 14, 1946; E. D. Domar, "Expansion and Employment", *American Economic Review*, Vol. 37, 1947;
R. F. Harrod, *Towards a Dynamic Economics*, London, 1948.

(3) We have to distinguish between capital widening and capital deepening. Capital widening extends productive capacity within the framework of given technology, leaving the average life of productive equipment unchanged. Pure capital deepening, however, does not increase productive capacity, but only increases the average life of productive equipment. In general capital widening and capital deepening occur together, so that in practice all positive net investment has an effect on productive capacity.

in an analysis of economic development over longer periods of time, we must consider the capacity-increasing effect of net investment, as well as the income-generating effect. This, in turn, poses a series of problems for a theory of long-term growth which do not arise in a short-run theory of income determination.

In this Introduction we restrict ourselves to the central problem, which emerges clearly if we start from the simple model of short-run income determination, discussed in § 1. In the initial situation the economy is in stationary equilibrium with normal or full utilization of productive capacity. We now assume that a given positive level of net investment takes places year after year from a certain period onwards. With a given propensity to save there will now be (as was shown in §1) a certain yearly equilibrium level of income, which is maintained as long as the level of net investment and the propensity to save do not change. While productive capacity expands year after year, real income and total demand remain constant. The possibilities of raising the social product grow continuously, while demand is lacking for the additional goods which could be produced; thus an ever increasing part of the constantly growing productive capacity remains unused. Now, firms undertake a certain yearly level of net investment only because they expect to use the additional stock of capital, i.e. because they expect to sell their planned increase in output. This in turn means that firms expect an appropriate increase in total demand. A rise in total demand, however, presupposes a rise in real income; given the propensity to save, this can only occur if there is an increase in net investment. Suppose net investment increases in such a way that the expansion in productive capacity which has taken place can be utilized in the manner planned by firms. This, however, leads to a further expansion in productive capacity; if the enlarged capacity is to be utilized as intended, there must be a further rise in income. An increase in income, however, requires a further rise in net investment, and so on. *It can be seen that a process of growth, once started, must continue ad infinitum if disturbances are to be avoided* (*i.e. if there are to be no disappointments in the expectations of firms regarding utilization of capacity and sales*). We can only speak of *disturbance-free growth*[1] if the increase in the capital stock, brought about by additional investment, can be utilized in conformity with the intentions and expectations of firms. *The central problem of the theory of long-run growth is to state the conditions for disturbance-free growth, in the sense just defined.*

(1) Translator's note: The German term is "Störungsfreies Wachstum". See footnote (2), p. 189.

2. Let K denote the capital stock, and P the potential output of this capital stock, given its degree of utilization.[1] Then the ratio:

$$\frac{K}{P} = \frac{1}{\sigma} \tag{85}$$

gives the capital stock required for the production of one unit of output at the assumed degree of utilization. This ratio is known as the "capital-output ratio.[2] The capital stock and production are a function of time. If we assume for the sake of simplicity that the capital output ratio is constant, it follows immediately from (85) that the rates of change of K and P with respect to time are directly proportional to the capital-output ratio:

$$\frac{dK}{dt} = \frac{1}{\sigma}\frac{dP}{dt}. \tag{86}$$

But the rate of change of the capital stock is identical with net investment I:

$$\frac{dK}{dt} = I. \tag{87}$$

Hence we can also write (86) in the following form:

$$\sigma \,.\, I = \frac{dP}{dt}. \tag{88}$$

Now, if the additional output dP, which is made possible by the net investment I, is to be sold, there must be an increase in real income exactly equal to dP. *In other words, the rate of growth of real income Y must be equal to the rate of growth of productive capacity* (assuming a constant degree of utilization):

$$\frac{dY}{dt} = \frac{dP}{dt}. \tag{89}$$

Equation (89) is the basic condition for disturbance-free growth. Using (88), we may write (89) in the following form:

$$\frac{dY}{dt} = \sigma \,.\, I. \tag{90}$$

If we rewrite (90) in the form:

$$\sigma \,.\, I = \frac{dY}{dt} \tag{90a}$$

[1] This degree of utilization may correspond to full utilization, but may also be less.

[2] The capital-output ratio has a time dimension. The variable σ denotes the reciprocal of the capital-output ratio, i.e. the "productivity of capital".

it possesses a *formal* similarity to the acceleration principle (75). But instead of the rate of growth of consumption we now have the rate of growth of income. It must be emphasized, however, that this similarity is *merely formal*. In fact, there is a crucial difference between equation (90a) and the acceleration principle. The acceleration principle describes the behaviour of firms regarding investment decisions (the reader should recall our discussion on p. 175). *Equation (90a), however, states a condition for disturbance-free growth. It links the rate of growth of income which is required for disturbance-free growth to the prevailing level of net investment.*

3. We are now in a position to state how income and investment must grow through time if disturbance-free growth is to be achieved (assuming a constant degree of utilization of the growing capital stock). Let us assume that the propensity to save is:

$$S = s \, . \, Y, \tag{91}$$

where s is the marginal propensity to save which, (for the sake of simplicity) is assumed to be constant. *It is obvious that disturbance-free growth presupposes the equality of voluntary savings and investment in each period.* Hence the second condition is that:

$$S = I. \tag{92}$$

The three equations (90a), (91), (92) determine national income and investment as a function of time. It should be noted that this system consists of one behaviour equation (91) and of two equations, (90a) and (92), which state conditions for disturbance-free growth.[1] In this growth model there is no investment function of the kind we had in the short-run models of income determination. Since equation (90a) is a dynamic relation, because it contains a rate of growth $\frac{dY}{dt}$, the growth model consisting of the three equations is a *dynamic model*.

Using (91) and (92), (90a) can be written:

$$\frac{dY}{dt} = s \, . \, \sigma \, . \, Y. \tag{93}$$

Our model thus reduces to this one homogeneous first-order differential equation. (93) states that disturbance-free growth requires that the rate of growth of income be proportional to the level of income, the factor of proportionality being $s \, . \, \sigma$, i.e. the product of the marginal

[1] Translator's note: we might call them "dynamic equilibrium conditions"; but see footnote 2, p. 189.

propensity to save and the reciprocal of the capital-output ratio. Solving this equation we obtain income as a function of time:

(94) $$Y = Y_0 \,.\, e^{s.\sigma.t},$$

where Y_0 is the initial income and e the base of the natural logarithms.[1] From (91) and (92) we derive the corresponding growth function for net investment:

(95) $$I = s \,.\, Y_0 \,.\, e^{s.\sigma.t}.$$

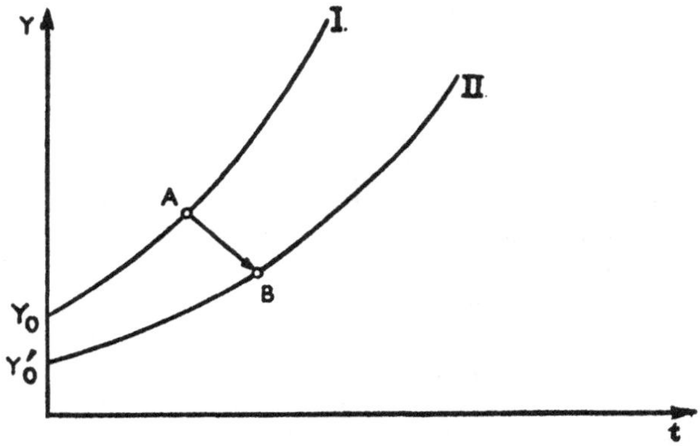

Fig. 52

Thus, income and net investment must grow exponentially if disturbance-free growth is to be ensured.

It should be noted that the rate of growth of income $\left(\frac{dY}{dt}\right)$ and of investment are directly proportional to the level of income and thus increase with rising income. This leads to an interesting result: *if the desired degree of utilization of the growing capital stock is to be realized, income must grow at an ever increasing rate.*

The curve of the growth of income given by (94) (and shown graphically in Fig. 52) may be denoted as the *path of disturbance-free long-run growth of income.*[2]

4. The rate of growth depends on the marginal propensity to

(1) $e = 2{\cdot}718\ldots$

(2) R. F. Harrod speaks of a "warranted" rate of growth of income. Occasionally the curve of disturbance-free growth is described as an equilibrium path, i.e. as a chain of successive equilibrium incomes in which each income necessarily follows from the income in the immediately preceding point of time. But it must be stressed that the concept of equilibrium in its usual form (as discussed in Vol. II) is not applicable to the relationships elucidated here. Even if each income which fulfils equation (94) also satisfies conditions (90a) and (92) (which are necessary conditions for equilibrium in the sense that no economic

save and on the capital-output ratio, and the position of the growth curve depends on the initial income Y_0. Fig. 52 shows the growth curves for the two initial incomes Y_0 and Y_0', s and σ being the same in each case. It can be seen from Fig. 52 that an accidental deviation of income from path I (say from A to B) will not lead back to path I; path II now represents disturbance-free growth, and income from now on remains lower than it would have been, had the accidental deviation from A to B not occurred.

The lower the marginal propensity to save and the larger the capital output-ratio, the smaller is the rate of growth at any given level of income. Given the capital-output ratio, a high marginal propensity to save requires high level of additional investment if equilibrium is to be maintained. This means that national income must also grow rapidly, if the larger capital stock is to be utilized in accordance with the intentions of firms. Given the capital-output ratio, a high marginal propensity to save is the *conditio sine qua non* for a rapid growth of real income. In this growth model the effect of a high marginal propensity to save is entirely different from that in the short-run theory of income determination, where a higher marginal propensity to save *ceteris paribus* leads to a reduction in income. But this is not contradictory. We must remember that the short-run theory analyses fluctuations of income on the assumption of *given* productive capacity, i.e. it neglects the capacity-increasing effect of investment. The theory of long-run growth, however, neglects those short-period fluctuations in income which occur within any given productive capacity, and concentrates on those effects on income which stem from the capacity-increasing effect of investment. The effects of additional savings appear in one way when we consider, as did the classics, only long-run development and assume that productive capacity is always fully employed; they appear entirely differently in an analysis restricted to the short-run effects

unit must experience surprises) each point on the curve of disturbance-free growth is, nevertheless, *not* an equilibrium position in the sense that no one has reason to alter his dispositions if disturbance-free growth is maintained. The income at the point of time t on the curve of disturbance-free growth necessarily generates a further growth of income and of investment. At each point of time firms have to increase the capital stock in order to be able to use the existing capital stock according to their intentions. Thus firms must continuously alter their dispositions with respect to investment, so that each point on the curve of disturbance-free growth fulfills certain equilibrium conditions *and* simultaneously represents a disequilibrium position. There is no objection to describing this peculiar situation by the term "dynamic equilibrium", provided one bears in mind the special character of this "equilibrium". (See: G. Bombach, "Zur Theorie des wirtschaftlichen Wachstums", *Weltwirtschaftliches Archiv*, Vol. 70, 1953, p. 129 ff.)

of additional savings. *When discussing savings, it is essential to indicate clearly whether one is considering long-run development with a constant degree of utilization of (the growing) productive capacity, or whether one is considering the short-run aspects of fluctuations in income within the framework of given productive capacity.* The theory

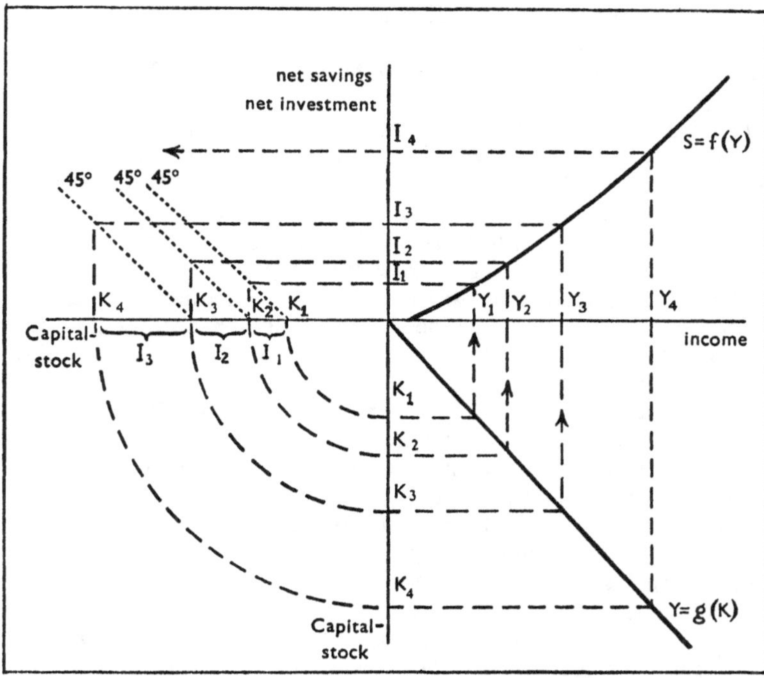

Fig. 53

of long-term growth explains the trend of national income, while the short-run theory of income determination explains the fluctuations of income around the trend. The latest development of the theory aims at combining both theories in an analysis which takes account of both aspects simultaneously.[1]

5. G. Bombach has given a simple diagrammatic representation of the process of growth analysed here.[2] In Fig. 53 the savings

(1) See especially: J. R. Hicks, *A Contribution to the Theory of the Trade Cycle*, Oxford 1950.

(2) G. Bombach *loc. cit.* p. 126–127. This work is especially recommended. The author introduces the degree of utilization of the capital stock as an explicit variable, and approaches as yet unsettled questions of growth theory.

function $S = f(Y)$ is drawn in quadrant I, which corresponds to the right-hand part of Fig. 39. Given the propensity to save, we can read off immediately what level of net investment is required if a given level of income is to be reached.

In quadrant IV the straight line through the origin represents the relationship between the capital stock, given its degree of utilization, and *potential* income. The capital stock K_1, K_2, . . . corresponds to the potential income Y_1, Y_2, ...

Quadrant II shows the addition to the capital stock, which is equal to prevailing net investment.

The process of growth takes place in the following way. Let the capital stock in the first period be K_1. If this capital stock is utilized to the degree intended by firms, the real income Y_1 can be produced. But this real income Y_1 can be absorbed only if net investment is at the level I_1, which leads to a rise in the capital stock from K_1 to K_2 (quadrant II). If the enlarged productive capacity is to be utilized to the degree intended by firms, the level of income Y_2 must be produced. The level of income Y_2 will only be absorbed if net investment is at the level I_2. This in turn leads to an increase in the capital stock, and so on.

It can be seen that the absolute increases in K, Y and I become ever larger, and that the process of growth never leads to a stationary position. The ratio of incomes at two successive points of time, however, remains constant, i.e. income grows in a geometric progression. With respect to this rate of growth the path of disturbance-free growth is an equilibrium path.

6. In conclusion we must emphasize that the growth model we have discussed states nothing about the forces which determine actual, observable growth. It merely elucidates the *conditions for disturbance-free growth* and shows what the path of income and investment must be if these conditions are to be fulfilled.(1)

(1) Regarding the relationship between growth models and cyclical models, see R. F. Harrod, *Towards a Dynamic Economics*, London, 1948.
G. Bombach, *loc. cit.* section 4.
For a criticism of the Harrod-Domar models, see J. Robinson, "The Model of an Expanding Economy," *Economic Journal*, 1952.
On growth theory in general see: J. Robinson, *The Accumulation of Capital*, London 1956.

Section B

THE CASE OF A CLOSED ECONOMY WITH GOVERNMENT ACTIVITY

§ 1. Introductory

1. The analysis of the preceding section referred to a closed economy without economic activity by the government. We next have to enquire how the economic activity of the government affects the formation of national income, i.e. how the economic dispositions of the government together with the dispositions of private economic units influence the level of national income. In Vol. I we discussed the various ways in which the government participates or interferes in the economic process of a modern economy. Here we shall not be concerned with all forms of governmental economic activity mentioned there. For example, we shall neglect such interventions as prohibitions of production, allocations and controls. We shall be concerned solely with those effects of governmental activity on national income which operate through government receipts and expenditures; for our purposes it is immaterial whether these are recurrent or non-recurrent receipts and expenditures.

2. Government expenditures and receipts (or payments by the government and payments to the government) may be divided into three groups:

	Expenditures	*Receipts*
(A)	Purchases of goods and services	Sales of goods and services
(B)	Transfer payments[1] and subsidies	Taxes
(C)	Repayment of debt	New Loans

These six groups comprise all governmental activities which give rise to payments and receipts. We now have to enquire how changes in governmental dispositions regarding these various groups affect the level of national income.

3. The scientific analysis of this range of problems has only begun during the last two decades. As long as the government's part in the economic process was relatively small, there was no reason to assume

[1] Transfer payments are payments to economic units, not being payments for goods and services rendered (for example, relief of all kinds, interest payments by the government, and pensions). See Vol. I. seventh ed. p. 91 ff.

Table 1. The National Product of the German Federal Republic, 1951–1955

	Billions DM at current prices					Billions DM at 1936 prices				
	1951	1952	1953	1954	1955	1951	1952	1953	1954	1955
Private Consumption	65·1	70·7	75·7	81·7	91·9	35·9	38·8	42·5	45·9	51·0
Government Expenditure[(1)]	18·4	22·6	22·5	24·0	25·3	11·3	12·8	12·7	13·5	13·9
Gross Investment	28·1	29·6	32·0	35·6	43·2	13·6	13·2	14·6	16·3	18·9
Domestic Expenditure	111·6	122·9	130·2	141·3	160·4	60·8	64·8	69·8	75·7	83·8
Net Foreign Investment	+2·0	+3·1	+4·2	+4·2	+3·6	+2·0	+1·9	+1·8	+1·8	+2·0
G.N.P. at market prices	113·6	126·0	134·4	145·5	164·0	62·8	66·7	71·6	77·5	85·8

Table 2. The Composition of the National Product (in %) 1951–1955

	1951	1952	1953	1954	1955
Private consumption	57·3	56·1	56·3	56·2	56·0
Government Expenditure	16·2	17·9	16·7	16·5	15·4
Gross Investment	24·7	23·5	23·8	24·5	26·3
Domestic Expenditure	98·2	97·5	96·8	97·2	97·7
Net Foreign Investment	1·8	2·5	3·2	2·8	2·3
G.N.P. at market prices	100·0	100·0	100·0	100·0	100·0

(1) Including occupation costs.
Source: Statistical Yearbook for the German Federal Republic, 1956, pp. 518, 521.

that government finance had a perceptible or important influence on economic activity. There was no reason to pay special attention to the effects of government financial transactions on the national income. Since the first world war, however, the governmental sector in the economy has expanded progressively. The order of magnitude of government financial transactions is nowadays such that government expenditures and receipts necessarily have a decisive influence on the economic process.[1] Once it is recognized that changes in government expenditures and receipts affect the course of the economy, it is a short step to the attempt to use fiscal policy deliberately as an instrument for influencing the course of the economy, e.g. to dampen fluctuations in employment, or to stabilize the level of employment. It is thus only natural that recent and current research should be occupied intensively with the questions with which we propose to deal. Important results have already been achieved, even though numerous questions are still open and await precise analysis. It is, therefore, necessary to stress that the subject we are about to discuss contains much unexplored matter, and that we are only providing an introduction to it, which will merely indicate the fundamental relationships involved.

4. An analysis of the effects of government expenditures and revenues (and changes in them) on national income requires at first a precise analysis of the effects of each factor separately. For example, if we wish to examine the effects of an increase in certain taxes on income, we have to assume that all other receipts as well as expenditures remain unchanged; the same applies when we examine the effects of raising a new loan. Again, when we examine the effects of changing a certain type of expenditure, we have to assume that all other expenditures as well as receipts remain constant. It must not be thought that an increase in taxes, for example, is *necessarily* linked to an increase in particular expenditures. *The raising of revenue must be separated sharply, on economic and conceptual grounds, from activities involving expenditure.* The government may increase taxes without increasing its expenditures; and it can increase its expenditures without raising taxes. It is important to realise that the government can combine the six instruments of fiscal policy in any way it likes. We can only ascertain the effects of a particular combination of receipts and expenditures after we have examined the effects of receipts and expenditures separately.

[1] The two tables on p. 194 show the absolute and relative shares of private consumption, private investment and government expenditure on goods and services in the German Federal Republic's G.N.P. at market prices for the years stated.

§ 2. Various Concepts of Income

1. It was shown in Vol. I that, as soon as we allow for government activities, we must distinguish between national income at market prices and national income at factor cost. These two concepts were explained in detail in Vol. I. If we denote private consumption during any period by C_{pr}, private net investment by I_{pr} and government expenditure on goods and services (i.e. government expenditure on consumption and investment) by A_{st}, the national income at market prices Y_m is given by:

(1) $$Y_m = C_{\text{pr}} + I_{\text{pr}} + A_{\text{st}}.$$

From (1) we derive the national income at factor cost Y_f:

(2) $$Y_f = Y_m - T_{\text{ind}} + Z_{\text{st}},$$

where T_{ind} are indirect taxes and Z_{st} indirect subsidies.

For our analysis, however, we need further concepts of income, which we now have to develop. If we add transfer payments T_r to national income at factor cost we obtain what is called *private income before taxes*:[1]

(3) $$Y_{\text{pr}} = Y_f + T_r.$$

If we subtract the undistributed profits of firms (U) from private income we obtain *personal income before taxes* (Y_p):

(4) $$Y_p = Y_{\text{pr}} - U.$$

By subtracting direct taxes (T_{dir}) from personal income we finally obtain personal disposable income (Y_d):

(5) $$Y_d = Y_p - T_{\text{dir}}.$$

Starting with personal disposable income, we have the following ordering of the various concepts of income:

(1) personal disposable income
+ direct taxes

(2) = personal income before taxes
+ undistributed profits

(3) = private income before taxes
− transfer payments

(4) = net national income at factor cost
+ (indirect taxes − subsidies)

[1] If we do not wish to include profits of public enterprises in indirect taxation, we must subtract them from income at factor cost in order to obtain private income.

(5) = net national income at market prices
+ depreciation

(6) = gross national income at market prices

Using equations (1)–(4) we can write (5) in the form:

(6) $$Y_d = C_{pr} + I_{pr} + A_{st} - T_{ind} + Z_{st} + T_r - U - T_{dir}.$$

If we denote by G all government expenditure on goods and services as well as on transfer payments and subsidies,

(7) $$G = A_{st} + Z_{st} + T_r$$

and all direct and indirect taxes by T,

(8) $$T = T_{dir} + T_{ind},$$

(6) becomes:

(9) $$Y_d = C_{pr} + I_{pr} + (G - T) - U.$$

In this expression the difference $G - T$ denotes the excess of all government expenditure on goods and services, as well as on transfer payments and subsidies, over all revenue from taxes (i.e. it denotes the *budget deficit or the budget surplus*).

If we denote the sum of personal disposable income and undistributed profits as private disposable income (Y_d^{pr}), then according to (9):

(10) $$Y_d^{pr} = C_{pr} + I_{pr} + (G - T).$$

The recipients of private disposable income can either spend it on consumption or save, hence:

(11) $$Y_d^{pr} = C_{pr} + S_{pr},$$

where S_{pr} obviously includes undistributed profits. From (10) and (11) we can derive the relation

(12) $$S_{pr} = I_{pr} + (G - T),$$

which was stated in Vol. I. *This equation states that private net saving during any period is equal by definition to the sum of private net investment and the budget deficit.*[1]

2. In the following analysis we shall understand by national income *national income at market prices*. Equation (1) shows that national income is equal to the sum of private consumption, private net investment and government expenditure on goods and services.

[1] Equation (12) is identical with equation (5) on p. 89 of Vol. I (7th ed.) and can easily be translated into the latter.

We have to examine what determines these three variables. We know that they are determined by the behaviour of economic units. In the context of macro-economic analysis the relevant units are: the group of households acting as consumers, the group of private firms acting as investors, and the government. The consumption decisions of households are expressed in the consumption function, which describes the dependence of consumption on the level of income. However, when we introduce the government into the analysis the question arises which income is relevant in determining the level of consumption and should therefore be inserted in the consumption function. Only private disposable income and personal disposable income are relevant, since households can make consumption decisions only within the limits set by these incomes. Which of these two incomes is to be used depends on the purposes at hand. *Usually private disposable income is taken as the independent variable in the consumption function.* We shall follow this practice and write the consumption function in the form:

(13) $$C_{pr} = C_{pr}(Y_d^{pr})$$

If we remember that:

(14)[1] $$(Y_d^{pr} = Y_m - T + T_r^1)$$

equation (13) can be written:

(15) $$C_{pr} = C_{pr}(Y_m - T + T_r).$$

In the following analysis we shall work with this function.

Since we regard private consumption as a function of private disposable income undistributed profits U do not appear explicitly in our analysis. If we wished to analyse the influence on national income of changes in the undistributed profits of firms, we should have to regard private consumption as a function of *personal* disposable income:

$$C_{pr} = C_{pr}(Y_m - T + T_r - U)$$

It is left to the reader to carry out the analysis on this alternative assumption.

§ 3. The Effect of Government Expenditure on the Level of National Income

National income at market prices is by definition:

(16) $$Y_m = C_{pr} + I_{pr} + A_{st}.$$

If we regard C_{pr} as a function of private disposable income, as we

[1] For the sake of brevity we shall henceforth denote the sum of transfer payments *and* subsidies by T_r.

decided to do at the end of § 2, we also have the relation (15):

$$C_{pr} = C_{pr}(Y_m - T + T_r). \quad (17)$$

We thus have two equations, one definitional and one behaviour equation, in six variables Y_m, C_{pr}, I_{pr}, A_{st}, T and T_r. Our system therefore possesses four degrees of freedom, i.e. four variables can be chosen arbitrarily.

1. At first we shall analyse our problem on the assumption that *total government revenue from taxation as well as private net investment are given constants*. By making these two assumptions we have

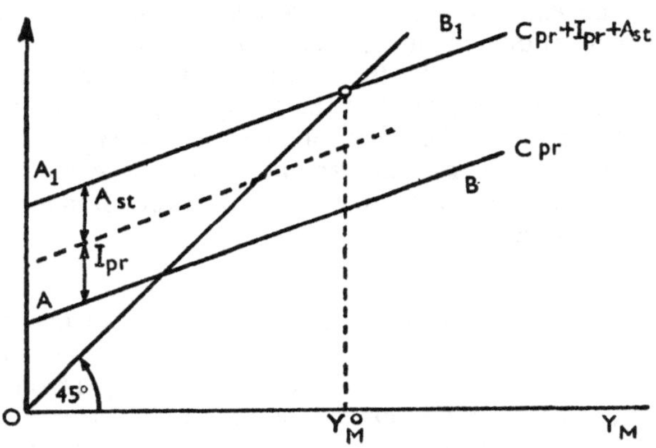

Fig. 54

reduced the number of degrees of freedom to two; now only A_{st} and T_r can be chosen arbitrarily. We are thus in a position to analyse the pure effects of government expenditure on national income.

2. Let us first consider a *variation in government expenditure on goods and services, transfer payments remaining constant.*

Using (17), (16) becomes:

$$Y_m = C_{pr}(Y_m - T + T_r) + I_{pr} + A_{st}. \quad (18)$$

In this equation T, T_r and I_{pr} are given constants. It follows from (18) that the level of A_{st} determines the level of Y_m. In equilibrium Y_m must be at that level at which private effective demand for consumption and investment and government demand for goods and services are exactly equal to income. This is the condition expressed in equation (18). We can ascertain this equilibrium income by the same simple graphical method which we used in Chapter III, Section A, § 1. In Fig. 54 the curve AB represents the consumption function, i.e. the dependence of private consumption on Y_m, T and T_r remaining constant. The curve A_1B_1 indicates total effective demand of the private and government sectors at alternative values of Y_m. On our assumptions the curve A_1B_1 is parallel to, and above, the curve AB, by an amount $I_{pr} + A_{st}$. The figure shows that the equilibrium income is Y_m^0; for only at this income is total effective demand exactly equal to income.

Fig. 54 shows that *ceteris paribus* an increase in A_{st} leads to a rise in Y_m; moreover it can also be seen that government expenditure on goods and services has the same effect on the level of national income as does private investment.[1] An increase (decrease) in A_{st} leads to an expansion (contraction) in national income. The extent to which national income rises (falls) as a result of an increase (decrease) in A_{st} depends on the multiplier, which in our simple model is equal to the reciprocal of the marginal propensity to save.

3. Now let us examine the effects of a change in *transfer payments, taxes T and government expenditure on goods and services A_{st} remaining constant*. For this purpose we write the expression for private disposable income in the form:

$$Y_d^{pr} = Y_m - (T - T_r).$$

The difference $T - T_r$ is the *net* amount received by, or taken from, private economic units by way of receipt of subsidies and payment of taxes. If $T = T_r$, payments of subsidies equal receipts from taxes; if $T < T_r$, transfer payments exceed receipts from taxes, i.e. payments made by the government to private economic units, which are not payments for currently produced goods and services, exceed similar payments made by private economic units to the government. If $T > T_r$, the situation is reversed. If we abbreviate by denoting

$$T - T_r = W,$$

then

$$W = 0 \quad \text{for} \quad T = T_r$$
$$W > 0 \quad \text{for} \quad T > T_r$$
$$W < 0 \quad \text{for} \quad T < T_r.$$

We can now write the consumption function as

$$C_{pr} = C_{pr}(Y_m - W). \tag{19}$$

The position of the consumption function thus depends on W. In Fig. 55 the curve AB represents the consumption function for $W = 0$. For $W > 0$ the consumption curve will lie below the curve AB and

[1] An attempt at a quantitative estimate of the direct employment-creating effects will be found in a special supplement to *Wirtschaft und Statistik* (published by the Statistisches Reichsamt) Nr 21, 1933.

parallel to it; it shifts by the horizontal amount W (curve A_1B_1 in Fig. 55). When W diminishes (increases), the consumption curve

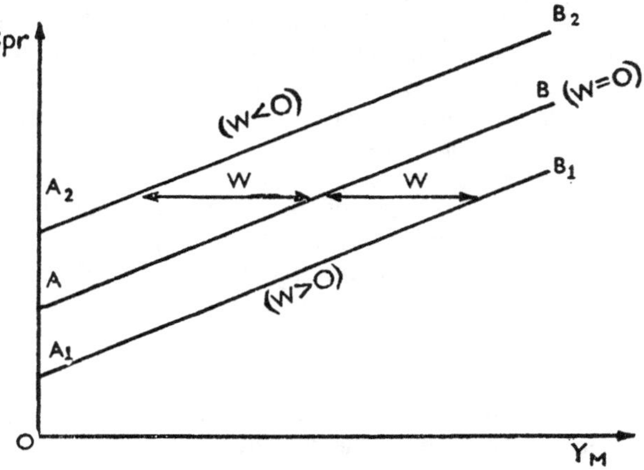

Fig. 55

shifts upwards (downwards). This immediately gives us the answer to our question. A change in transfer payments, taxes remaining

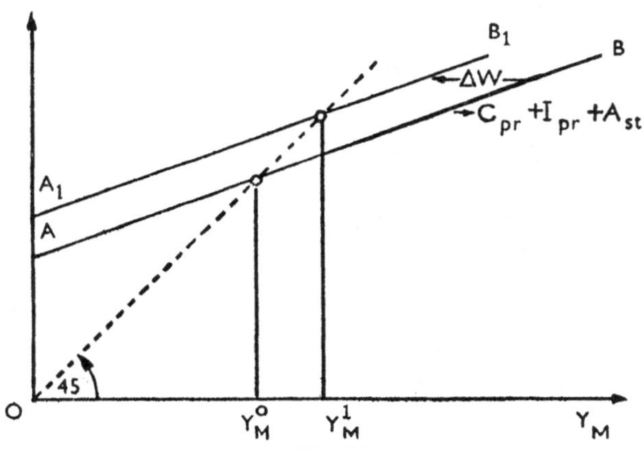

Fig. 56

constant, means a change in W and thus a parallel shift in the consumption function. When T_r rises, T remaining constant, W becomes smaller, and the consumption function shifts upwards. In Fig. 56 the curve AB represents total effective demand as a function of Y_m

before the increase in transfer payments. When transfer payments are increased by the amount ΔT_r, W changes by the amount $\Delta W = -\Delta T_r$, so that the consumption function AB shifts to the left by the amount ΔW. The equilibrium income rises to Y_m^1. *Thus, an increase in transfer payments, ceteris paribus, has an expansionary effect; and a fall in transfer payments leads to a contraction in income.*

It can be seen that an increase in government expenditure on goods and services, ceteris paribus, has a stronger expansionary effect than an increase in transfer payments of the same amount. An increase in A_{st} of £1 million shifts the curve of total effective demand vertically upwards by £1 million, while a rise in transfer payments shifts the curve of effective demand horizontally upwards by £1 million. A *numerical* example will clarify this. Let us assume a linear consumption function:

$$C_{pr} = a + b(Y_m - W),$$

and for the sake of simplicity let us also assume $I_{pr} = 0$. Then the equilibrium income is given by the condition:

$$Y_m = a + b(Y_m - W) + A_{st},$$

or:

$$Y_m = \frac{a + A_{st} - bW}{1 - b}. \tag{20}$$

It follows from (20) that:

$$\Delta Y_m = \frac{1}{1 - b} \cdot \Delta A_{st}, \quad (W \text{ constant}) \tag{21}$$

and

$$\Delta Y_m = -\frac{b}{1 - b} \cdot \Delta W, \quad (A_{st} \text{ constant}) \tag{22}$$

where ΔA_{st} and ΔW are partial differences in A_{st} and W respectively. In (21) and (22) b is the marginal propensity to consume. The fraction $\frac{1}{1 - b}$ is thus the reciprocal of the marginal propensity to save. If $0 < b < 1$ the reciprocal value of the marginal propensity to save is greater than 1, and

$$\frac{b}{1 - b} < \frac{1}{1 - b}.$$

An increase in A_{st} of £1 million thus raises income by more than an increase in transfer payments of £1 million. The multiplier effect of a change in government expenditure on goods and services is thus larger than that of an equal change in transfer payments. For example, if $b = \frac{2}{3}$, $\Delta Y_m = 3$ for $\Delta A_{st} = 1$. For $\Delta W = -1$, however, $\Delta Y_m = 2$.

The reason for the stronger expansionary effect of government expenditure on goods and services can be seen easily when we consider the process of expansion in terms of dynamic analysis. If A_{st} increases by £1 million, *ceteris paribus*, income in the first period rises immediately by £1 million. In the second, third, etc. periods there is a further increase in income due to the secondary, tertiary, etc. increases in consumption which take place in the course of the multiplier process. For $b = \frac{2}{3}$ the series of income changes is:

$$1, \tfrac{2}{3}, (\tfrac{2}{3})^2, (\tfrac{2}{3})^3, \ldots,$$

the sum of which is 3. But if transfer payments are increased by £1 million there is no change in income in the first period.[1] In the second period income increases only by £1 million multiplied by the marginal propensity to consume of the recipients of the transfer payments, and the series of income changes is:

$$\tfrac{2}{3}, (\tfrac{2}{3})^2, (\tfrac{2}{3})^3, \ldots,$$

the sum of which is 2.

4. Finally, let us consider the effect of repaying loans.[2] The repayment of loans to the public or the banks simply means an exchange of assets as far as the owners of government securities are concerned. Instead of claims against the government they now hold claims against commercial banks or the central bank (depending on whether the government securities were owned by the public or by the commercial banks). If the government redeems securities held by the banks, the liquidity of the banks increases. This will have no direct effect on national income. If the government redeems securities held by the public, the public now holds more cash, while at the same time the liquidity of the banks is raised. As a rule, the public does not use the added cash to purchase goods and services, so that in this case also the exchange of assets does not lead to a direct increase in effective demand and an expansion in national income.

But the repayment of debt may have an indirect expansionary influence on private effective demand through its effect on the rate of interest. The relationships relevant here were discussed previously, in connection with the effects of open market policies on national

(1) Translator's note: assuming consumption in one period depends on disposable income in the preceding period.

(2) For the sake of simplicity we assume that the government keeps an account only with the central bank.

income (pp. 153–154). The repayment of debt, considered by itself, always increases the quantity of money in the private sector of the economy. If the demand for money is perfectly interest-elastic the increase in the quantity of money does not lead to a change in the rate of interest and thus does not affect economic activity. However, if the demand for money is not perfectly interest-elastic, the increased quantity of money can be absorbed only at a lower rate of interest. If private investment is completely interest-inelastic there is still no change in activity. However, if private investment is interest-elastic, the fall in the rate of interest stimulates private investment activity, and thus brings about an expansionary process.

The repayment of debt to the central bank entails a destruction of money (a reduction in the liabilities and assets of the central bank.)

§ 4. The Effect of Taxes and Government Borrowing on National Income

1. Let us next consider the effects of *changes in taxation.* We assume that the total amount of taxation T changes by the given amount ΔT. Government expenditure on goods and services, transfer payments and private net investment are assumed to remain constant.

From the analysis in § 3 it follows that, *ceteris paribus*, a rise in taxation means an increase in W and hence a parallel shift downwards of the consumption curve. This reduces the equilibrium level of income. An increase in taxation thus leads to a contraction in income. In equation (22) ΔW is now positive and ΔY_m correspondingly negative. The "taxation-multiplier" is the same as the multiplier for transfer payments, and is determined by the marginal propensity to consume of households, taken as a group. The larger the part of an increase in taxation which falls on consumption, the stronger is the contractionary effect of the rise in taxation; conversely, the expansionary effect of a reduction in taxation is the larger, the larger the part of the additional disposable income which is devoted to consumption.

This, of course, gives only a crude picture of the effects of changes in taxation. The reader may justifiably object that the expansionary or contractionary effect will differ, depending on which taxes are changed. Indeed, the expansionary or contractionary effect of a change in taxation depends not only on the total change in taxation but also to a large extent on the incidence of the change in taxation. But a macro-economic analysis, which uses such broad aggregates as those in our first simplest model, cannot deal with these effects.

To take them into account we would have to split up the broad aggregates, and give a detailed micro-economic analysis of the reactions of individual economic units to given changes in particular taxes. We can only give a few examples: if the additional taxation is raised solely through an increase in income tax on high incomes, the larger part of this additional taxation will fall on savings, and the contractionary effect resulting from the reduction in consumption will be small. But this does not exhaust the effects of the increase in taxation. Further effects depend to a large extent on how the rise in income tax affects the firms' demand for factors of production. The reader might consider what happens when the increase in income tax falls mainly on the low income groups. An increase in death-duties does not as a rule influence consumption, so that there will be no (or only a small) contractionary effect. A detailed analysis of the effect on consumption of changes in various kinds of taxes is not yet available; this is a wide field for fruitful future research. Nevertheless, macro-economic analysis retains its value, even though it indicates the relevant relationships only in the broadest outline.

2. Finally let us briefly consider the effects, *ceteris paribus*, of *the raising of loans by the government*. The government can borrow from (a) the public, (b) the commercial banks, (c) the central bank. If the government borrows on the open market, the amounts subscribed by the public will come from the savings of the same and (or) preceding periods. This will have no *direct* effect on economic activity. But the raising of a loan on the open market reduces the quantity of money in the private sector. If this leads to a rise in the rate of interest, (whether and to what extent this happens depends on the interest-elasticity of liquidity preference) and if the rise in the rate of interest reduces net investment, a process of contraction ensues.

A loan from the central bank has no immediate effect on the rate of interest. A change in the rate of interest may result, but only when the government spends the proceeds of the loan. This will be discussed further in § 6.

§ 5. The Combined Effect of Changes in Government Expenditure and Revenue

1. The results obtained in the preceding paragraphs enable us to state the combined effect of changes in government expenditure and revenue. The basis of our analysis is once more equation (18):

$$Y_m = C_{\text{pr}}(Y_m - T + T_r) + I_{\text{pr}} + A_{\text{st}}, \tag{23}$$

As before, we assume private net investment to be a given constant. Let us consider a series of possible combinations of changes in revenue and expenditure.

2. Let the government simultaneously increase taxes by the amount ΔT and transfer payments by the same amount, so that $\Delta T = \Delta T_r$, A_{st} remaining constant. It is clear that this leaves private disposable income unchanged and therefore, in our macro-economic model, consumption and income Y_m remain unchanged. This conclusion rests on the assumption, contained in (23), that the aggregate marginal propensity to consume is unaffected by this transaction, which is equivalent to the assumption that those who pay the additional taxes have the same marginal propensity to consume as those who receive the increase in transfer payments. If this assumption is not fulfilled the result will be different. For example, if the marginal propensity to consume of the recipients of the additional transfer payments is larger than that of those who pay the added taxes (i.e. if there is a redistribution of income in favour of the lower income groups) there will be an expansion in income, resulting from the change in the propensity to consume.

3. Let the government simultaneously increase taxation by the amount ΔT and expenditure on goods and services by the same amount, so that $\Delta A_{st} = \Delta T$. As in the previous case, the budget deficit (or surplus) $A_{st} + T_r - T$ remains unchanged. The difference between this and the preceding case is that *now the equilibrium income rises by the amount* ΔA_{st}. This can be proved in several ways. Given a marginal propensity to consume b $(0 < b < 1)$, an increase in taxation of £1 leads to a successive series of income changes equal to:

$$-b, -b^2, -b^3, \ldots$$

£1 of additional government expenditure on goods and services, however, leads to a series of successive income changes equal to:

$$1, b, b^2, b^3, \ldots$$

Hence there is a net increase in income of £1.

We may also say that the shift in effective demand is $\Delta T \,.\, (1 - b)$ and hence, through the multiplier effect, the final increase in income is:

$$\Delta T \,.\, (1 - b) \,.\, \frac{1}{1 - b} = \Delta T$$

This result derives from the fact that an increase in A_{st}, financed by additional taxation, leaves private disposable income unchanged, and from the assumption that the (aggregate) marginal propensity to consume is unaffected by the distribution of income. This can be seen clearly from the following proof. We write (23) in the form:

$$Y_m - W^{(1)} = C_{\mathrm{pr}}(Y_m - W) + I_{\mathrm{pr}} + A_{\mathrm{st}} - W$$

Since $Y_m - W$ denotes private disposable income Y_d^{pr}, we may also write:

$$Y_{\mathrm{d}}^{\mathrm{pr}} = C_{\mathrm{pr}}(Y_{\mathrm{d}}^{\mathrm{pr}}) + I_{\mathrm{pr}} + A_{\mathrm{st}} - W. \tag{24}$$

Given I_{pr}, A_{st} and W, this equation determines the equilibrium value of private disposable income. Now, when an increase in A_{st} is financed by additional taxes, the budget surplus (deficit) $A_{\mathrm{st}} - W$ remains unchanged, and therefore private disposable income also remains unchanged. But if private disposable income remains unchanged, Y_m must change by an amount equal to the change in W, i.e. by an amount equal to the additional taxes ΔT. This proposition, known as the *Haavelmo theorem*, is valid on the assumptions we have stated, no matter what the form of the consumption function.[2]

Briefly, the theorem states that an increase in government expenditure on goods and services which is financed by taxation has a multiplier effect of 1.

The expansionary effect of such a balanced increase in expenditure and revenue remains even if the marginal propensity to consume of those who pay the additional taxes is different from that of those whose incomes rise because of the additional government expenditure.[3] If we denote the marginal propensity to consume of those who pay the taxes by b_1, and the marginal propensity to consume of all other economic units by b_2, the shift in effective demand is $\Delta T(1 - b_1)$.

(1) $W = T - T_r$

(2) T. Haavelmo, "Multiplier Effects of a Balanced Budget", *Econometrica*, Vol. 13. 1945, p. 311 ff.
See also the subsequent discussion of this article by G. Haberler, R. M. Goodwin, E. E. Hagen and T. Haavelmo in *Econometrica*, Vol. 14, 1946.
See further: R. Turvey, "Some Notes on Multiplier Theory", *American Economic Review*, Vol. 43, 1953.
W. J. Baumol and M. H. Peston, "More on the Multiplier Effects of a Balanced Budget", *American Economic Review*, Vol. 45, 1955.
A. T. Peacock, "A Note on the Balanced-Budget Multiplier", *Economic Journal*, Vol. 66, 1956.
E. Schneider, "Bemerkungen zum Haavelmo-Theorem" in *Festschrift für Erik Lindahl*, Stockholm, 1956.

(3) See: E. Schneider, "Zur Frage der Wirkung finanzpolitischer Massnahmen auf die wirtschaftliche Aktivität", *Finanzarchiv*, New Series, Vol. 10, 1944 p. 277 ff.

Through the multiplier effect, this leads to a final rise in income of:

$$\Delta Y_m = \Delta T \,.\, \frac{1 - b_1}{1 - b_2}\,.$$

For $b_1 = b_2$ we have the Haavelmo theorem. If $b_1 < b_2$, $\Delta Y_m > \Delta T$; i.e. the expansionary effect is stronger than in the Haavelmo case. This situation arises when the government raises the additional revenue ΔT through an increase in income taxation which is progressive. If $b_1 > b_2$, $\Delta Y_m < \Delta T$, i.e. the expansionary effect is weaker than in the Haavelmo case.

It should be noted that these statements about the expansionary effects of a balanced budget ($\Delta A_{st} = \Delta T$) refer to the final outcome, i.e. to the expansion in income which has taken place when the multiplier process is completed. If we wished to follow the individual phases of the expansionary process we should have to analyse it in terms of the kind of dynamic analysis we used in Section A, § 1.[1]

4. Now let us consider the case in which a change in government expenditure on goods and services or (and) on transfer payments, as well as a change in taxation, leads to a *budget deficit or surplus.*

(a) Let the government reduce taxation by the amount ΔT, with A_{st} and T_r remaining unchanged. There is now a budget deficit equal to the reduction in taxation. In the first instance consumption rises by $b \,.\, \Delta T$ $(0 < b < 1)$. Through the multiplier the final rise in income is $\frac{b}{1 - b} \,.\, \Delta T$[2] .

(b) Let the government increase expenditure on goods and services by the amount ΔA_{st}, with T and T_r remaining unchanged. There is now a budget deficit equal to ΔA_{st}. Income rises by $\frac{\Delta A_{st}}{1 - b}$.

(c) Let the government increase transfer payments by ΔT_r, which is larger than the additional taxation ΔT, expenditure on goods and services remaining unchanged. The budget deficit is $\Delta T_r - \Delta T$. W is reduced, so that the consumption function shifts to the left and there is an expansion in income.

(d) Let the government increase its expenditure on goods and services by an amount greater than the simultaneous increase in taxation, T_r remaining unchanged. The budget deficit is now equal to $\Delta A_{st} - \Delta T$. In the first instance income rises by $\Delta A_{st} - b \,.\, \Delta T$,

(1) In this connection, see the works of Goodwin and Hagen mentioned above.

(2) We assume that the multiplier is the same in all periods. But even without this assumption there will be an expansionary effect.

and, through the multiplier effect, the final expansion in income is $\frac{1}{1-b} \cdot (\Delta A_{st} - b \,.\, \Delta T)$.

(e) Let the government reduce taxation by an amount larger than the simultaneous reduction in expenditure on goods and services, T_r remaining unchanged. The budget deficit is now equal to $\Delta T - \Delta A_{st}$. In the first round effective demand increases by $\Delta A_{st} - b \,.\, \Delta T$, resulting in a final change in income of $\frac{\Delta A_{st} - b \,.\, \Delta T}{1-b}$. This change in income will be expansionary if $|\Delta A_{st}| < |b \,.\, \Delta T|$, i.e. if the ratio of the change in expenditure on goods and services to the change in taxation is smaller than the marginal propensity to consume. *Thus, a budget deficit is not necessarily expansionary, and there is no unique deficit multiplier.*

5. Finally, let us briefly consider the opposite *case of a budget surplus.*

(a) Let the government increase taxation, *ceteris paribus*, by the amount ΔT. Such a measure always has a contractionary effect. The final reduction in income is $\frac{b}{1-b} \,.\, \Delta T$.

(b) Let the government reduce its expenditure on goods and services, *ceteris paribus*, by ΔA_{st}. This always leads to a contraction in income by $\frac{\Delta A_{st}}{1-b}$.

(c) *Ceteris paribus*, let the government reduce transfer payments. This increases W, the consumption function shifts to the right, and there is a contraction in income.

(d) Let the government reduce taxation by an amount smaller than the simultaneous reduction in expenditure on goods and services, T_r remaining unchanged. The resulting budget surplus is $\Delta T - \Delta A_{st}$. In the first round income falls by $\Delta A_{st} - b \,.\, \Delta T$, and the final reduction in income is $\frac{\Delta A_{st} - b \,.\, \Delta T}{1-b}$.

(e) Let the government increase its expenditure on goods and services, but by an amount smaller than the simultaneous increase in taxation, transfer payments remaining unchanged. The resulting budget surplus is $\Delta T - \Delta A_{st}$. In the first round the change in effective demand is $\Delta A_{st} - b \,.\, \Delta T$, which leads to a final change in income of $\frac{\Delta A_{st} - b \,.\, \Delta T}{1-b}$.

The resulting change in income is contractionary if

$$\Delta A_{st} < b \,.\, \Delta T$$

i.e. if the ratio of ΔA_{st} to ΔT is smaller than the marginal propensity to consume. *Thus, a budget surplus is not necessarily contractionary.*

6. It should be emphasized once again that the theorems we have derived refer to *national income at market prices.* Different results are obtained for *national income at factor cost,* and hence one must always specify the relevant income. Let us demonstrate this in connection with the Haavelmo theorem. *The change in national income at factor cost is:*

$$(*)\ \Delta Y_f = \Delta Y_m - (\Delta T_{ind} - \Delta Z_{st}).$$

The Haavelmo theorem states that:

$$(**)\ \Delta Y_m = \Delta A_{st} = \Delta T.$$

Using (**) and remembering that in the special case of the Haavelmo theorem $\Delta Z_{st} = 0$, (*) becomes:

$$\Delta Y_f = \Delta A_{st} - \Delta T_{ind} = \Delta T_{dir}.$$

On the assumptions of the Haavelmo theorem the change in national income at factor cost is not equal to the change in government expenditure on goods and services, but is smaller. *Only if* $\Delta T_{ind} = 0$, *i.e. only if the increase in government expenditure on goods and services is financed exclusively by an increase in direct taxation, is the change in national income at factor cost equal to the change in national income at market prices.*

If $\Delta T_{ind} \neq 0$ the change in national income at factor cost, on the assumptions of the Haavelmo theorem, may be positive, negative or zero, depending on whether $\Delta A_{st} \gtrless \Delta T_{ind}$ or $\Delta A_{st} = \Delta T_{ind}$.

The usual formulation of the Haavelmo theorem, however, applies only to national income at market prices; and given the assumptions of the Haavelmo theorem, the change in national income at market prices is always

$$\Delta Y_m = \Delta A_{st}$$

irrespective of which taxes are raised to finance the increase in government expenditure on goods and services.

§ 6. The Case When Taxation Varies with the Level of Income

1. So far we have assumed that the total amount raised by taxation is an instrument of fiscal policy. But this assumption does not correspond to reality. While the government does fix the level of expenditure on goods and services, it does not fix the total amount to be raised by taxation. Instead, the government determines the bases

of assessment and *tax rates; given the bases of assessment and tax rates*, total tax receipts vary with the level and composition of national income. A more realistic analysis thus requires that we regard T as a rising function of Y_m:

$$(25) \qquad T = T(Y_m).$$

Similarly, it is more realistic to regard the total sum of net transfer payments, W, as a rising function of income:

$$(26) \qquad W = W(Y_m).$$

A change in tax rates or in the rates of transfer payments will mean a shift in the curve representing the function (25) or (26).

Our basic equation (23) now becomes:

$$(27) \qquad Y_m = C_{\text{pr}}[Y_m - T(Y_m) + T_r(Y_m)] + I_{\text{pr}} + A_{\text{st}}$$

or, if we abbreviate again by denoting

$$W = T - T_r,$$

we may write:

$$(28) \qquad Y_m = C_{\text{pr}}[Y_m - W(Y_m)] + I_{\text{pr}} + A_{\text{st}}.$$

This equation will now be the basis of our analysis, in which we continue to assume that private net investment is a given constant. Since we are interested solely in the effects of *changes* in certain variables we may neglect the existence of private net investment altogether, and assume $I_{\text{pr}} = 0$.

2. Since $W(Y_m)$ is an increasing function of Y_m, the consumption function will not show parallel shifts. For positive values of W we now have the picture shown in Fig. 57. The horizontal shift of the consumption function corresponding to $W = 0$ becomes larger with rising Y_m, because W is increasing. This has important consequences, as we shall show.

3. Let us next consider the *marginal propensity to consume* with respect to income Y_m. Since the difference $Y_m - W(Y_m)$ denotes private disposable income Y_d^{pr}, i.e:

$$(29) \qquad Y_d^{\text{pr}} = Y_m - W(Y_m),$$

we may also write the consumption function:

$$(30) \qquad C_{\text{pr}} = C_{\text{pr}}(Y_d^{\text{pr}}),$$

where Y_d^{pr} is given by (29). Thus, private consumption is a function of Y_m. The marginal propensity to consume with respect to Y_m is:

$$(31) \qquad \frac{dC_{\mathrm{pr}}}{dY_m} = \frac{dC_{\mathrm{pr}}}{dY_d^{\mathrm{pr}}} \cdot \frac{dY_d^{\mathrm{pr}}}{dY_m}.$$

According to (29) we have:

$$(32) \qquad \frac{dY_d^{\mathrm{pr}}}{dY_m} = 1 - \frac{dW}{dY_m},$$

and therefore:

$$(33) \qquad \frac{dC_{\mathrm{pr}}}{dY_m} = \left(1 - \frac{dW}{dY_m}\right) \cdot \frac{dC_{\mathrm{pr}}}{dY_d^{\mathrm{pr}}}.$$

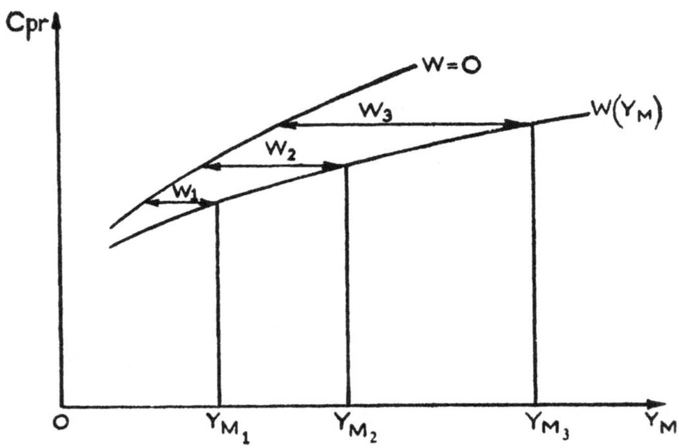

Fig. 57

$\frac{dW}{dY_m}$ denotes the net marginal rate of taxation of national income at market prices. When there are no transfer payments, or when these are constant, this expression is identical with the marginal rate of taxation of Y_m i.e. it represents the amount of taxation taken from an additional income of £1 million. As a rule, this expression increases progressively with rising income.

In the cases considered in the preceding paragraphs W was assumed to be independent of the level of income, which means that the marginal rate of net transfer payments was assumed to be zero. In this special case:

$$(34) \qquad \frac{dC_{\mathrm{pr}}}{dY_m} = \frac{dC_{\mathrm{pr}}}{dY_d^{\mathrm{pr}}},$$

i.e. the marginal propensity to consume with respect to Y_m is the same as the marginal propensity to consume with respect to private disposable income. But if we assume W to be a rising function of Y_m this equality no longer holds. Since $\frac{dW}{dY}$ is usually positive, it follows (as can be seen from (33)) that the marginal propensity to consume with respect to Y_m is smaller than the marginal propensity to consume with respect to private disposable income.

A simple example may help to clarify this. Let the consumption function (30) be:

$$C_{pr} = a + b \, . \, Y_d^{pr}. \tag{35}$$

and let the relationship between W and national income at market prices be given by:

$$W = d \, . \, Y_m \quad (0 < d < 1). \tag{36}$$

On these assumptions the relation (33) becomes:

$$\frac{dC_{pr}}{dY_m} = (1 - d) \, . \, b, \tag{37}$$

while for the case $W =$ constant, we have

$$\frac{dC_{pr}}{dY_m} = b. \tag{37a}$$

4. *What effect has a change in government expenditure on goods and services on national income, given the assumption that W depends on Y_m?* We know the answer to this question if we know the multiplier for changes in A_{st}. This multiplier is simply:

$$\mu = \frac{1}{1 - \frac{dC_{pr}}{dY_m}} \tag{38}$$

Since in our basic equation (28) private consumption appears as a function of Y_m, each change in A_{st} affects consumption through its effect on Y_m, and this change in consumption in turn affects income, and so on, so that the multiplier for A_{st} is of the form with which we are already familiar, since changes in A_{st} are economically equivalent to changes in autonomous private net investment. Using (33) the multiplier is:

$$\mu = \frac{1}{1 - \left(1 - \frac{dW}{dY_m}\right) \cdot \frac{dC_{pr}}{dY_d^{pr}}} \, . \tag{39}$$

A change in A_{st} by the amount ΔA_{st} thus leads to a final change in Y_m of:

$$\Delta Y_m = \mu \,.\, \Delta A_{st}, \tag{40}$$

where μ denotes the expression given by (39). *Expression (39) shows that the multiplier is smaller when W rises with Y_m than it is when W is constant. The expansionary effect of a given change in A_{st} is now smaller than in the case considered in 3.* The reason for this is simply that now marginal net taxation is subtracted from successive increments in income, in addition to marginal savings. A taxation system so constructed that W increases with rising Y_m thus contains an *automatic brake* on expansion. This brake is stronger, the larger $\frac{dW}{dY_m}$ i.e. the larger the net marginal rate of taxation, and the more this rate increases with rising income. Conversely, the fact that when income falls tax receipts decline and transfer payments increase (e.g. for unemployment payment) leads to an automatic dampening of the decline in income. *Thus the increase in W with rising Y_m to a certain extent acts as an automatic stabilizer of economic activity.* In this connection the following comment is made in the *Report of the Sub-committee on Monetary, Credit, and Fiscal Policies of the Joint Committee on the Economic Report* (Congress of the U.S.A., Document No. 129, Washington 1950)—the so-called Douglas Report.[1]

"The maintenance of unchanged tax rates and expenditure programmes will produce, as a response to fluctuations in the national income, an 'automatic flexibility' of revenues and actual expenditures, which will exert a stabilizing effect on the economy. . . . We believe that this automatic flexibility is a valuable contribution to stability, and that the degree of automatic flexibility in our fiscal system should, if possible, be increased." (p. 16). But the Report justifiably adds that the limitations of this automatic flexibility must not be overlooked: ". . . though it can retard or perhaps even stop a decline of business activity or a rise of prices . . . it cannot by itself re-establish full-employment conditions or push prices back to a pre-inflation level . . . it is almost certain to be inadequate in the face of a serious depression or inflation." (p. 16). In the event of a serious

[1] H. S. Ellis has called this important document the "Magna Carta of Modern Monetary Policy" and rightly adds: the report" deserves to be put on the same plane as the Bullion Report which 125 years ago became a milestone in English monetary history, and its positive contributions are much greater than those of the famous Macmillan Report two decades ago." (H. S. Ellis, "Die Wiederentdeckung des Geldes" in a collection of essays *Vollbeschäftigung Inflation und Planwirtschaft*, ed. A. Hunold, Erlenbach-Zurich, 1951, p. 124–125.)

depression or inflation automatic flexibility must be supplemented by expansionary or contractionary changes in tax rates and (or) government expenditure.

5. It is interesting to see what effect an increase in government expenditure on goods and services has on the budget when there is automatic flexibility in W. The budget deficit (B) is:

$$B = A_{st} - W$$

If W is constant, any change in A_{st} clearly alters B by the same amount. But if W is a rising function of Y_m, an increase in A_{st}, by raising income, also increases W. The effect on the budget now depends on the quantitative relationship between changes in W to changes in A_{st}. If we denote changes in B, A_{st} and W by ΔB, ΔA_{st} and ΔW respectively, then

(41) $$\Delta B = \Delta A_{st} - \Delta W.$$

Now, the change in income resulting from a change in A_{st} is given by (40); and the change in W corresponding to this change in income is:

$$\Delta W = \frac{dW}{dY_m} \,.\, \Delta Y_m,$$

so that (41) becomes:

$$\Delta B = \Delta A_{st} - \frac{dW}{dY_m} \,.\, \Delta Y_m$$

$$= \Delta A_{st} - \mu \,.\, \frac{dW}{dY_m} \,.\, A_{st}$$

(42) $$= \left(1 - \mu \,.\, \frac{dW}{dY_m}\right) .\, \Delta A_{st}.$$

Equation (42) *shows that the change in the budget deficit resulting from an increase in government expenditure on goods and services may be positive, zero or negative, depending on whether:*

(43) $$\mu \,.\, \frac{dW}{dY_m} \lesseqgtr 1$$

or:

(44) $$\frac{dW}{dY_m} \lesseqgtr \frac{1}{\mu}$$

Given the marginal propensity to consume, the multiplier μ depends solely on the net marginal rate of taxation, as can be seen from (39). *Hence the value of the net marginal rate of taxation determines the* *effect of a change in A_{st} on the budget deficit.* The reader might construct a numerical example to help clarify these relationships. It is also instructive to examine how a change in the structure of tax rates, i.e. a shift in the W-function, alters the expansionary effect of a given change in A_{st} and the budget.

6. Our basic equation (28):

$$Y_m = C_{pr}[Y_m - W(Y_m)] + I_{pr} + A_{st} \tag{45}$$

contained one degree of freedom. We asked how a change in A_{st} affects the level of income Y_m. Private net investment was assumed to be autonomously given, and the value of A_{st} could be chosen arbitrarily. *We shall now restrict the range of variation of A_{st} by the requirement that the budget must always be balanced,* i.e. that:

$$A_{st} = W. \tag{46}$$

We have added an equation to our system, so that *no degrees of freedom* remain. *The two equations* (45) *and* (46) *now determine the values of all the variables.*

The following *numerical example* may help to clarify this. Let:

$$W = \tfrac{1}{6}Y_m,$$
$$I_{pr} = 10,$$
$$C_{pr} = 10 + \tfrac{4}{5} . (Y_m - W).$$

Using (46), (45) now becomes:

$$Y_m = 10 + \tfrac{4}{5}(Y_m - \tfrac{1}{6}Y_m) + 10 + \tfrac{1}{6}Y_m. \tag{47}$$

Solving this linear equation for Y_m we obtain:

$$Y_m = 120$$

The corresponding values for A_{st} and W are:

$$A_{st} = W = 20$$

Now suppose that for some reason private net investment falls to $I_{pr} = 5$. The propensity to consume remaining unchanged, this leads to a contraction in income. Assuming that the budget must be balanced, the equilibrium level of income is now:

$$Y_m = 90.$$

If we drop the assumption of a balanced budget, and if government expenditure A_{st} is maintained at the level prior to the decline in private net investment ($A_{st} = 20$) the equilibrium level of income will be:

$$Y_m = 105$$

The contraction in income is smaller than when the budget is balanced.

The argument also applies when the decline in income is brought about by a fall in the propensity to consume.

The results derived from this numerical example possess general validity: a fall in private investment and (or) the private propensity to consume always leads to a stronger contraction in income if we require a balanced budget than it does if this requirement is not made, and a budget deficit is permitted to arise; conversely, an expansionary process leads to a larger rise in income when the budget is balanced than it does if a budget surplus is permitted to arise. A balanced budget reinforces expansionary or contractionary tendencies. The reason for this can easily be seen when one considers the problem in terms of process analysis. When private investment declines during any period the fall in national income during the same period is equal to the decline in investment. In the second period consumption declines as do net tax receipts and therefore government expenditure on goods and services falls, so that the decline in income is stronger than it would be if government expenditure on goods and services remained unchanged. In the third period there is a further decline in consumption, net tax receipts, and government expenditure on goods and services, and so on, until the new equilibrium is reached.

This theorem—that a balanced budget reinforces expansionary or contractionary tendencies—is of fundamental importance from the point of view of a fiscal policy which aims at the stabilization of income and employment. *It follows from the theorem that the aim of income stabilization is incompatible with the requirement that the budget be balanced in each period.* This point is expressed particularly clearly in the *Douglas-Report* mentioned above:

"We recommend that Federal fiscal policies be such as not only to avoid aggravating economic instability but also to make a positive and important contribution to stabilization, at the same time promoting equity and incentives in taxation and economy in expenditures. A policy based on the principle of an annually balanced budget regardless of fluctuations in the national income does not meet these tests, for if actually followed it would require drastic increases of tax rates or drastic reductions of Government expenditures during periods of deflation and unemployment, thereby aggravating the decline, and marked reductions of tax rates or increases of expenditures during periods of inflationary boom, thereby accentuating the inflation." (pp. 11–12).

From this the following conclusion follows:

"A policy that will contribute to stability must produce a surplus of revenues over expenditures in periods of high prosperity and comparatively full employment and a surplus of expenditures over revenues in periods of deflation and abnormally high unemployment." (p. 12.) This conclusion follows from our previous analysis and needs no further explanation. But it should be remembered that a change in the budget surplus can be brought about by a change in expenditures and (or) revenues, and that the extent of the contractionary or expansionary effect of any given change depends on the way it is brought about.

Of course, we must not expect of a fiscal policy aimed at stabilising economic activity at a high level more than it can achieve. Its effectiveness is limited, as the *Douglas Report* notes, due to the fact that "... economic forecasting is highly imperfect at present and tax and expenditure policies under present procedures are very inflexible." The *Report* therefore recommends an examination of the question of how fiscal policy can be rendered more flexible, and then observes: "... until this greater flexibility is actually achieved it will be well to recognise this limitation on the effectiveness of fiscal policy as a stabilization device, and not to discard or weaken monetary policy, which, despite its shortcomings, does have the great merit of flexibility." (p. 15.) It should be emphasized that the choice between monetary policy on the one hand, and fiscal policy on the other, is not mutually exclusive. This is clearly stated in the *Report*: "We recommend that an appropriate, flexible, and vigorous monetary policy, *employed in co-ordination with fiscal and other policies*, (our italics) should be one of the principal methods used to achieve the purposes of the Employment Act[(1)] ... For several reasons we reject the idea, held by a few economists and others, that for stabilization purposes little or no reliance should be placed on monetary policy and that we should rely exclusively on other measures, such as fiscal policies .... Monetary policy is strong precisely where fiscal policy is weakest; it is capable of being highly flexible. It can be altered with changes in economic conditions on a monthly, daily or even hourly basis." (pp. 17–18.) We have mentioned the limitations on fiscal policy which are due to imperfect economic forecasting and the resulting difficulties of discovering the appropriate time for, and extent of, fiscal measures. It should be emphasised that these limitations also apply to monetary policy.[(2)]

(1) The Employment Act of 1946 declares that the aim of American economic policy is the maintenance of a high level of employment, production and purchasing power. See: *The Employment Act: Past and Future*, Edt. Gerhard Colm, National Planning Association, Washington, D.C. 1956.

(2) See the essay by F. A. Lutz, "Arbeitslosigkeit und Kreditexpansion" in the collection of essays *Vollbeschäftigung, Inflation und Planwirtschaft*, p. 246, ff., mentioned above.

7. So far we have assumed private net investment to be autonomously given and constant. This assumption, too, needs to be revised. In the first place, besides autonomous investment, we can take account of induced private investment with the help of the acceleration principle. Furthermore, we can build into our model assumptions about the possible influence of government expenditure on goods and services and of taxation policy on the level of private investment. But these questions lie outside the scope of an introductory book; moreover, they are questions which have yet to be clarified by extensive research.

In this connection, however, we have to consider another factor which may influence private investment. A budget surplus during any period leads to a diminution in the quantity of money in the private sector during the same period. If the *budget surplus* leads to a contraction in income, there is a decline in the transactions demand for money; i.e. simultaneously with the decline in the quantity of money there is a shift to the left in the liquidity-preference curve. Depending on the extent to which the demand for money and the quantity of money decline, the rate of interest may rise, fall, or remain unchanged. If there is a fall in the rate of interest which stimulates private investment, the contractionary effect of the budget surplus may be neutralized. If a contractionary effect is to be achieved, the fall in the rate of interest must be prevented by appropriate open market operations by the central bank. If there is a rise in the rate of interest which reduces private net investment, this will strengthen the contractionary effect of the budget surplus.

Next let us consider the case of a budget deficit. Let the government finance additional expenditure on goods and services by borrowing on the open market. In this case the quantity of money remains unchanged.[1] The expansionary effect of the added expenditure will increase the transactions demand for money, and there may be a rise in the rate of interest. This may reduce private investment, so that the expansionary effect of the additional government expenditure may be neutralized. The expansionary effect of the added government expenditure will be fully realized only if private investment is completely interest-inelastic.

If the added government expenditure is financed by borrowing from the central bank, there is an increase in the quantity of money. Furthermore, the liquidity of the commercial banks increases. But there is also an increase in the transactions demand for money, because of the rise in effective demand; and the rate of interest may

[1] We assume once again that the government keeps an account only with the central bank.

fall, rise or remain unchanged. If there is a fall in the rate of interest which stimulates private investment, the expansionary effect may be strengthened.

The effects which operate through the rate of interest may also occur in the case of a balanced budget. Let the government finance additional expenditure on goods and services by additional taxation. We have seen that this may have an expansionary effect (*the Haavelmo theorem*). In this case the quantity of money remains unchanged; but because of the expansion in income there is an increase in the transactions demand for money, and hence the rate of interest may rise. If this reduces private investment, the expansionary effect of the balanced budget may be neutralized.

The way in which the budget affects the quantity of money and liquidity preference in the private sector is thus of considerable importance in determining the total effect of a given combination of government expenditure and revenue on national income.[1]

8. The importance of applying complementary monetary and fiscal policies should now be clear. For example, assume the government attempts to deal with a depression by public works financed by borrowing from the public. If this borrowing leads to a rise in the rate of interest which reduces private investment, the central bank must prevent this rise in the rate of interest by appropriate open market operations. Thus, if a government is to overcome a depression it must conduct monetary and fiscal policies in such a way that their effects are complementary, and not contradictory; and the same applies when the aim of policy is to slow down or stop an inflationary process. In the course of our analysis we have indicated the instruments of monetary and fiscal policy which are available for bringing about an expansion or contraction in income. How and when these instruments are to be used depends on the prevailing economic situation, and on the aims of economic policy. If the aim of economic policy is a high and stable level of employment, the instruments of monetary and fiscal policy must be used in conformity with that aim. As regards the budget this means that the effects of any proposed composition of expenditure and revenue must be assessed according to their consistency with overall economic policy.

(1) See: K. Philip, "Finanzpolitik und Zins", *Weltwirtschaftliches Archiv*, Vol. 62, 1949, p. 214 ff.

Section C

THE BALANCE OF PAYMENTS AND NATIONAL INCOME

We shall now apply to an open economy parts of the analysis developed in section A of this chapter. For the sake of simplicity we shall once more neglect the economic activity of the government; but after reading this section the reader should be able to build the results of section B into the analysis.

§1. The Determinants of National Income in an Open Economy

1. In section A, §§1 and 2 of this chapter it was shown that, with given propensities to consume and invest, we can find a certain equilibrium level of income which is characterized by the equality of *voluntary savings and voluntary investment*. In the simplest case, in which net investment is assumed to be autonomous and constant, this equilibrium level of income was given by the equation:

(1) $$C(Y) + I_0 = Y$$

or

(2) $$S(Y) = I_0,$$

2. We first have to show how this fundamental theorem is modified when we drop the assumption of a closed economy. It was shown in Volume 1[1] that, for any period, the *ex-post* national income of an open economy without government activity is:

(3) $$Y = C + I + (Ex - Im),$$

where Ex denotes exports, Im imports, and hence $Ex - Im$ the export or import surplus (i.e. the balance of payments surplus)[2]

We also know that consumption during any period depends mainly on the level of income (*the consumption function*), and also that intended investment by firms is a function of several variables (income, the rate of interest, profits) (*the investment function*). In the

[1] Vol. I, seventh edn., 1958, chapter IV.

[2] It should be remembered (see Vol. I seventh edn., pp. 71–72) that exports and imports contain not only visible but also invisible exports and imports, and also interest and dividends paid or received from abroad. In the following analysis, however, mainly visible and invisible exports and imports are relevant.

theory of income determination in an *open* economy we add a third important behaviour equation to the above two, namely the so called *import function.* This function describes the *dependence of the level of imports on the level of income:*

$$Im = Im(Y). \tag{4}$$

As a rule imports are a rising function of income; and the increase in imports associated with a unit rise in income is called the *marginal propensity to import.*[1] Mathematically, the marginal propensity to import q is the first derivative of the import function:

$$q = \frac{dIm}{dY}. \tag{5}$$

As a rule, the marginal propensity to import is not a constant function of income, but for the sake of simplicity we shall assume it to be constant. Countries which are heavily dependent on imports, such as Sweden, and Denmark, have a high marginal propensity to import, while the U.S.A. and the U.S.S.R. have a low marginal propensity to import.[2]

3. To begin with let us assume that the *levels of exports and net investment are autonomously given.* Given this assumption, it follows from the considerations outlined in section A that the income given by (3) will be an *equilibrium income* if, and only if, consumption and imports have the values corresponding to the consumption and import functions. Thus, the equilibrium income must satisfy the condition:

$$Y = C(Y) + I + Ex - Im(Y) \tag{6}$$

If investment and exports are autonomously given, this equation determines a unique equilibrium income. (6) is now the equilibrium condition which replaces condition (1) for the closed economy.

[1] Y, I, C, Ex and Im are measured in real terms or in terms of money at constant prices.

[2] The marginal propensity to import will differ for the individual sectors of the economy, and therefore the value given by (5) must be understood as an average of the marginal propensities to import of the various sectors.

It should be noticed that we cannot draw any conclusions about the size of the marginal propensity to import from the published estimates of the *average propensity to import* $\left(\frac{Im}{Y}\right)$ for various countries. The average propensity to import may be low (high) while the marginal propensity to import is high (low). According to Chang's estimates, for example, Australia had an average propensity to import of 15·5% and a marginal propensity to import of 35% during the inter-war period.

Condition (6) may be expressed in another way if we use the savings function instead of the consumption function. It then becomes:

(6a) $$S(Y) - I = Ex - Im(Y)$$

This condition states that *the equilibrium level of income is reached when the difference between voluntary savings (at that level of income) and voluntary net investment is equal to the export surplus (at that*

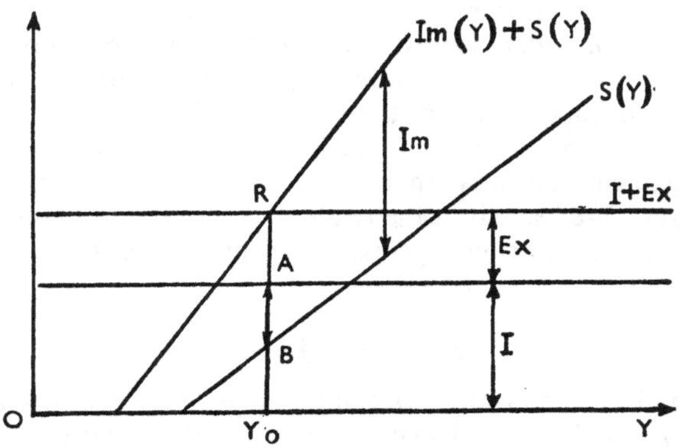

Fig. 58

level of income). In a closed economy the difference between voluntary savings and voluntary net investment must be zero. We must once again distinguish carefully between equation (6a) and the *ex-post* equation developed in volume I which is always valid.[1]

(6b) $$S = I + (Ex - Im)$$

In this equation S and I represent the *actual* savings and investment of any period; *hence they contain both the intended and the unintended components of S and I.* Equation (6a) however is an *equilibrium condition*, which is only satisfied at a particular level of income.

Condition (6a) can be presented in a simple diagram if we write it in the form:

(6c) $$S(Y) + Im(Y) = I + Ex$$

In Fig. 58 the line $I + Ex$ represents the sum of autonomous investment and exports. The line $Im(Y) + S(Y)$ represents the sum of the savings and import functions. The abscissa of the intersection point R of the two lines $I + Ex$ and $Im + S$ gives the equilibrium level of income Y_0. The distance AB is the difference between

[1] 7th edn., p. 73.

exports and imports (the balance of payments deficit) at the level of income Y_0.[1] It can easily be seen that any level of income other than Y_0 can not be an equilibrium level. At any level of income which is either smaller or larger than Y_0 the difference between voluntary savings and voluntary investment is not equal to the difference between exports and imports.

4. The equilibrium condition (6) may also be expressed in yet another way, with which we are familiar from section A: *at the equilibrium income total monetary demand must be equal to total monetary supply at ruling prices.* Monetary demand now consists of the sum: $C + I + Ex$, and monetary supply consists of home production and imports, i.e. of the sum $Y + Im$.

5. The preceding analysis can easily be extended to the case in which investment depends on national income and (or) on the rate of interest. We leave it to the reader to carry out the appropriate analysis, using the relationships explained in section A.

§2. The Export Multiplier

1. We shall now consider how national income is affected by a *change in exports.* This problem corresponds to the one we considered in section A, §3, when we analysed the effects of a change in the propensitites to consume and invest in a closed economy. *We assume that prices of goods, wage rates, rates of interest and exchange rates remain constant. This assumption will enable us to analyse the pure income effects, i.e. to neglect the simultaneously occurring price effects.*[2] The effect of price changes will be analysed below (§5).

Let us assume that, for some reason, exports fall during a boom. Production and employment in the export industries decline, as does the income earned in those industries. Given the propensity to consume, consumption falls, which in turn leads to further declines in production and employment in the consumption goods industries, and so on. The reduction in exports generates a cumulative downward process which gradually extends throughout the whole economy. Let us investigate this process in detail.

[1] Obviously, a balance of payments surplus or balanced trade are also possible.

[2] Each acquisition of a claim against foreign countries, arising from foreign trade, leads to the creation of money by the central bank. The assumption of constant rates of interest thus means that either the increase in the quantity of money resulting from an increase in exports does not affect the rate of interest, because liquidity preference is perfectly interest-elastic, or that the central bank carries out neutralizing open market operations.

2. We begin with *comparative static analysis*. Let the consumption function be:

$$C = a + b \,.\, Y,$$

and the import function:

$$Im = \alpha + q \,.\, Y.$$

The marginal propensity to consume is b, and the marginal propensity to import q. Equation (6) now becomes:

$$Y = a + b \,.\, Y + I + Ex - \alpha - q \,.\, Y.$$

Solving for Y we obtain the equilibrium income Y_0:

$$Y_0 = \frac{a - \alpha}{1 - b + q} + \frac{1}{1 - b + q} \,.\, (I + Ex). \tag{7}$$

Since $1 - b$ is the marginal propensity to save, s, we may also write (7) in the form:

$$Y_0 = \frac{a - \alpha}{s + q} + \frac{1}{s + q} \,.\, (I + Ex). \tag{7a}$$

It follows from (7a) that if exports change by dEx the equilibrium income changes by:

$$dY_0 = \frac{1}{s + q} \,.\, dEx. \tag{8}$$

The change in the equilibrium income is thus determined by the reciprocal of the sum of the marginal propensities to save and import. We therefore denote the ratio $\frac{1}{s + q}$ as the *export multiplier with respect to income*. On the usual assumptions $(s + q)$ is less than 1, and therefore this multiplier is larger than 1. The larger s, given the marginal propensity to import, or the larger q, given the marginal propensity to save, the smaller is the export multiplier, i.e. the smaller the contraction (expansion) in income resulting from a fall (rise) in exports.[1]

The export multiplier (8), which we have derived from linear consumption and import functions, is generally valid. By differentiating (6) with respect to Ex we have:

$$\frac{dY}{dEx} = \frac{dC}{dY} \cdot \frac{dY}{dEx} + 1 - \frac{dIm}{dY} \cdot \frac{dY}{dEx},$$

[1] On the assumption of constant prices, a *rise* in exports is possible only if there are unused resources. Therefore, in analysing *expansionary processes* we must assume that unused resources are available.

therefore:

(9) $$\frac{dY}{dEx} = \frac{1}{1 - \frac{dC}{dY} + \frac{dIm}{dY}}$$

or:

(9a) $$dY = \frac{1}{1 - \frac{dC}{dY} + \frac{dIm}{dY}} \, . \, dEx$$

where $\frac{dC}{dY}$ is the marginal propensity to consume b, and $\frac{dIm}{dY}$ is the marginal propensity to import q.

Since

$$1 - b = s,$$

we have

(10) $$dY = \frac{1}{s + q} \, . \, dEx.$$

(10) can be derived simply from the equilibrium condition:

(6a) $$S(Y) = I + (Ex - Im).$$

Net investment remaining constant, the change in S is:

(11) $$dS = dEx - dIm.$$

If the changes in S and Im are to be equilibrium changes they must satisfy the condition that

$$dS = s \, . \, dY$$

and

$$dIm = q \, . \, dY$$

so that, for equilibrium changes, (11) becomes:

$$s \, . \, dY = dEx - q \, . \, dY,$$

and therefore:

$$dY = \frac{1}{s + q} \, . \, dEx.$$

3. From Fig. 58 we can ascertain the new equilibrium income corresponding to a change in exports. All we need to do is to shift the $I + Ex$ line upwards or downwards and observe the resulting shifts in R. It can be seen that the change in income is smaller the steeper the $Im + S$ line, i.e. the larger the sum of the marginal propensities to save and import.

4. The next question relates to the comparative static effect of a change in exports on the *balance of payments surplus* (i.e. on the

difference between exports and imports). The balance of payments surplus, Z, is:

$$Z = Ex - Im \tag{12}$$

and the change in Z is:

$$dZ = dEx - dIm. \tag{13}$$

Now, the change in imports associated with a change in income is:

$$dIm = q \, . \, dY,$$

and for the change in the equilibrium income given by equation (10) it is:

$$dIm = \frac{q}{s + q} \, . \, dEx = \frac{1}{1 + \frac{s}{q}} \, . \, dEx. \tag{14}$$

(13) now becomes:

$$dZ = \frac{s}{s + q} \, . \, dEx = \frac{1}{1 + \frac{q}{s}} \, . \, dEx. \tag{15}$$

The ratio $\frac{q}{s+q}$ in (14) is called the *export multiplier with respect to imports*, and the ratio $\frac{s}{s+q}$ is the *export multiplier with respect to the balance of payments*. Both multipliers are always less than 1. The larger $\frac{q}{s}$, i.e. the larger q and the smaller s, the smaller (larger) is the export multiplier with respect to the balance of payments (with respect to imports).

Numerical example: If $s = 0{\cdot}1$ and $q = 0{\cdot}3$, the income-multiplier (10) is 2·5, the import-multiplier $\frac{3}{4}$, and the balance of payments multiplier $\frac{1}{4}$. Assuming constant marginal propensities to save and import, a rise (fall) in exports of £1 would raise (lower) real income by £2·5; imports would change by £$\frac{3}{4}$, and the balance of payments surplus by £$\frac{1}{4}$. But if $s = 0{\cdot}4$ and $q = 0{\cdot}2$, the income-multiplier would be smaller ($1\frac{2}{3}$), and the balance of payments surplus would change by £$\frac{2}{3}$.

5. We have yet to analyse the *path of movement from one equilibrium situation to the next*. This, however, can be done only in terms of *process analysis*. Let us begin with an example in which we merely indicate the *changes* in the relevant variables. We assume that exports contain no imports, which is equivalent to taking exports net of their import content. We assume further that consumption in period t depends on the income of the *preceding* period

$t - 1$. Similarly, a change in income in period t induces a change in imports only in the *following* period $t + 1$. Thus we have:

(16) $$dC = b \,.\, dY_{t-1}$$

and

(17) $$dIm_t = q \,.\, dY_{t-1}$$

Further, let:

$$s = 0.1; \qquad q = 0.3.$$

In the course of the successive periods the *changes* in the relevant variables will be as follows:

Period	dC	dS	dIm	dEx	$dEx - dIm$	dY
1	—	—	—	100	100	100
2	90	10	30	100	70	160
3	144	16	48	100	52	196
4	176·4	19·6	58·8	100	41·2	217·6
5	.	.	.	.	.	.
↓	.	.	.	.	.	.
∞	225	25	75	100	25	250

Out of the increase in income (100) in the first period 90 is spent on consumption in the second period, and 10 is saved. At the same time the increase in income in the first period leads to an increase in imports of 30 in the second period,[1] so that the balance of payments surplus changes by 70, and so on. The final result is that income increases by 250, consumption by 225, savings by 25, imports by 75 and the balance of payments surplus by 25. The sequence in the table shows clearly that the system remains in a state of expansion (or contraction, if $dEx = -100$) as long as the change in the balance of payments surplus is larger than the change in voluntary savings (both changes measured in relation to the original situation). An export surplus always has an expansionary effect on income, while an increase in voluntary savings has a contractionary effect. As long as the export surplus in any period is larger than voluntary savings, the expansionary effect of the export surplus is not fully compensated. In the course of time, however, the dampening effect of the rise in imports and savings becomes ever stronger. The increase in the export surplus (measured in relation to the original situation)

[1] Since we have assumed net investment to remain constant, the additional imports are used solely for consumption.

becomes smaller; the increase in savings (measured in relation to the original situation) becomes larger. *Thus, rising savings and imports ultimately bring to a halt the expansionary process resulting from the increase in exports, and establish a new equilibrium. The new equilibrium situation is reached when the expansionary (contractionary) effect of the change in the export surplus is precisely compensated by the contractionary (expansionary) effect of the change in savings.*

6. The analysis of this process can easily be generalized. Using (16) and (17) we obtain the income for any period t from (6):

$$Y_t = (b - q) \,.\, Y_{t-1} + I + Ex. \tag{18}$$

The change in income in period t resulting from a change in exports, investment remaining constant, is therefore:

$$dY_t = (b - q) \,.\, dY_{t-1} + dEx. \tag{19}$$

This so-called difference equation links the income of period t to the income of the preceding period $t - 1$, and thus enables us to find the changes in income in the successive periods:

1st period: $dY_1 = dEx$

2nd period: $dY_2 = (b - q) \,.\, dEx + dEx$

3rd period: $dY_3 = (b - q)^2 \,.\, dEx + (b - q) \,.\, dEx + dEx$

. . . .

nth period: $dY_n = (b - q)^{n-1} \,.\, dEx + \ldots + (b - q) \,.\, dEx + dEx$

$$= \frac{1 - (b - q)^n}{1 - b + q} \,.\, dEx$$

or, since $1 - b = s$

$$dY_n = \frac{1 - (b - q)^n}{s + q} \,.\, dEx. \tag{20}$$

The expression by which dEx is multiplied is the *multiplier for the nth period.*

Similarly, *the multiplier with respect to the balance of payments surplus for the nth period is:*

$$dZ_n = dEx - q \,.\, dY_{n-1} \tag{21}$$

$$= \frac{s + q \,.\, (b - q)^{n-1}}{s + q} \,.\, dEx.$$

Since the marginal propensity to consume is usually smaller than 1, and the marginal propensity to import always smaller than 1, the sequence of income changes and changes in the balance of payments surplus approaches the limit:

$$\lim_{n\to\infty} dY_n = \frac{1}{s+q} \, . \, dEx$$

and

$$\lim_{n\to\infty} dZ_n = \frac{s}{s+q} \, . \, dEx.$$

From (21) we can ascertain after how many periods the initial increase in the balance of payments surplus, brought about by the increase in exports, is reduced to a given level. This question is not without interest. Assume we start from a situation of under-employment and balance of payments equilibrium (i.e. the balance of payments surplus = zero). If an autonomous rise in exports now occurs, a surplus on the balance of payments results, which is automatically reduced in the way described above. Conversely, if a reduction in exports takes place in a situation of high employment and equilibrium on the balance of payments, the balance of payments deficit which results in the first period is automatically reduced in the course of time. *It is important to emphasize that the balance of payments surplus or deficit is not completely eliminated. The balance of payments does not return to what it was in the initial position; a surplus or deficit remains.*[1] Thus the effect on income of a change in exports does not restore the original equilibrium on the balance of payments. *This effect brings about only a partial correction of the balance of payments, which is given by (15) and depends on s and q.* How quickly the initial surplus or deficit is removed, i.e. after how many periods perhaps 50% or 70% of it disappears, can be ascertained from (21). For example, if 50% of the initial surplus is to be removed, the number of requisite periods n can be found from the equation:

$$\frac{s + q \, . \, (b - q)^{n-1}}{s+q} = \frac{1}{2},$$

by solving it for n. It can be seen that the speed of the automatic adjustment process depends on s and q.

7. The case of an autonomous change in imports, exports remaining constant, can be analysed similarly. For example, Fig. 58 shows that, *ceteris paribus*, a rise in the propensity to import leads to a fall

[1] Only in the special case $s = 0$ is there an automatic equalization of exports and imports at a new level.

in the equilibrium level of income. The path to the new equilibrium can again be analysed in terms of period analysis.

8. So far we have assumed net investment to be constant, in order to isolate the effects of a change in exports. Using the acceleration principle, we can easily take account of the investment induced by changes in income. Now, however, an increase in exports may lead *directly* to an increase in investment in the export industries. This gives rise to certain special characteristics of the "foreign trade accelerator", which we cannot discuss here.[1]

9. An *autonomous change in net investment, ceteris paribus*, has the same effects on national income as an autonomous change in exports. *But the effect on the balance of payments is different.* Consider an economy with under-employment and balanced trade. If there is a rise in domestic investment, income and employment increase; but a simultaneous increase in imports also occurs. Exports remaining constant, the domestic expansionary process leads to a deficit on the balance of payments which continues to grow until the expansionary process is ended. The reader might find it useful to analyse the process of adjustment and derive the multiplier with respect to the balance of payments.

§3. The Export Multiplier in the Case of a Two-Country Model

1. Each increase in the exports of a country A is identical with an increase in the imports of other countries B. An expansionary process takes place in country A, due to the increase in exports; simultaneously a contractionary process takes place in countries B, due to an increase in imports. The contraction in income in countries B in turn leads to a fall in imports and hence possibly to repercussions on country A. So far we have neglected such repercussions, which is permissible if (a) country A's share in world trade is so small that changes in its exports have no perceptible contractionary effects on the rest of the world, or (b) the countries affected by the contractionary process neutralize it by internal fiscal or monetary policy. In all other cases these repercussions cannot be neglected, and we have to analyse the effects of a country's changes in exports (or imports), taking account of such repercussions. For this purpose we shall consider only two countries, 1 and 2. Even this simplest case will indicate the complexity of the problem.

Let us consider two countries, 1 and 2, which have unused resources and whose balances of payments are in equilibrium. There

[1] See: H. Giersch, "The Acceleration Principle and the Propensity to Import", *International Economic Papers*, Vol. 4, 1954.

is an autonomous increase in exports in country 1, i.e. an autonomous rise (a rise which is not the result of a change in income) in imports in country 2. This results in the following chain of effects:

Country 1	Country 2
autonomous rise in exports	autonomous rise in imports
↓	↓
rise in income	fall in income
↓	↓
induced increase in imports	induced decrease in imports
↙	↘
reduction in income	rise in income
↓	↓
induced decrease in imports	induced increase in imports
↙	↘

and so on

We now have to analyse this process in detail. Instead of starting from a situation of under-employment and balance of payments equilibrium, we can of course start from a situation of high employment with balance of payments equilibrium, and ask how an autonomous decline in the imports of country 1 affects the system as a whole. In both cases we once again assume constant prices (including rates of exchange) in order to be able to analyse the pure income effects of autonomous changes in exports. We begin by *stating the equilibrium conditions for incomes in both countries.*

2. For the sake of simplicity, let us again regard net investment in both countries as autonomously given. The equilibrium conditions for the incomes of the two countries then are:

$$(22) \qquad Y_1 = C_1(Y_1) + I_1 + Ex_1(Y_2) - Im_1(Y_1)$$
$$Y_2 = C_2(Y_2) + I_2 + Ex_2(Y_1) - Im_2(Y_2).$$

Since the imports of one country are identically equal to the exports of the other country, we have:

$$Ex_1(Y_2) \equiv Im_2(Y_2)$$

and

$$Ex_2(Y_1) \equiv Im_1(Y_1).$$

Hence the system (22) can also be written as:

$$(22a) \qquad \begin{aligned} Y_1 &= C_1(Y_1) + I_1 + Ex_1(Y_2) - Im_1(Y_1) \\ Y_2 &= C_2(Y_2) + I_2 + Im_1(Y_1) - Ex_1(Y_2). \end{aligned}$$

It should be noted that the balance of payments surplus now depends on the incomes of *both* countries.

Given net investment and the propensities to consume and import of both countries, these two equations determine the equilibrium levels of income in both countries. The equilibrium incomes can be ascertained geometrically in the following way. The first equation in (22a) gives the income of the first country as a function of the income of the second country:

$$(23) \qquad Y_1 = \varphi_1(Y_2).$$

Any given income Y_2 is associated with a certain income in country 1. It is clear that the income in country 1 is higher the higher the income in country 2.

If we differentiate the first equation in (22a) with respect to Y_2, we obtain:

$$(24) \qquad \frac{dY_1}{dY_2} = \frac{q_2}{s_1 + q_1},$$

in which q_1, q_2 denote the marginal propensities to import of the two countries respectively, and s_1 denotes the marginal propensity to save of country 1. Since all the constants are positive $\frac{dY_1}{dY_2}$ is always positive, i.e. Y_1 rises with rising Y_2.

Similarly, the second equation in (22a) gives the income of the second country as a function of the income of the first country:

$$(25) \qquad Y_2 = \varphi_2(Y_1).$$

Here also the income Y_2 rises with increasing Y_1.

Differentiating the second equation in (22a) with respect to Y_1 we obtain:

$$(26) \qquad \frac{dY_2}{dY_1} = \frac{q_1}{s_2 + q_2}.$$

If we assume that the marginal propensities to save and import are constant, (23) and (25) will be linear functions, whose position is that given in Fig. 59. The slope of (23) with respect to the Y_2-axis is always smaller than the slope of (25) with respect to the Y_2 axis.[1] Hence, an intersection point R of the two lines always exists. The co-ordinates of R give the equilibrium incomes in both countries, assuming that, at ruling prices, both incomes do not exceed the productive capacity of the respective economies.[2]

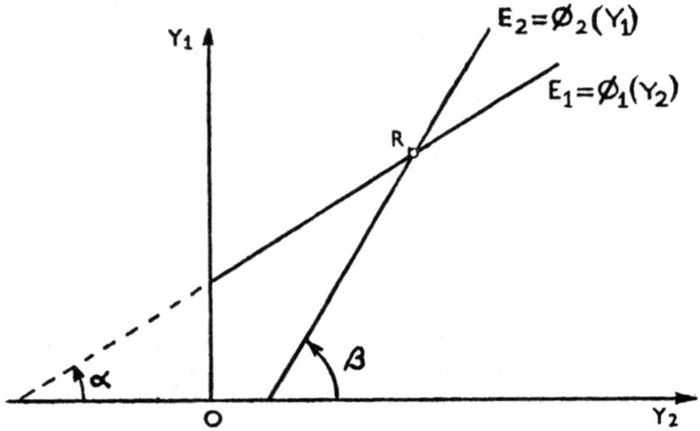

Fig. 59

Numerical example: Let:

$$C_1(Y_1) + I_1 = a_1 + \tfrac{1}{2} \cdot Y_1$$

$$C_2(Y_2) + I_2 = a_2 + \tfrac{3}{4} \cdot Y_2$$

$$Ex_1(Y_2) = \alpha_2 + \tfrac{1}{4} Y_2$$

$$Im_1(Y_1) = \qquad \tfrac{1}{8} \cdot Y_1.$$

(1) The slope of (23) with respect to the Y_2-Axis is given by (24):

$$\tan \alpha = \frac{q_2}{s_1 + q_1}.$$

The slope of (25) with respect to the Y_2-axis is equal to the reciprocal of (26):

$$\tan \beta = \frac{s_2 + q_2}{q_1}$$

It is clear that $\tan \alpha < \tan \beta$ because

$$\frac{q_2}{s_1 + q_1} < \frac{s_2 + q_2}{q_1}$$

(2) The reader might consider the case in which the maximum potential real income in each country is smaller than the income corresponding to point R.

The first equation in (22a) now becomes:

$$Y_1 = a_1 + \tfrac{1}{2}Y_1 + \alpha_2 + \tfrac{1}{4}Y_2 - \tfrac{1}{8} \,.\, Y_1,$$

from which (23) becomes:

$$Y_1 = \tfrac{1}{5} \,.\, (8a_1 + 8\alpha_2 + 2\,Y_2). \tag{27}$$

The second equation in (22a) becomes:

$$Y_2 = a_2 + \tfrac{3}{4} \,.\, Y_2 + \tfrac{1}{8} \,.\, Y_1 - \alpha_2 - \tfrac{1}{4} \,.\, Y_2,$$

from which (25) becomes:

$$Y_2 = \tfrac{1}{4} \,.\, (Y_1 - 8\alpha_2 + 8a_2). \tag{28}$$

Thus:

$$\tan \alpha = \tfrac{2}{5}$$

and

$$\tan \beta = 4.$$

For $a_1 = 10$, $a_2 = 12$ and $\alpha_2 = 5$, we have:

$$Y_1 = 24 + \tfrac{2}{5} \,.\, Y_2$$

$$Y_2 = 14 + \tfrac{1}{4} \,.\, Y_1.$$

The equilibrium incomes are:

$$Y_1 = \tfrac{296}{9}; \qquad Y_2 = \tfrac{200}{9}.$$

In equilibrium the balance of payments surplus is:

$$Z = 6\tfrac{4}{9}.$$

Thus the equilibrium income is not associated with balanced trade.

Generally, for the equilibrium values of the two incomes we have:

$$Y_1 = \tfrac{1}{9} \,.\, (16a_1 + 8a_2 + 8\alpha_2)$$

$$Y_2 = \tfrac{1}{9} \,.\, (20a_2 + 4a_1 - 16\alpha_2)$$

and for the balance of payments surplus:

$$Z = \tfrac{1}{9}(4a_2 - a_1 + 4\alpha_2).$$

3. Now let us consider the changes in the equilibrium values of income and of the balances of payments when the exports of country 1 to country 2 increase, i.e. when *the export function $Ex_1(Y_2)$ shifts*. Consider our numerical example. An autonomous increase in the exports of country 1 means an increase in α_2. This increase in α_2 shifts the function (27) *as well as* function (28); the function (27)

shifts parallel upwards (from I to I' in Fig. 60) and the function (28) parallel to the left (from II to II' in Fig. 60). The new equilibrium incomes are given by point R′. The equilibrium level of income of country 1 rises and that of country 2 declines. The balance of payments of country 1 improves.[1]

We may consider these relationships more generally. For this purpose we write the export function of country 1 (= the import function of country 2) as: $Ex_1(Y_2) + \alpha$ in which α gives the position

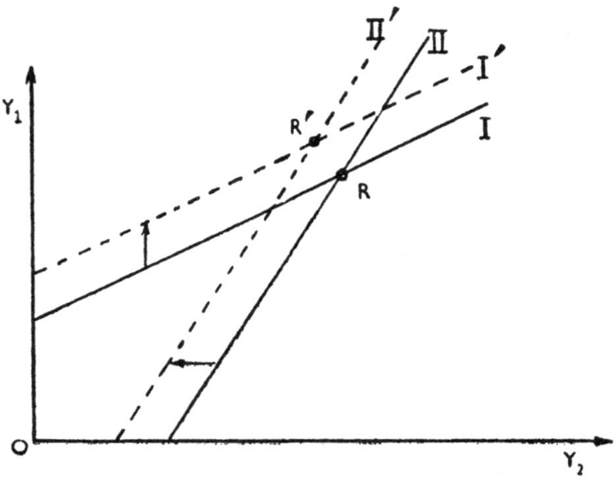

Fig. 60

of the function in the Ex_1, Y_2 system of co-ordinates. A shift in the export function is expressed as a change in α. Equations (22a) now become:

$$(29) \qquad \begin{aligned} Y_1 &= C_1(Y_1) + I_1 + Ex_1(Y_2) + \alpha - Im_1(Y_1) \\ Y_2 &= C_2(Y_2) + I_2 + Im_1(Y_1) - Ex_1(Y_2) - \alpha. \end{aligned}$$

Given net investment in both countries, these two equations determine *both* equilibrium incomes as functions of α. If α changes by $d\alpha$, i.e. if the export function of country 1 shifts by $d\alpha$, the equilibrium incomes change by dY_1 and dY_2 respectively. We now have to show what determines these changes. It follows from (29) that:

$$(30) \qquad \begin{aligned} dY_1 &= dC_1 + dEx_1 + d\alpha - dIm_1 \\ dY_2 &= dC_2 - dEx_1 - d\alpha + dIm_1. \end{aligned}$$

[1] See R. Robinson, "A Graphical Analysis of the Foreign Trade Multiplier", *Economic Journal*, Vol. 62, 1952.

Now, the change in consumption is equal to the change in income multiplied by the marginal propensity to consume; and similarly, the change in the imports of a country is equal to the change in that country's income multiplied by the marginal propensity to import. Hence:

(31)
$$dC_1 = b_1 \,.\, dY_1; \qquad dEx_1 = q_2 \,.\, dY_2$$
$$dC_2 = b_2 \,.\, dY_2; \qquad dEx_2 = q_1 \,.\, dY_1.$$

Using (31), (30) becomes:

(32)
$$dY_1 = b_1 \,.\, dY_1 + q_2 \,.\, dY_2 + d\alpha - q_1 \,.\, dY_1$$
$$dY_2 = b_2 \,.\, dY_2 - q_2 \,.\, dY_2 - d\alpha + q_1 \,.\, dY_1$$

or:

(32a)
$$s_1 \,.\, dY_1 = \quad q_2 \,.\, dY_2 + d\alpha - q_1 \,.\, dY_1$$
$$s_2 \,.\, dY_2 = -\, q_2 \,.\, dY_2 - d\alpha + q_1 \,.\, dY_1,$$

where s_1 and s_2 denote the marginal propensities to save. (32) and (32a) are systems of two linear equations for dY_1 and dY_2, the solution of which yields:

(33) (a)
$$dY_1 = \frac{1}{s_1 + q_1 + \frac{s_1}{s_2} \cdot q_2} \,.\, d\alpha$$

(b)
$$dY_2 = \frac{1}{s_2 + q_2 + \frac{s_2}{s_1} \cdot q_1} \,.\, (-d\alpha).$$

The expressions by which $d\alpha$ is multiplied are the *export multipliers in the two-country case*. They indicate by how much the equilibrium incomes of both countries change as a result of a shift in the import function of one country. Income rises in the country whose exports increase, and falls in the country in which the propensity to import rises, *assuming, of course, that net investment and the propensity to consume remain unchanged*. The importance of the export multipliers is that they indicate the factors which *determine the extent of the change in income in both countries. As can be seen, the determining factors are the marginal propensities to save and import in both countries. The rise in income in country 1, resulting from an increase in exports, is larger, the smaller the marginal propensity to save in country 1, the smaller the marginal propensities to import in both countries and the larger the marginal propensity to save in country 2, where imports have risen.*

4. If we insert the values of dY_2 and dY_1 from (33) into the expression:

$$dZ = q_2 \, . \, dY_2 + d\alpha - q_1 \, . \, dY_1$$

we obtain the change in the balance of payments surplus dZ:

$$dZ = \frac{1}{1 + \frac{q_1}{s_1} + \frac{q_2}{s_2}} \, . \, d\alpha. \tag{34}$$

The change in the balance of payments thus depends on the ratio of the marginal propensity to import to the marginal propensity to save in both countries. The smaller the ratio the larger is dZ. It can be seen from (34) that the *balance of payments multiplier is always smaller than 1.* Thus, if an initial situation of balanced payments is disturbed by an autonomous rise in exports, this disturbance will *not* be *completely* removed by the income changes resulting in both countries.

5. Equations (33) have some interesting implications. First, it follows from them that:

$$dY_1 : dY_2 = s_2 : s_1. \tag{35}$$

The ratio of the income changes in the two countries is equal to the inverse ratio of their respective marginal propensities to save. The value of the marginal propensities to import only affects the size of the income changes in both countries, but not their ratio.

It also follows that the change in income in one country depends only on the *ratio* of the marginal propensity to import to the marginal propensity to save *in the foreign country.* If the propensities in the foreign country vary in such a way that their ratio remains unchanged, *ceteris paribus*, there will be no change in the multiplier.

Finally, it can be seen that the income multipliers may be smaller than, equal to or larger than 1.

6. In conclusion, let us consider the process of income changes in the two-country case in terms of sequence analysis. We shall illustrate this process with a numerical example. As in § 2, we assume that consumption in any one period depends on the income of the *preceding* period, and that a change in income in any one period induces a change in imports only in the *following* period. Let:

$$s_1 = 0{\cdot}2; \qquad q_1 = 0{\cdot}4$$
$$s_2 = 0{\cdot}1; \qquad q_2 = 0{\cdot}2.$$

In the first period there is an autonomous increase of 100 in the exports of country 1, so that the income of country 1 (2) rises (falls)

Period	Country 1 $s_1 = 0{\cdot}2$; $q_1 = 0{\cdot}4$							Country 2 $s_2 = 0{\cdot}1$; $q_2 = 0{\cdot}2$						
	dC	*dS*	*dIm* in-duced	*dEx* auto-nomous	*dEx* in-duced	*dZ*	*dY*	*dC*	*dS*	*dIm* auto-nomous	*dIm* in-duced	*dEx* in-duced	*dZ*	*dY*
1	—	—	—	+100	—	+100	+100	—	—	+100	—	—	−100	−100
2	+80	+20	+40	+100	−20	+ 40	+120	− 90	−10	+100	−20	+40	− 40	−130
3	+96	+24	+48	+100	−26	+ 26	+122	−117	−13	+100	−26	+48	− 26	−143
4	+97·6	+24·4	+48·8	+100	−28·6	+ 22·6	+120·2	−128·7	−14.3	+100	−28·6	+48·8	− 22.6	−151·3
⋮	⋮	⋮	⋮	⋮	⋮	⋮	⋮	⋮	⋮	⋮	⋮	⋮	⋮	⋮
↓	↓	↓	↓	↓	↓	↓	↓	↓	↓	↓	↓	↓	↓	↓
∞	+80	+20	+40	+100	−40	+ 20	+100	−180	−20	+100	−40	+40	− 20	−200

The changes in any period are changes from the initial situation.

by 100. In the second period the increase in income leads to a rise in consumption of 80, a rise in savings of 20 and an induced increase in imports of 40 in country 1. The fall in income in country 2 leads, in the second period, to a reduction in consumption of 90, a reduction in savings of 10 and an induced reduction in imports of 20. In the second period income in country 1 is 120 higher, and in country 2 130 lower than in the initial situation. Country 1's balance of payments surplus of 100 in period 1 is reduced to 40 in period 2. The same process is repeated in subsequent periods. The increase in income in country 1 finally reaches the equilibrium value of +100, and that in country 2 the equilibrium value −200. If payments were balanced in the initial situation, there will now be a permanent deficit of 20 on the balance of payments of country 2. The initial deficit of −100 is only partially removed. The sequence of the relevant variables will vary with the numerical values of the marginal propensities to save and import.[1]

§4. The Investment Multiplier in the Case of a Two-Country Model

1. We now assume that there is an *autonomous* change in net investment in country 2. What is the resulting effect on the income and the balance of payments of *both* countries? Clearly, there is a rise in income in country 2, which in turn induces increased imports from country 1, i.e. induces an increase in exports in country 1. In practice it is not easy to distinguish between induced and autonomous increases in exports (i.e. between increases in exports which are, and those which are not, brought about by changes in income). This distinction is nevertheless of the greatest importance in theoretical analysis. The direct effect of an autonomous increase in exports (brought about, for example, by the removal of a tariff on a desired article) is different from that of a change in exports induced by a rise in income in the foreign country. If, at the *existing* level of income, country 2 purchases more exports from country 1 (because of a reduction in tariffs) there is a reduction in internal demand and hence in the income of country 2. But if country 2 increases its imports from country 1 because of a rise in income resulting from an increase in investment, there is no initial fall in internal demand in country 2. This difference has an important effect on the final outcome. We therefore have to examine the effects of a change in net investment in one country on the incomes of both countries.

(1) See: F. Machlup, *International Trade and the National Income Multiplier*, 1943, pp. 64 ff. Appendix A of this book contains the formula for the level of income in both countries after *n* periods.

2. Let us assume that net investment in country 2 changes by $d\alpha$. It follows from (22a) that:

$$(36) \qquad \begin{aligned} dY_1 &= dC_1 + dEx_1 - dIm_1 \\ dY_2 &= dC_2 + d\alpha + dIm_1 - dEx_1. \end{aligned}$$

Substituting from (31) we have:

$$(37) \qquad \begin{aligned} dY_1 &= b_1 \,.\, dY_1 \qquad + q_2 \,.\, dY_2 - q_1 \,.\, dY_1 \\ dY_2 &= b_2 \,.\, dY_2 + d\alpha - q_2 \,.\, dY_2 + q_1 \,.\, dY_1 \end{aligned}$$

or:

$$(38) \qquad \begin{aligned} (s_1 + q_1) \,.\, dY_1 - q_2 \,.\, dY_2 &= 0 \\ -q_1 \,.\, dY_1 + (s_2 + q_2) \,.\, dY_2 &= d\alpha. \end{aligned}$$

Solving both equations for dY_1 and dY_2 we obtain:

$$(39a) \qquad dY_1 = \frac{q_2}{(s_1 + q_1)(s_2 + q_2) - q_1 q_2} \,.\, d\alpha = \frac{\frac{q_2}{s_1}}{s_2 + q_2 + \frac{s_2}{s_1} \cdot q_1} \,.\, d\alpha$$

$$(39b) \qquad dY_2 = \frac{s_1 + q_1}{(s_1 + q_1)(s_2 + q_2) - q_1 q_2} \,.\, d\alpha = \frac{1 + \frac{q_1}{s_1}}{s_2 + q_2 + \frac{s_2}{s_1} \cdot q_1} \,.\, d\alpha.$$

A comparison of (39b) with (33b) shows that *the multiplier effect of an autonomous increase in investment is larger than the multiplier effect of anautonomous rise in exports, because in the former case repercussions through the foreign country reinforce the expansionary effect of the increase in domestic investment, while in the latter case these repercussions work against it.* In this case, as before, income grows in both countries until the export surplus is equal to the additional voluntary saving.

The final change in the balance of payments of country 1 is:

$$(40) \qquad dZ = q_2 \,.\, dY_2 - q_1 \,.\, dY_1 = \frac{q_2}{s_2 + q_2 + \frac{s_2}{s_1} \cdot q_1} \,.\, d\alpha.$$

Since the "balance of payments multiplier" is always positive, the balance of payments of country 1 improves with an increase in net investment in country 2. The balance of payments of country 2, where the increase in net investment takes place, deteriorates. *If country 2 has an initial balance of payments deficit, this deficit may be reduced or removed by an appropriate reduction in domestic effective demand.* If prices remain constant, balanced payments are then achieved through a fall in income and employment. The amount by which domestic investment has to be reduced (assuming the propensity to consume remains unchanged) in order to achieve balanced payments depends on the size of the marginal propensities to save and import in *both* countries.

(40) also shows that the balance of payments multiplier is always smaller than 1. It thus remains true in this case that, if payments are initially balanced, a disturbance resulting from a change in investment in one of the countries is not removed by the resulting changes in income. *The income effects resulting from a disturbance do not by themselves restore balanced payments.*

§5. The Balance of Payments and the Rate of Exchange[1]

So far we have assumed constant prices and rates of exchange. This assumption was necessary in order to isolate the relationship between income and the balance of payments. We now have to consider how the results so far established are modified when we combine these income-effects with the effects resulting from the relationships between the balance of payments, prices and rates of exchange. In this context it is again useful to analyse the *pure price effects*; only afterwards will we present an analysis of the combined income and price-effects. In the following, we restrict ourselves to a consideration of the main aspects of the problem; a complete analysis, so far as it is possible at the present stage of knowledge, lies outside the scope of this book.

1. Let us assume that the rate of exchange has been fixed politically

[1] See espec.: H. v. Stackelberg, "The Theory of Foreign Exchanges under Perfect Competition", *International Economic Papers*, Vol. 1, 1951.
P. T. Ellsworth, "Exchange Rates and Exchange Stability", *Review of Economics and Statistics*, Vol. 32, 1950.
G. Haberler, "The Market for Foreign Exchange and the Stability of the Balance of Payments", *Kyklos*, Vol. 3, 1949.
F. Machlup, "The Theory of Foreign Exchanges", *Economica* 1939.
J. Robinson, "The Foreign Exchanges" in *Essays on the Theory of Employment*, Oxford, 1947.
J. Meade, *The Balance of Payments*, London, 1951.

at a certain level and that it is now changed,[1] domestic and foreign prices remaining constant. How will this affect the balance of payments surplus?

The effect of a change in the rate of exchange on the balance of payments clearly depends on how the *value* of exports and imports is affected by this change; i.e. on whether the rate of change in the value of exports (with respect to the rate of exchange) is larger, smaller or equal to the rate of change in the value of imports. That is, the effect depends on whether:

$$\frac{dEx}{dw} \gtreqless \frac{dIm}{dw}, \tag{41}$$

Using elasticities instead of rates of change, (41) becomes:

$$\eta Ex, w \gtreqless u \,.\, \eta_{Im,w}. \tag{42}$$

A devaluation, i.e. an increase in w[2] *improves (worsens) the balance of payments (measured in terms of domestic currency) if the ratio of the elasticity of the value of exports to the elasticity of the value of imports (both with respect to the rate of exchange) is larger (smaller) that the ratio of the value of imports to the value of exports.*

When a devaluation improves the balance of payments we say the balance of payments reacts normally to the devaluation; when it worsens the balance of payments, we say the reaction of the balance of payments is perverse.

2. We must now examine in greater detail what determines the elasticities of the value of exports and imports.

Consider a certain commodity which is supplied and demanded both in the home and in the foreign country. Fig. 61 indicates the market situation for the commodity in both countries *at a given rate of exchange*. The right-hand side of the diagram gives the demand and supply in the home country (say Germany) as functions of price in DM (German marks). The left-hand side of the diagram shows the demand and supply situation for the same good in the foreign country (say England) as functions of the price of the good in marks, on the assumption that transport costs between the home and foreign country are zero.[3] Demand and supply in England, of course,

[1] The fixing of the rate of exchange at a particular level implies the willingness of the central bank to buy or sell foreign currency at the fixed rate in whatever amounts may be necessary (to do this sufficient reserves of foreign currency must be available).

[2] More domestic currency is now paid per unit of foreign currency.

[3] The following analysis can easily be extended to the case when transport costs are not zero.

depend on the £-price of the good. But at a given rate of exchange each price expressed in £s corresponds to a given price expressed in marks; hence, *when the rate of exchange is given*, we can express supply and demand in *both* countries as functions of price expressed in terms of the currency of *one* of the countries. If we are interested in the value of exports and imports in terms of the foreign currency, we must express supply and demand in both countries as functions of the £-price (the price in terms of the foreign currency). If we are interested in the value of exports and imports in terms of the domestic currency, we must express supply and demand in both countries as

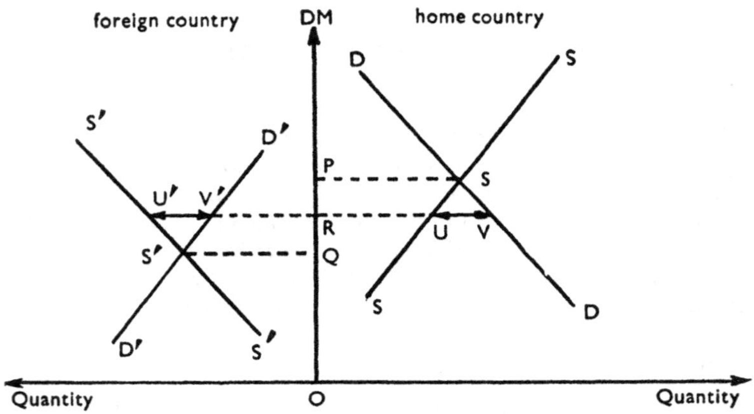

Fig. 61

functions of the mark-price (the price in terms of the domestic currency). Let us first consider the *balance of payments surplus in terms of the domestic currency.*

The market situation in both countries shown in Fig. 61 is such that at all prices between *OQ* and *OP* (i.e. at all prices lying between the equilibrium prices in both countries) Germany has excess demand and England excess supply. The excess demand in Germany can thus be met by imports from England. There is a certain price between *OQ* and *OP* (in Fig. 61 the price *OR*) at which the excess demand *UV* in the home country and the excess supply *U'V'* in the foreign country are just equal.(1) This price can be found easily by plotting the curves

(1) The reader might consider how Fig. 61 would have to be modified if transport costs between the home and foreign country are not zero (see: E. Barone, *Grundzüge der theoretischen Nationalökonomie*, Bonn, 1927, p. 102 ff).
H. Cunynghame (*A Geometrical Political Economy*, Oxford, 1904) appears to have been the first to develop the graphical method used in Fig. 61.

of excess demand in the home country and of excess supply in the foreign country in the same diagram (Fig. 62). These curves are derived from the supply and demand curves of each country respectively. The excess demand curve *PP'* represents the import demand of the home country as a function of price in terms of the home currency (DM). The curve *QQ'* shows the supply of foreign exporters as a function of price in DM. *OR* is the price in terms of home currency at which the home demand for imports is equal to the foreign supply of exports.

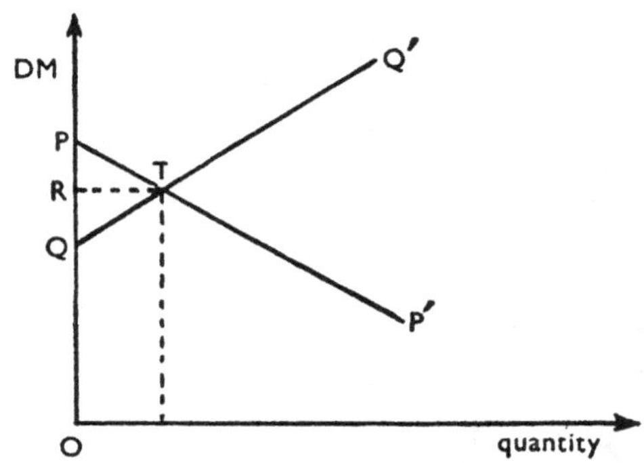

Fig. 62

It should be noted that the German demand for imports is derived from the *total* home demand and the *total* home supply; and similarly, the supply of English exporters is derived from the *total* English home demand and *total* English supply. The elasticity of the German demand for imports with respect to price in DM thus depends on the elasticity of total home demand and on the elasticity of home supply; and the elasticity of supply of English exports with respect to price in DM depends on the elasticity of English home demand and on the elasticity of English supply. It should be clear that the elasticity of German import demand is greater than the elasticity of total home demand, because, with a fall in the home price, home demand increases and home supply decreases. Similarly, the elasticity of supply of English exports is greater than the elasticity of total English supply.

So far we have assumed a given rate of exchange. When there is a change in the rate of exchange, the system of curves of the home country (the right-hand side in Fig. 61) obviously remains unchanged, and hence the import demand of the home country, as a function of price in the home currency, also remains unchanged. The curves of the foreign country, however, shift, because the same price in DM is now associated with a different price in £s. Fig. 63 shows the shifts in the English curves when there is a depreciation of the mark: demand increases and supply decreases. Hence the supply curve of English exports (as a function of price in DM) also shifts. The supply of English exporters, as a function of price in £s, is obviously unaffected by the alteration in the rate of exchange.

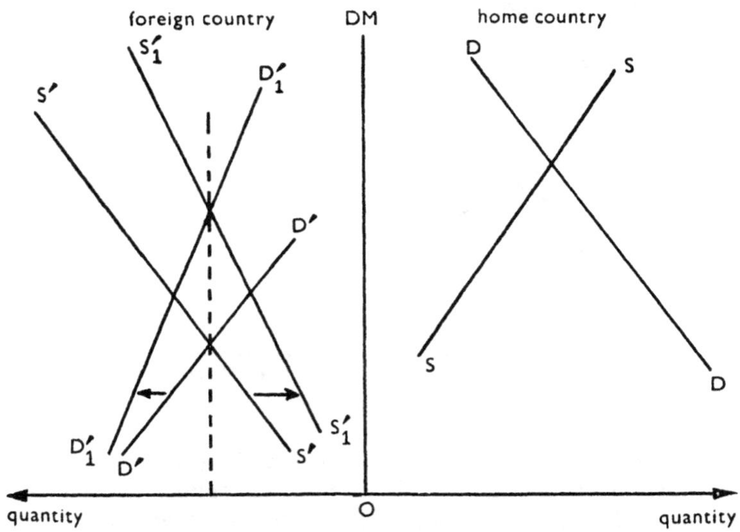

Fig. 63

Since the curves in the foreign country (Fig. 61) shift vertically upwards or downwards with alterations in the rate of exchange, it follows that the rate of exchange determines whether a good, which is demanded and supplied in both the home and the foreign country, is imported or exported by the home country (or, in the limiting case, is neither exported not imported).[1]

[1] When transport costs are above zero, export goods and import goods "are separated by a band of neutral goods (i.e. potential export and import goods, [E.S.]) which is smaller, the smaller the domestic and foreign costs of transport plus tariffs". (H. v. Stackelberg, "The Theory of Foreign Exchanges under Perfect Competition"
The existence of neutral goods, i.e. of goods which do not enter international trade, thus depends on the existence of transport costs (including tariffs). Which particular goods fall into the category of neutral goods at any time

What we have said so far refers to *one particular* good. For each good exported or imported we can construct a diagram like Figs. 61 and 62. In order to be able to speak of *the* demand for imports and *the* supply of imports of a country, we shall regard the quantity of imports and exports of all goods as being expressed by a quantity index. The demand and supply of imports as well as the demand and supply of exports then refers to the total quantity of imports and exports.

We are now in a position to state the effect of a devaluation, or, more generally, of a change in the rate of exchange, on the *balance of payments in terms of the home currency.* We use the following notation:

Prices in home currency (DM)	Prices in foreign currency (£)
Imports $p_{im}^{\,i}$ $(= p_{im}^{\,a} \,.\, w)$	$p_{im}^{\,a}$
Exports $p_{ex}^{\,i}$ $(= p_{ex}^{\,a} \,.\, w)$	$p_{ex}^{\,a}$

As we have seen, a devaluation of the domestic currency leaves the import demand curve *PP′* (Fig. 62) unchanged, while the import supply curve *QQ′* shifts. The way this curve shifts can be seen if we remember that a devaluation reduces any given mark-price in terms of pounds. For example, if the DM is devalued by 50% (i.e. if the pound appreciates by 100%) any given quantity of English exports will now be supplied only at double the previous mark-price. Thus, a devaluation of the domestic currency shifts the supply curve (as a function of the DM-price) of English exports in such a way that, in the case of a devaluation of 50% (20%), the ordinates of any given quantities (along the abscissa) double (increase by ¼) (Fig. 64). Fig. 64 shows that, as a rule, a devaluation leads to a reduction in the quantity of imports and to a rise in their price in terms of the domestic currency.[1]

The same considerations apply when we consider a country's exports. Fig. 65 shows the German supply of exports as a function of price in DM and the demand for German goods abroad also as a function of price in DM.[2] A devaluation of the domestic currency

depends to a large extent on the rate of exchange. "The list of actual import and export commodities cannot be treated as given once and for all" (G. Haberler, "The Market for Foreign Exchange", *Kyklos*, Vol. 3, 1949, p. 209).

(1) If the import-elasticity of demand is zero, price rises and the quantity remains unchanged; if import-demand is completely elastic, the quantity of imports falls while their price remains unchanged.

(2) As an exercise the reader might derive both curves from a system corresponding to that in Fig. 61.

clearly leaves the export supply curve unchanged. But the demand curve for exports shifts, because foreign buyers of German goods are

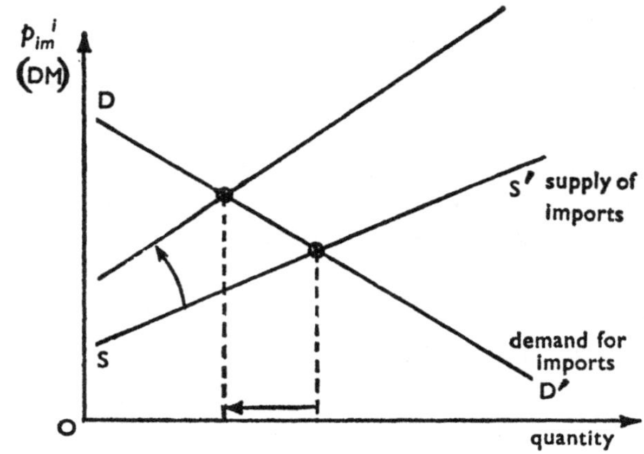

Fig. 64

concerned with the price in terms of foreign currency, and this price is reduced by a devaluation. At any given mark-price a larger

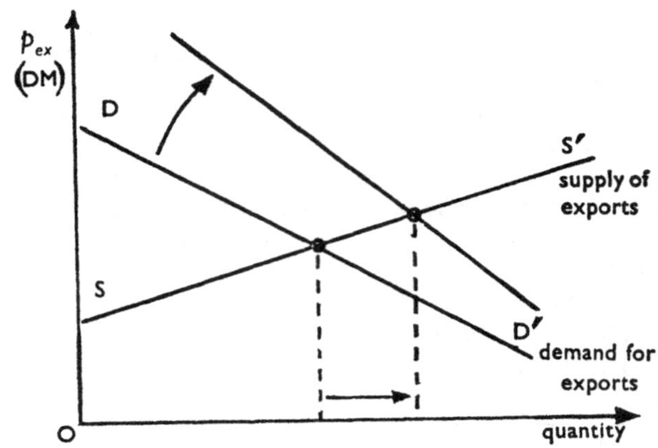

Fig. 65

quantity is now demanded; in other words, the same quantity as before is now demanded at a higher domestic price. For example, if the mark is devalued by 20%, the new export demand curve is obtained by raising all ordinates by 25% (Fig. 65). Fig. 65 shows that as a rule the quantity of exports and their price in terms of domestic currency increase as a result of a devaluation.[1]

The reaction of the balance of payments to a devaluation, however, depends, not on the change in the *quantity* of exports and imports, but on the change in the value of exports and imports. From the results we have reached so far we can see how the value of exports and imports, in terms of domestic currency, is affected by a devaluation.

Since a devaluation leads to an increase in the quantity and the price (in terms of domestic currency) of exports, the value of exports in terms of domestic currency usually increases. The value of exports also increases in the two limiting cases of perfectly elastic or perfectly inelastic supply of exports.

Since a devaluation normally leads to a fall in the quantity of imports, but to a rise in prices in terms of domestic currency, the value of imports in terms of domestic currency may fall, rise or remain unchanged. When the demand for imports is completely inelastic (elastic) the value of imports rises (falls). *Which case occurs depends on the elasticity of supply of imports with respect to the foreign price and on the elasticity of demand for imports with respect to the domestic price.*

If we denote

η_m as the elasticity of demand for imports with respect to their price in terms of domestic currency,

ε_m as the elasticity of supply of imports with respect to their price in terms of foreign currency[2] then

the elasticity of the value of imports in terms of domestic currency with respect to the rate of exchange is given by:

(43) $$\eta_{Im,\,w} = \frac{\varepsilon_m \cdot (\eta_m + 1)}{\varepsilon_m - \eta_m}.$$

This relation plays an important part in the modern theory of exchange-rates. Its derivation is as follows:

If we denote the domestic demand for imports by m, the supply of imports by a_m, then m is a function of $p_{im}{}^a \cdot w$:

(44a) $$m = m(p_{im}{}^a \cdot w) = m(p_{im}{}^i)$$

and a_m is a function of $p_{im}{}^a$:

(44b) $$a_m = a_m(p_{im}{}^a)$$

[1] When the supply of exports is completely inelastic (elastic) only price (quantity) rises.

[2] It should be noted that each of these two elasticities in turn depends on two elasticities, namely on the elasticities of the curves in the two systems of Fig. 61.

We then have:

(45) $$\eta_m = \frac{dm}{m} \div \frac{dp_{im}{}^i}{p_{im}{}^i} = \frac{p_{im}{}^i}{m} \cdot \frac{dm}{dp_{im}{}^i}$$

$$\varepsilon_m = \frac{da_m}{a_m} \div \frac{dp_{im}{}^a}{p_{im}{}^a} = \frac{p_{im}{}^a}{a_m} \cdot \frac{da_m}{dp_{im}{}^a}.$$

Since, in equilibrium

(46) $$m = a_m$$

it follows from (45) that:

(47) $$\frac{\eta_m}{\varepsilon_m} = w \cdot \left(\frac{dm}{dp_{im}{}^i} \div \frac{da_m}{dp_{im}{}^a}\right)$$

Using (44a), (46) becomes:

$$m(p_{im}{}^a \cdot w) = a_m(p_{im}{}^a)$$

or:

$$m(p_{im}{}^i) = a_m\left(\frac{p_{im}{}^i}{w}\right).$$

This equation determines $p_{im}{}^i$ as a function of w. Differentiating for w we obtain:

$$\frac{dp_{im}{}^i}{dw} = \frac{p_{im}{}^i}{w} \cdot \frac{1}{1 - w \cdot \left(\frac{dm}{dp_{im}{}^i} \div \frac{da_m}{dp_{im}{}^a}\right)}$$

or, because of (47),

(48) $$\frac{dp_{im}{}^i}{dw} = \frac{p_{im}{}^i}{w} \cdot \frac{1}{1 - \frac{\eta_m}{\varepsilon_m}}.$$

But

(49) $$Im = m \cdot p_{im}{}^a \cdot w = p_{im}{}^i \cdot m(p_{im}{}^i)$$

and therefore:

$$\frac{w}{Im} \cdot \frac{d\,Im}{dw} = \frac{w}{m \cdot p_{im}{}^i} \cdot \frac{d\,(m \cdot p_{im}{}^i)}{dp_{im}{}^i} \cdot \frac{dp_{im}{}^i}{dw}$$

$$= \frac{w}{m \cdot p_{im}{}^i} \cdot \left(m + p_{im}{}^i \cdot \frac{dm}{dp_{im}{}^i}\right) \cdot \frac{dp_{im}{}^i}{dw}$$

$$= \frac{w}{p_{im}{}^i} \cdot (1 + \eta_m) \cdot \frac{dp_{im}{}^i}{dw}.$$

Substituting (48) we obtain:

$$\text{(43)} \qquad \eta_{Im,\,w} = \frac{w}{p_{im}{}^{i}} \cdot \frac{p_{im}{}^{i}}{w} \cdot \frac{1}{1 - \dfrac{\eta_m}{\varepsilon_m}} \cdot (1 + \eta_m)$$

$$= \varepsilon_m \cdot \frac{1 + \eta_m}{\varepsilon_m - \eta_m}.$$

(43) shows the following: since ε_m is not negative and usually positive, and η_m not positive and usually negative, the reaction of the value of imports, in terms of domestic currency, to a devaluation depends on whether $|\eta_m| \gtreqless 1$.

For $|\eta_m| < 1$ $\eta_{Im,\,w} > 0$. The value of imports in terms of domestic currency rises.

For $|\eta_m| > 1$ $\eta_{Im,\,w} < 0$. The value of imports in terms of domestic currency falls.

For $|\eta_m| = 1$ $\eta_{Im,\,w} = 0$. The value of imports in terms of domestic currency remains constant.

Thus, the reaction of the value of imports in terms of domestic currency depends solely on the elasticity of the demand for imports.

In the special case $\varepsilon_m = \infty$ (43) becomes:

$$\eta_{Im,\,w} = 1 + \eta_m.$$

When the supply of imports is perfectly elastic, the elasticity of the value of imports (in terms of domestic currency) with respect to the rate of exchange is greater by 1 than the elasticity of the quantity of imports with respect to price in terms of domestic currency.[1]

We can similarly derive *the elasticity of the value of exports in terms of domestic currency with respect to the rate of exchange.* Let us denote

- η_x as the elasticity of demand for export goods with respect to the price in the importing country,
- ε_x as the elasticity of supply of export goods with respect to the price in the exporting country.

We then have:

$$\text{(50)} \qquad \eta_{Ex,w} = \frac{-\eta_x \cdot (1 + \varepsilon_x)}{\varepsilon_x - \eta_x}.$$

Since ε_x is not negative and as a rule positive and η_x not positive and as a rule negative, $\eta_{Ex,w}$ is not negative. Thus, the value of

[1] It is easily seen that the elasticity of the quantity of imports with respect to price in terms of domestic currency is equal to the elasticity of the quantity of imports with respect to the rate of exchange.

exports in terms of domestic currency usually increases. In the most unfavourable case it remains constant ($\eta_x = 0$).

In the special case of $\varepsilon_x = \infty$ (50) becomes:

$$\eta_{Ex,w} = -\eta_x.$$

When the supply of exports is completely elastic, the elasticity of the value of exports (in terms of domestic currency) with respect to the rate of exchange is equal but of opposite sign to the elasticity of supply of exports with respect to price in the exporting country.[1]

The following table summarises the results we have established.

Domestic Currency

	(A) Price	(B) Quantity	(C) Value	(D) Balance of payments surplus
I Exports	increase	increase or no change	increase	
II Imports	increase	decrease or no change	1. increase 2. decrease 3. no change	1. improvement, deterioration or no change 2. improvement 3. improvement

We are now in a position to state how a devaluation affects the balance of payments surplus in terms of domestic currency. The answer emerges from column C and is indicated in column D of the table. It can be seen that *as a rule the balance of payments improves as a result of a devaluation. It can deteriorate only if* $|\eta_m| < 1$ *i.e. only if the demand for import goods is inelastic.*

We have seen that the balance of payments improves, remains constant or deteriorates depending on whether:

(41) $$\frac{dEx}{dw} \gtreqless \frac{dIm}{dw}$$

or:

(42) $$\eta_{Ex,w} \gtreqless u \cdot \eta_{Im,w}$$

Using (50) and (43), (42) becomes:

(51) $$\frac{-\eta_x \cdot (1 + \varepsilon_x)}{\varepsilon_x - \eta_x} \gtreqless u \cdot \frac{\varepsilon_m \cdot (1 + \eta_m)}{\varepsilon_m - \eta_m}.$$

(1) We leave it to the reader to prove that:

$$\eta_{x, P_{ex}{}^i} = \eta_{x,w}$$

A devaluation thus increases the balance of payments surplus if:

$$\text{(51a)} \qquad \frac{-\eta_x \cdot (1 + \varepsilon_x)}{\varepsilon_x - \eta_x} > u \cdot \frac{\varepsilon_m \cdot (1 + \eta_m)}{\varepsilon_m - \eta_m}$$

After some manipulation this condition can be written in the form:

$$\text{(51b)} \quad u \cdot \varepsilon_x \cdot \varepsilon_m \cdot \left(\frac{1}{u} \cdot \eta_x + \eta_m + 1\right) < \eta_m \cdot \eta_x \cdot (u \cdot \varepsilon_m + \varepsilon_x + 1) + \varepsilon_m \cdot \eta_x \cdot (u - 1).$$

For $\varepsilon_x = \varepsilon_m = \infty$ (51b) becomes:

$$\frac{1}{u} \cdot \eta_x + \eta_m + 1 < 0.$$

Condition (51b) is always satisfied when $u < 1$, i.e. in the case of an export surplus, if

$$\text{(52a)} \qquad \frac{1}{u} \cdot \eta_x + \eta_m + 1 < 0$$

Thus an import elasticity in each country of greater than 1 (in absolute terms) is a sufficient condition for the balance of payments to react normally to a devaluation. But condition (52a) *may* also be fulfilled if $|\eta_m| > 1$ and $|\eta_x| < 1$, or $|\eta_m| < 1$ and $|\eta_x| < 1$.

A *necessary* condition for a perverse reaction of the balance of payments to a devaluation, is:

$$\text{(52b)} \qquad \frac{1}{u} \cdot \eta_x + \eta_m + 1 > 0$$

For this condition to be fulfilled when $u < 1$ it is necessary, *but not sufficient*, that both import elasticities, in absolute terms, be less than 1.

Thus, a devaluation may result in a deterioration of the balance of payments. This may happen if the quantity of imports is highly inelastic with respect to price expressed in terms of the currency of the importing country and, especially if, in addition, $u < 1$, i.e. if there is an initial export surplus. Whether or not such an "elasticity pessimism" (Machlup) is justified has recently been the subject of extensive discussion,(1) but we cannot discuss this issue here. It must be pointed out, however, that, in this context, it is important to

(1) See: F. Machlup, "Elasticity Pessimism in International Trade", *Economia Internazionale*, 1950; and G. Orcutt, "Measurement of Price Elasticities in International Trade", *Review of Economics and Statistics*, 1950. An exhaustive bibliography will be found in G. Haberler, *A Survey of International Trade Theory*, Princeton University Press, 1955.

distinguish between the short-run and the long-run effects of a change in the rate of exchange. In both cases the order of magnitude of the elasticities is decisive; and hence the great importance of measuring import elasticities.[1]

In the special case in which payments are balanced before the devaluation, i.e. $u = 1$, condition (51b) for the normal reaction of the balance of payments becomes:

$$(53) \qquad \varepsilon_x \cdot \varepsilon_m \cdot (\eta_m + \eta_x + 1) < \eta_m \cdot \eta_x \cdot (\varepsilon_m + \varepsilon_x + 1).$$

This condition is always fulfilled if:

$$(54) \qquad \eta_m + \eta_x + 1 < 0$$

i.e. if the sum of the import elasticities of both countries is smaller than −1. If both import elasticities regardless of sign are greater than 1, (54) is certainly fulfilled, and the balance of payments reacts normally to a devaluation when $u = 1$.

A perverse reaction of the balance of payments occurs if:

$$(55) \qquad \eta_m + \eta_x + 1 > 0,$$

i.e. if the sum of the two import elasticities is greater than −1.

If

$$(56) \qquad \eta_m + \eta_x + 1 = 0,$$

the balance of payments is unaffected by a devaluation.

The conditions (54)–(56) are called the *Marshall-Lerner conditions.* It should be noted that they are valid only for $u = 1$. For $u \neq 1$ they are replaced by the conditions (52).

3. What we have said so far applies to the balance of payments in terms of the domestic currency. We obtain *entirely different results when we express the value of imports and exports in terms of the foreign currency.* In Fig. 66 the curve DD' represents domestic demand for foreign goods as a function of price in terms of the foreign currency, the rate of exchange being given. The curve SS' shows the supply of foreign exports as a function of price in the foreign currency. A devaluation of the domestic currency leaves the supply curve unchanged; but the demand curve swivels anti-clockwise about point D′. This is so because any given £-price is now associated with a higher price in DM, so that any given quantity is now demanded in Germany at a correspondingly lower price expressed in £s. For example, if the mark is devalued by 50 %, i.e. the pound appreciated by 100 %, the new import-demand curve is obtained by halving

[1] See: J. Tinbergen, *Econometrics*, London, 1951, p. 177.

all the ordinates of the old demand curve. A glance at Fig. 66 shows that as a rule the quantity of imports and their price, expressed in the foreign currency, declines.[1]

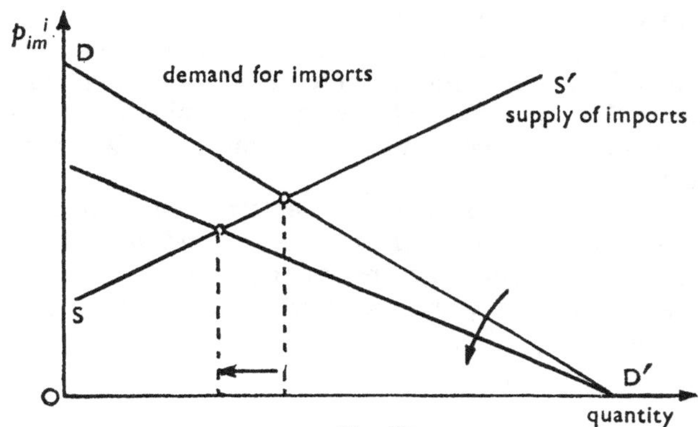

Fig. 66

Fig. 67 shows the demand for export-goods in the foreign country as a function of price in the foreign currency (curve DD')

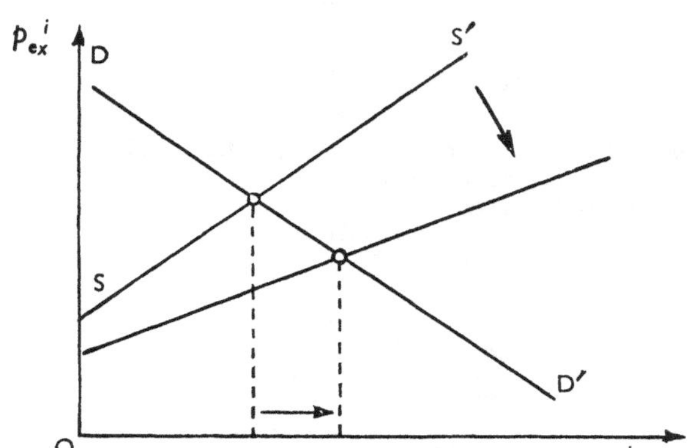

Fig. 67

and the supply of export-goods in the exporting country also as a function of price in terms of the foreign currency (curve SS'). A devaluation of the domestic currency leaves the demand curve

[1] When supply is perfectly elastic, only prices in terms of foreign currency fall. When supply is perfectly inastic only the quantities fall.

unchanged; but the supply curve shifts downwards. For example, when there is a devaluation of 50% all the ordinates of the previous supply curve are halved. Fig. 67 shows that as a rule a devaluation leads to an increase in the quantity of exports but to a fall in their price in terms of foreign currency.(1)

It follows, therefore, that a devaluation of the domestic currency always lowers the value of imports in terms of the foreign currency (let us denote this value by *Im'*) and that the value of exports in terms of the foreign currency (which we denote by *Ex'*) may fall, rise or remain constant.

The elasticities of imports and exports in terms of foreign currency with respect to the rate of exchange ($\eta_{Im',w}$ and $\eta_{Ex',w}$) can be derived immediately from the corresponding elasticities of imports and exports in terms of domestic currency ($\eta_{Im,w}$ and $\eta_{Ex,w}$) if we remember that

$$\eta_{Ex',w} = \eta_{Ex,w} - 1$$

and

$$(57)^{(2)} \qquad \eta_{Im',w} = \eta_{Im,w} - 1$$

Using (43) and (50) we have:

$$(58) \qquad \eta_{Im',w} = \frac{\eta_m \cdot (\varepsilon_m + 1)}{\varepsilon_m - \eta_m}$$

$$(59) \qquad \eta_{Ex',w} = \frac{-\varepsilon_x \cdot (\eta_x + 1)}{\varepsilon_x - \eta_x}\,.$$

(1) When demand is completely inelastic only price falls, and when demand is completely elastic only quantity rises.

(2) The proof is simple: We have:

$$Ex' = \frac{Ex}{w}\,.$$

Thus:

$$\frac{dEx'}{dw} = \frac{w \cdot \dfrac{dEx}{dw} - Ex}{w^2}$$

$$= \frac{1}{w} \cdot \frac{dEx}{dw} - \frac{Ex}{w^2}$$

$$= \frac{Ex}{w^2}\left(\frac{w}{Ex} \cdot \frac{dEx}{dw} - 1\right)$$

$$= \frac{Ex'}{w} \cdot (\eta_{Ex,w} - 1)$$

or:

$$\frac{w}{Ex'} \cdot \frac{dEx'}{dw} = \eta_{Ex',w} = \eta_{Ex,w} - 1$$

Since as a rule $\varepsilon_m > 0$ and $\eta_m < 0$, it follows from (58) that $\eta_{Im',w} < 0$, *that is, a devaluation lowers the value of imports in terms of the foreign currency* (as we already know).

Since as a rule $\varepsilon_x > 0$ and $\eta_x < 0$, $\eta_{Ex',w} \lesseqgtr 0$ depending on whether $|\eta_x| \lesseqgtr 1$. *Thus, whether the value of exports in terms of foreign currency rises, remains constant or falls depends solely on the elasticity of demand for exports with respect to price in the foreign currency.*

4. The following table summarises the results we have reached so far regarding the effects of a devaluation of the domestic currency.[1]

	Imports			Exports		
	Price	Quantity	Value	Price	Quantity	Value
Domestic Currency	rises	falls	rises falls no change	rises	rises	rises
Foreign Currency	falls	falls	falls	falls	rises	rises falls no change

It is important for the reader to understand these relationships. The analysis of these questions requires the most precise formulation, since the reactions of price, quantities and values are completely different, depending on whether the price and values of imports and exports are expressed in terms of the domestic or in terms of the foreign currency.

5. If we compare the reaction to a devaluation of the balance of payments in terms of the domestic currency with the reaction in terms of foreign currency, we see that there are *important differences* between them. A devaluation of the domestic currency improves or worsens the balance of payments in terms of the foreign currency depending on whether:

(60)
$$\frac{dEx'}{dw} \gtrless \frac{dIm'}{dw}$$

or, in terms of elasticities,

(61)
$$\eta_{Ex',w} \gtrless u \cdot \eta_{Im',w}$$

where

$$u = \frac{Im}{Ex} = \frac{Im'}{Ex'}$$

Substituting (57), (61) becomes:

(62)
$$\eta_{Ex,w} - 1 \gtrless u \cdot (\eta_{Im,w} - 1).$$

[1] The table gives only the normal cases.

A comparison of (62) with condition (42) for the balance of payments in terms of the domestic currency shows *that the conditions for an increase (decrease) in the balance of payments surplus in terms of the foreign currency are different from those for an increase (decrease) in the balance of payments surplus in terms of the domestic currency.*

Let us pursue this a little further.[1] We turn first to the case in which *the balance of payments in terms of the domestic currency reacts normally to a devaluation.* This means that the balance of

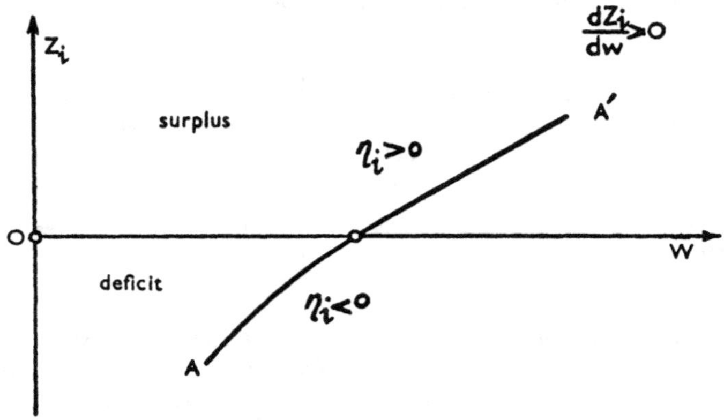

Fig. 68

payments surplus, Z_i, increases as a result of the devaluation, (a deficit decreases) (curve AA' in Fig. 68). From curve AA' we can easily derive the curve for the balance of payments in terms of the foreign currency. Since:

$$Z_a = \frac{Z_i}{w} = \frac{BC}{OB} = \tan \alpha^{(2)}$$

(Fig. 69) we only need observe how the angle changes with a devaluation (an increase in w). It can be seen that as w rises, Z_a increases at first, reaches a maximum at $w = OT$, and subsequently declines. It follows that for $0 < w \leq OT$ a devaluation improves the balance

[1] See: E. Schneider, "De l'influence de variations du taux de change sur la balance des paiements", *Bulletin d'information et de Documentation de la Banque Nationale de Belgique*, 32nd year, Vol. II, No. 6, Dec. 1957.

[2] Translator's note: Z_i = balance of payments surplus in terms of the domestic currency;
Z_a = balance of payments surplus in terms of the foreign currency.

of payments both in terms of the domestic and in terms of the foreign currency. For $w > OT$, however, a devaluation (appreciation) leads to an improvement (deterioration) of the balance of payments in terms of the domestic currency and to a deterioration (improvement) of the balance of payments in terms of the foreign currency.

This can be easily stated by using the elasticity of the balance of payments, Z_i, with respect to the rate of exchange. We have:

$$\eta_{Z_i,w} = \frac{dZ_i}{dw} \cdot \frac{w}{Z_i} = \frac{dZ_i}{dw} : \frac{Z_i}{w}.$$

Now $\frac{dZ_i}{dw}$ is the slope of curve AA' and $\frac{Z_i}{w}$ the slope of the radius

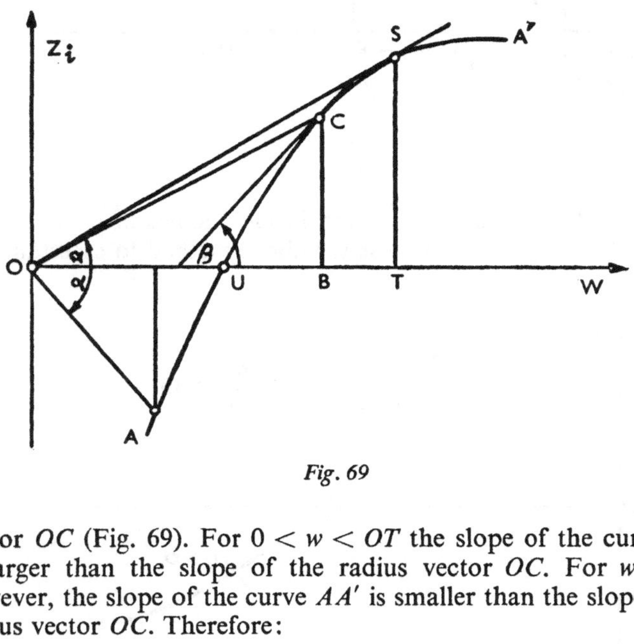

Fig. 69

vector OC (Fig. 69). For $0 < w < OT$ the slope of the curve AA' is larger than the slope of the radius vector OC. For $w > OT$, however, the slope of the curve AA' is smaller than the slope of the radius vector OC. Therefore:

For	$w > OT$	$0 < \eta_{Z_i,w} < 1$
and for	$OU < w < OT$	$\eta_{Z_i,w} > 1.$

The balances of payments Z_i and Z_a thus move in opposite directions when the elasticity of the balance of payments in terms of the domestic currency is positive and smaller than 1.

We ma / now consider the case in which the balance of payments in terms of the domestic currency reacts perversely, i.e. when a

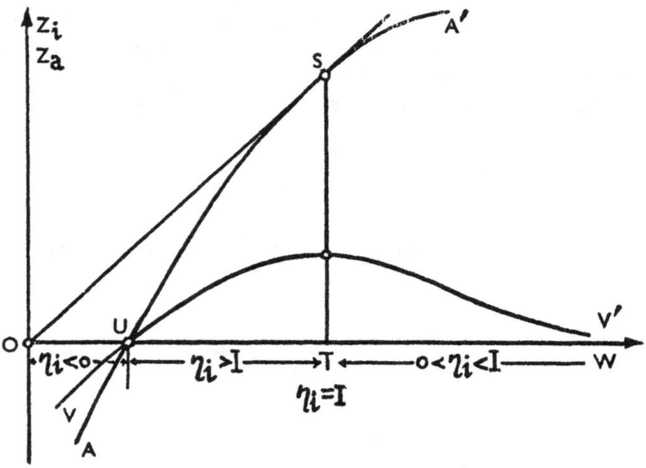

Fig. 70

devaluation leads to a deterioration in the balance of payments Z_i (curve AA' in Fig. 71). If we use the above method to ascertain the

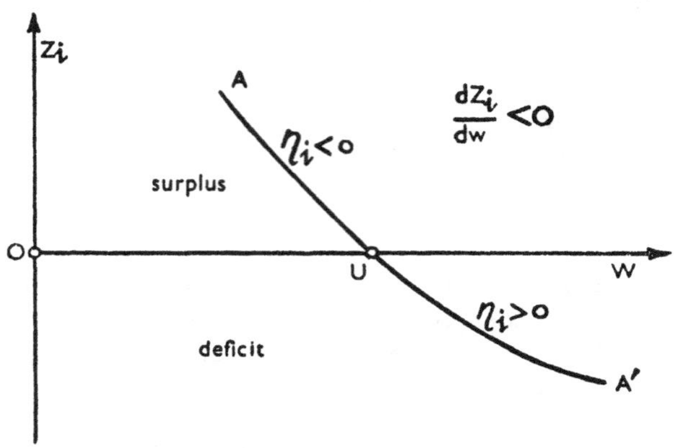

Fig. 71

reaction to a devaluation of the balance of payments in terms of the foreign currency we find (Fig. 72) that in the range $0 < w < OT$, Z_a reacts in the same way as Z_i, i.e. both the balance of payments surplus in terms of the domestic currency and the balance of payments surplus in terms of the foreign currency diminish as a result of a devaluation. For $w > OT$, however, the two balances of payments react in opposite directions, i.e. a devaluation increases a deficit in terms of the domestic currency but reduces a deficit in terms of the foreign currency. Thus, for $w > OT$ the balance of payments in terms of the domestic currency reacts perversely, while the balance of payments in terms of the foreign currency reacts normally.

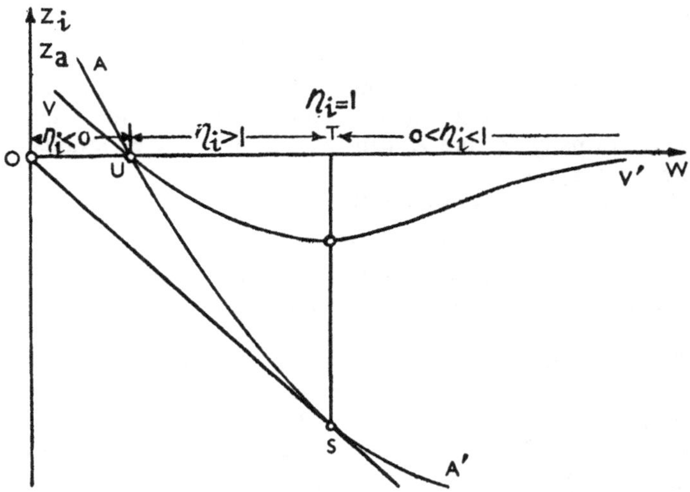

Fig. 72

In the range $w > OT$, i.e. for $0 < \eta_{Z_i,w} < 1$, and given Z_i reacts normally, a devaluation has an expansionary effect on national income but worsens the foreign exchange position of a country. For $w > OT$, i.e. for $0 < \eta_{Z_i,w} < 1$, and given that the balance of payments reacts perversely, a devaluation has a contractionary effect on national income but improves the country's foreign exchange position.

We have shown above (p. 258) that the balance of payments in terms of the domestic currency reacts normally to a devaluation if:

(63) $$\eta_{Ex,w} > u \cdot \eta_{Im,w}$$

where

(63a) $$u = \frac{Im}{Ex}$$

Now:

(64)[1]
$$\eta_{Z_i,w} = \frac{1}{1-u} \cdot \eta_{Ex,w} - \frac{u}{1-u} \cdot \eta_{Im,w}$$

or:

(64)
$$\eta_{Z_i,w} = \frac{1}{1-u} \cdot (\eta_{Ex,w} - u \,.\, \eta_{Im,w}).$$

If the two balances of payments Z_i and Z_a are to react in opposite directions when Z_i reacts normally, then, as we have shown, the condition $0 < \eta_{Zi,w} < 1$, must be fulfilled, i.e.

(65)
$$0 < \eta_{Ex,w} - u \,.\, \eta_{Im,w} < 1 - u$$

This inequality can be fulfilled only if $0 < u < 1$, i.e. only if there is an export surplus, which confirms our previous result that, when Z_i reacts normally, Z_i and Z_a can react in opposite directions only if there is a surplus.

If Z_i reacts perversely to a devaluation, the condition:

(66)
$$\eta_{Ex,w} < u \,.\, \eta_{Im,w}$$

must be fulfilled. It follows from (64) that, given Z_i reacts perversely, Z_i and Z_a can react in opposite directions only if there is a balance of payments deficit.

6. The way in which the balance of payments reacts to a devaluation of the domestic currency can be shown geometrically, and given a slightly different interpretation. To do so, let us assume that each value of exports is associated with an equal supply of foreign exchange (= the demand for marks) and that each value of imports is associated with an equal demand for foreign exchange (= the supply of marks); and that the rate of exchange is determined freely on the foreign exchange market.

[1] The proof is as follows: We have:

$$Z_i = Ex - Im$$

and therefore:

$$\frac{dZ_i}{dw} = \frac{dEx}{dw} - \frac{dIm}{dw}$$

or:

$$\frac{w}{Z_i} \cdot \frac{dZ_i}{dw} = \frac{Ex}{Z_i} \cdot \frac{w}{Ex} \cdot \frac{dEx}{dw} - \frac{Im}{Z_i} \cdot \frac{w}{Im} \cdot \frac{dIm}{dw}$$

or:

$$\eta_{Z_i,w} = \frac{Ex}{Z_i} \cdot \eta_{Ex,w} - \frac{Im}{Z_i} \cdot \eta_{Im,w}$$

Substituting (63a) the last equation becomes:

$$\eta_{Z_i,w} = \frac{1}{1-u} \cdot \eta_{Ex,w} - \frac{u}{1-u} \cdot \eta_{Im,w}$$

Fig. 73 shows the value of exports and imports in terms of the foreign currency as a function of the rate of exchange, for the case when the value of exports rises with an increase in the rate of exchange, i.e. when the balance of payments reacts normally, (a devaluation reduces an import surplus and increases an exports surplus). There is an import surplus when $w < w_0$, and an export surplus when $w > w_0$. Let the rate of exchange w_0 be the equilibrium rate of exchange, i.e. the rate of exchange at which the balance of

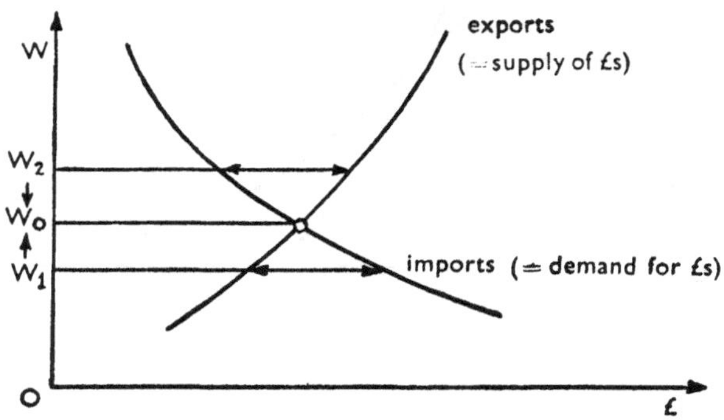

Fig. 73

payments surplus is zero, (i.e. no international gifts or voluntary long-term capital movements take place). Thus, there will be an import surplus when the pound is under-valued, and an export surplus when the pound is overvalued.(1) On our assumptions, when there is an import surplus more £s are demanded than supplied. On a free foreign exchange market, this leads to a rise in the pound-rate, so that the demand for pounds decreases and the supply of pounds increases. Thus the rate of exchange automatically moves in the direction of the equilibrium rate. Again, if there is an initial export surplus the pound-rate falls, so that the rate of exchange moves in the direction of an equilibrium rate. Thus the market mechanism restores equilibrium whenever there is a deviation from it. If the balance of payments reacts normally, the equilibrium of the foreign exchange market is stable. For this reason, we often say that the balance of payments is stable, by which we mean that the balance of payments reacts normally to changes in the rate of exchange.

(1) It should be noted that the concepts of "over- and under-valuation of a currency" makes sense only in the context of an equilibrium rate of exchange.

Let us consider the case in which the value of exports in terms of the foreign currency decreases. We then have the two possibilities shown in Figs. 74a and 74b. In the first case (Fig. 74a) the value of

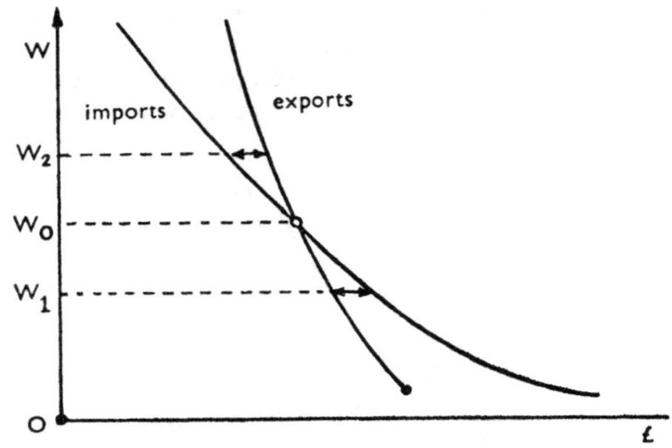

Fig. 74a

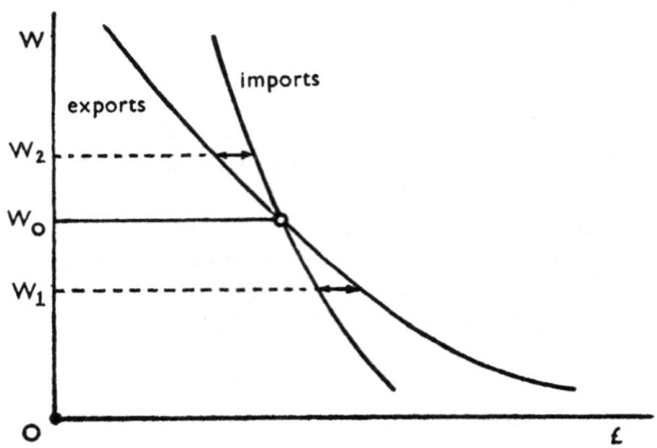

Fig. 74b

imports falls more than the value of exports when the rate of exchange increases. In the second case (Fig. 74b) the value of imports falls less than the value of exports when the rate of exchange increases. As can be seen, the equilibrium exchange-rate is stable in the first case but unstable in the second. In the second case there is an export surplus at the rate w_1 ($<w_0$) so that the market mechanism brings about

a fall in the pound-rate and thus a movement away from the equilibrium rate. At the rate w_2 ($>w_0$) there is an import surplus, so that the market mechanism brings about a rise in the pound-rate and thus once again a movement away from the equilibrium rate. On the assumptions we have made, an abnormal reaction of the balance of payments is identical with an unstable equilibrium in the foreign exchange market. For this reason we speak of an "unstable balance of payments" when the reaction is abnormal.

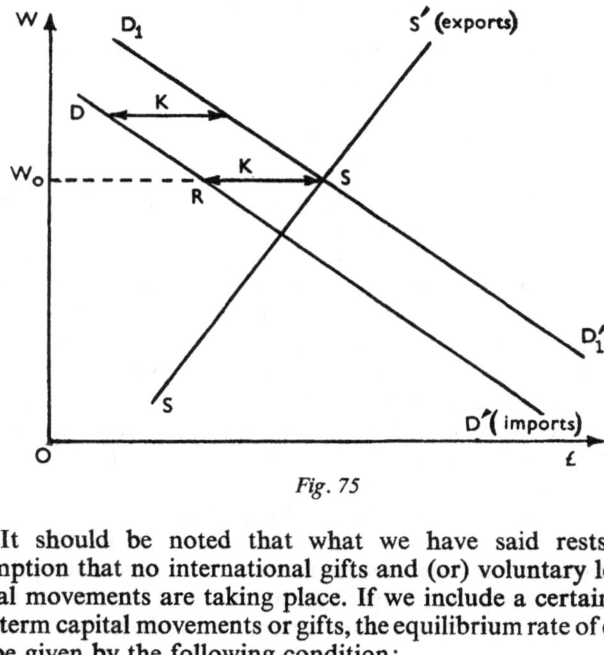

Fig. 75

7. It should be noted that what we have said rests on the assumption that no international gifts and (or) voluntary long-term capital movements are taking place. If we include a certain level of long-term capital movements or gifts, the equilibrium rate of exchange will be given by the following condition:

Demand for foreign exchange for imports
\+ Demand for foreign exchange for capital exports
= Supply of foreign exchange from exports

or more simply:

value of imports + capital exports = value of exports,

or: value of exports − value of imports = capital exports.

In Fig. 75 the curve DD' shows the demand for foreign exchange for purposes of imports, and the curve D_1D_1' shows the demand for foreign exchange for imports and for voluntary capital exports of k £s. The equilibrium rate of exchange w_0 is given by the intersection point S of the curve D_1D_1' with the supply curve SS'. At this rate of exchange, and only at this rate of exchange, is the balance of trade surplus just equal to *desired* capital exports. At any rate of exchange other than w_0 there is disequilibrium on the balance of payments.

§ 6. Devaluation and the Terms of Trade

Finally, we may briefly consider how the terms of trade of the devaluing country change, i.e. how the expression

$$\lambda = \frac{p_{ex}{}^{i}}{p_{im}{}^{a}.w} = \frac{p_{ex}{}^{i}}{p_{im}{}^{i}} = \frac{p_{ex}{}^{a}}{p_{im}{}^{a}} \tag{67}$$

changes. The change in λ clearly depends on how the prices of import goods and export goods (both expressed in the same currency) change as a result of a devaluation. Now, we have seen that the prices of both export and import-goods rise in terms of the domestic currency as a result of a devaluation. The change in λ thus depends on the extent to which both sets of prices rise. If the prices of export goods (in terms of domestic currency) rise more (less) than the prices of import goods (in terms of the domestic currency) λ increases (decreases). An increase (decrease) in λ means that one unit of exports fetches a larger (smaller) quantity of import goods. In the first (second) case the terms of trade move in favour of (against) the devaluing country. If the prices of export goods rise in the same proportion as the prices of import goods, λ remains unchanged.

It follows from what we have said that the changes in the prices of import and export-goods (expressed in the same currency) depend on the elasticities of supply and demand of imports and exports. Let us consider this in greater detail. The change in λ associated with a devaluation of the domestic currency is given by the derivative $\frac{d\lambda}{dw}$. It follows from (67) that:

$$\frac{d\lambda}{dw} = \frac{1}{(p_{im}{}^{a})^2}\left(p_{im}{}^{a}\,\frac{dp_{ex}{}^{a}}{dw} - p_{ex}{}^{a}\,\frac{dp_{im}{}^{a}}{dw}\right), \tag{68}$$

from which it follows that $\frac{d\lambda}{dw} \gtreqless 0$ depending on whether

$$p_{im}{}^{a}\,\frac{dp_{ex}{}^{a}}{dw} \gtreqless p_{ex}{}^{a}\,\frac{dp_{im}{}^{a}}{dw}$$

or

$$\frac{w}{p_{ex}{}^a} \cdot \frac{dp_{ex}{}^a}{dw} \gtreqless \frac{w}{p_{im}{}^a} \cdot \frac{dp_{im}{}^a}{dw}$$

or

(69) $$\eta_{p_{ex}{}^a,w} \gtreqless \eta_{p_{im}{}^a,w}$$

Now:

(70) $$\eta_{p_{ex}{}^a,w} = \frac{-\varepsilon_x}{\varepsilon_x - \eta_x}$$

and

(71)[1] $$\eta_{p_{im}{}^a,w} = \frac{\eta_m}{\varepsilon_m - \eta_m}.$$

Substituting (70) and (71), (69) becomes:

$$\frac{-\varepsilon_x}{\varepsilon_x - \eta_x} \gtreqless \frac{\eta_m}{\varepsilon_m - \eta_m}$$

or:

$$-\varepsilon_x \cdot (\varepsilon_m - \eta_m) \gtreqless \eta_m \cdot (\varepsilon_x - \eta_x)$$

or:

(72) $$\varepsilon_x \cdot \varepsilon_m \gtreqless \eta_m \cdot \eta_x.$$

The terms of trade move in favour of (against) the devaluing country if the mathematical product of the elasticities of supply of exports of both countries is smaller (larger) than the mathematical product of the elasticities of demand for imports of both countries. The actual change in the terms of trade thus depends on the numerical values of the four elasticities ε_x, ε_m, η_x, η_m. In an article which appeared in

[1] The proof for (71) is as follows:
Let m be the demand for imports, and a_m the supply of imports. Then

$$\text{(x)} \quad m = m(p_{im}{}^a \,.\, w)$$
$$a_m = a_m(p_{im}{}^a).$$

In equilibrium

$$\text{(xx)} \quad m(p_{im}{}^a \,.\, w) = a_m(p_{im}{}^a)$$

This condition determines $p_{im}{}^a$ as a function of w. If we differentiate (xx) with respect to w we have:*

$$\text{(xxx)} \quad m' \,.\, p_{im}{}^a \,.\, (1 + \eta_{p_{im}{}^a,w}) = a_m' \,.\, \frac{dp_{im}{}^a}{dw}$$

Now

$$\frac{\eta_m}{\varepsilon_m} = w \,.\, \frac{m'}{a_m'},$$

(See equation (47)). Using the last equation and simplifying, (xxx) becomes:

$$\eta_{p_{im}{}^a,w} = \frac{\eta_m}{\varepsilon_m - \eta_m}.$$

* m' and a_m' denote the first derivatives of (x) with respect to $p_{im}{}^a \,.\, w$ and $p_{im}{}^a$ respectively.

1954[1] K. Rothschild has shown that the elasticity of demand for the exports of small or medium-sized industrial states of the European type is small, while the elasticities of supply are relatively large, so that a devaluation may well worsen the terms of trade. While Rothschild regards an improvement in the terms of trade as improbable, Haberler regards it as quite possible.[2] Much more empirical research is required before we can come to any firm conclusions in this matter.[3]

§ 7. The Effects of Changes in the Conditions of Demand and Supply on the Balance of Payments

So far we have assumed that the demand and supply curves, both in the home and in the foreign country, remain unchanged. Let us now briefly consider the effects on the balance of payments of shifts in the demand and supply curves in the domestic and foreign country, the rate of exchange being given. The relevant relationships can be seen easily with the aid of the analytical apparatus developed in § 5.

We shall first consider the case in which there is an increase in effective demand in the home country. The demand curves DD (Fig. 76) for the various commodities will shift to the right by varying amounts. Some new commodities will now be imported, and commodities already being imported will be imported in larger quantities. That is to say, while the supply curve of imports remains unchanged, the demand curve for imports shifts to the right (Fig. 76). This usually leads to a rise in the prices and quantities of imports (Fig. 76).[4] The value of imports in terms of the home currency always increases. Due to the shift of the demand curves to the right (Fig. 76) the domestic supply of exports is reduced; the curve SS' (Fig. 77) shifts upwards. Some commodities hitherto exported cease to be internationally traded, and the quantities of other goods available for export are reduced (Fig. 77). As a rule the quantity of exports falls, and the prices of exported goods rise.[5] The value of exports in terms of the domestic currency may rise, fall or remain constant.[6]

[1] K. Rothschild, "The Effects of Devaluation on the Terms of Trade", *International Economic Papers*, Vol. 5, 1955.

[2] G. Harberler, "Currency Depreciation and the Terms of Trade", in: *Weltwirtschaftliche Entwicklung und Soziale Ordnung*, Vienna 1952, p. 149 ff.

[3] Regarding the difficulties inherent in such empirical enquiries see K. Rothschild *loc. cit.*, pp. 235–36.

[4] If supply is perfectly elastic only quantities increase.

[5] If demand is perfectly inelastic only prices rise.

[6] The reader may wish to apply the results derived in § 5, to the present case.

It can be easily seen that the value of exports remains constant if the elasticity of the demand for exports with respect to price in terms of the domestic currency equals 1. The value of exports rises (falls) if this elasticity is smaller (larger) than 1. It follows that the balance of

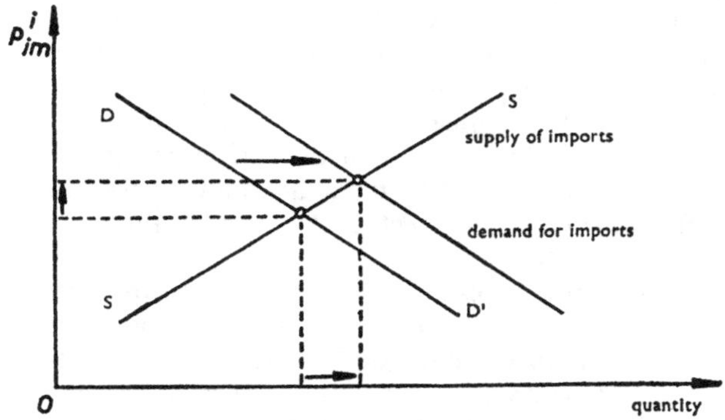

Fig. 76

payments deteriorates when the value of exports falls or remains constant. If the value of exports increases, the balance of payments may improve, deteriorate or remain unchanged.

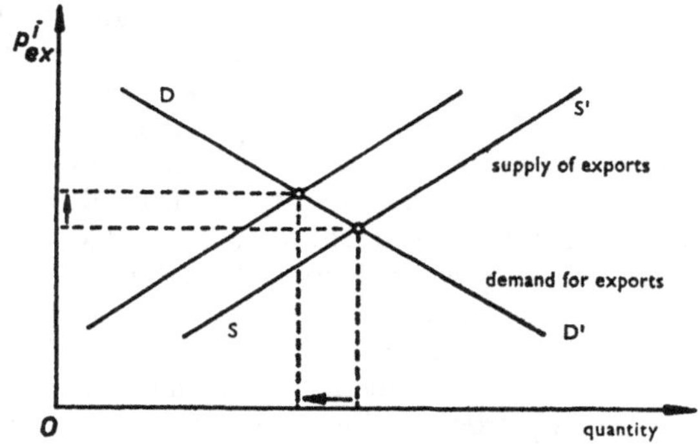

Fig. 77

If we bear in mind these relationships it is evident that, in order to obtain a complete picture of the effects of a change in domestic effective demand on national income, we have to take account not only of the income effects, which were considered above, but also of price effects. Let us assume, for example, that the price-elasticity of the demand for exports is greater than 1. If now there is a rise in domestic real income (due, perhaps, to a rise in domestic investment), the operation of the resulting income effects alone leads to a deterioration in the balance of payments, as was shown above. If payments were initially balanced there will now be a deficit. If domestic prices rise during this expansionary process the deficit on the balance of payments will be larger than it would be if prices remained constant, i.e. if only the income effect were operative, since both the price and income effects of the expansionary process operate in the same direction. However, if the price-elasticity of the demand for exports is smaller than 1, the deficit-creating income effect, resulting from the rise in income, may be reduced by the concomitant price effects. But it may also be reinforced. The effect depends on the numerical values of the relevant elasticities.

Let us also consider the case when money wage rates rise in the home country. In this case the curves of domestic demand and supply in Fig. 61 for all, or only some, goods shift upwards. The result is always a rise in prices and a simultaneous increase in the demand for imports. The value of imports in terms of the domestic currency therefore increases. The supply curve of exports, however, shifts upwards, so that exports usually decline. The value of exports in terms of the domestic currency may thus rise, fall or remain constant. The effect on the balance of payments, therefore, is the same as in the case of an increase in domestic effective demand, which was discussed above.

We are now in a position to state the effects of a change in the rate of exchange on the balance of payments together with the effects of changes in income and other price effects. We shall merely give a few examples. Consider a country with under-employment and balanced payments. Domestic investment is increased in order to raise the level of employment. As we know, the income effect of the resulting internal expansion leads to a balance of payments deficit. In order to remove the deficit, the home currency is devalued. If the balance of payments reacts normally, this in fact reduces the deficit. Moreover, the devaluation reinforces the internal expansionary process. Thus both aims are achieved: the deficit is reduced and the level of income raised. If the expansionary process raises domestic prices, the resulting effects on the balance of payments must be taken into account.

Again, consider an economy with full employment and a deficit on the balance of payments. If the currency is devalued in order to reduce the deficit, this leads to an excess of effective demand at prevailing prices, i.e. to an inflationary gap. The effects of the gap can be avoided only if the increase in effective demand which results from the devaluation is counteracted by contractionary monetary and (or) fiscal measures which reduce consumption and (or) investment.

§ 8. Concluding Remarks

Our analysis has been restricted to a two-country model, and its extension to a three-country model is outside the scope of this *Introduction.* Although valuable contributions have been made to the study of these problems,[1] we here reach the frontiers of research. Much remains to be done before these difficult questions can be completely clarified. Even our treatment of the basic relationships between the balance of payments and national income has shown how complicated are the inter-connections and how many variables have to be considered. The formulae we have derived thus *must not* be applied *mechanically* to concrete problems. Although our analysis rested on the simplest assumptions, and though we have reduced the problem to its simplest dimensions, the results we have established are nevertheless of the utmost importance if we are to understand concrete situations.[2] Our analysis shows the effect of certain central variables in the relevant context. Moreover, these theoretical analyses yield questions for empirical enquiry. It must never be forgotten that facts alone are silent; we can hope to discover the inter-relationships among facts only by posing meaningful questions. Meaningful questions, however, can only be derived from theoretical reasoning, i.e. by reasoning in terms of a model which contains the relevant aspects extracted from a far more complex reality. Only thus is it possible to obtain knowledge of economic relationships; and all theoretical economists proceeded in this way, from Adam Smith to Ricardo, Thünen, Marx, Menger, Wieser, Walras, and so on, to modern theorists.[3] The various theoretical constructions which have emerged in the course of the development of economic theory differ only as regards the kinds of models used. Either known

(1) See: S. Laursen and L. Metzler, "Flexible Exchange Rates and the Theory of Employment", *Review of Economics and Statistics*, Vol. 32, 1950.
A. C. Harberger, "Currency Depreciation, Income, and the Balance of Trade", *Journal of Political Economy*, Vol. 58, 1950.
W. Stolper, "Stand und ungelöste Probleme der Theorie des Aussenhandelsmultiplikators", *Zeitschrift für die gesamte Staatswissenschaft*, Vol. 108, 1952.
J. Meade, *The Balance of Payments*, London 1951.

(2) E.g. see: B. B. Metelius, *Utlandstransaktionerna och den Svenska Ekonomi*, Stockholm, 1955.

(3) Anyone who wishes to see an example, in a classical work, of reasoning in terms of models and of its power (and each student should read at least one classic) should consult the work of J. H. von Thünen, *Der isolierte Staat in Beziehung auf Landwirtschaft und Nationalökomie*. Reprinted Jena 1910.
Fruitful model building and reasoning in terms of models, as well as the practical relevance of theoretical analysis, is nowhere as clearly illustrated as in the case of this master, who not only leads the reader to the results, but reveals the process of his creative thinking.

models were improved by taking account of new knowledge gained from experience, or new models were created to deal with certain problems. Progress in economic theory takes place through the development of ever more powerful models for the analysis of economies which are themselves changing as time passes. Although theoretical constructions can therefore never reach a final form, they can help to give us a deeper understanding of economic forces, which in turn increases the possibilities of effective control through economic policy.

APPENDIX I

(to Chapter III, Section A, § 3)

The Multiplier in Conditions of Under-employment and Full Employment

We still have to consider a problem to which we alluded above (p. 116), namely the effect of the level of employment on the size of the investment multiplier. If C_r denotes real consumption, Y_r real income, C consumption in money terms, Y money income, and P an index of the general price level, we have:

$$(1) \qquad C_r = \frac{C}{P} \qquad \text{and} \qquad Y_r = \frac{Y}{P}.$$

In accordance with our previous discussion, the consumption function then takes the form:

$$(2) \qquad C_r = f(Y_r)$$

or

$$(3) \qquad \frac{C}{P} = f\left(\frac{Y}{P}\right).$$

We thus have two marginal propensities to consume: the real marginal propensity to consume, and the marginal propensity to consume in money terms. The former is given by: $\frac{dC_r}{dY_r}$, and the latter by: $\frac{dC}{dY}$. Between the two marginal propensities to consume we have the simple relationship:

$$(4) \qquad \frac{dC}{dY} = \frac{C_r}{Y_r} \cdot \varepsilon_P + \frac{dC_r}{dY_r} \cdot \varepsilon_r,$$

in which

$$(5) \qquad \varepsilon_P = \frac{dP}{P} \div \frac{dY}{Y}$$

represents the elasticity of the price level with respect to changes in money income, and

$$(6) \qquad \varepsilon_r = \frac{dY_r}{Y_r} \div \frac{dY}{Y}$$

represents the elasticity of real income with respect to changes in money income. Both elasticities show the extent to which a change in money income consists of a change in the price level or of a change in real income. It is easily seen that the sum of the two elasticities equals 1:

(7) $$\varepsilon_P + \varepsilon_r = 1.$$ [(1)]

Equation (4) is derived in the following way. It follows from (3) that:

(8) $$C = P \,.\, C_r(Y_r).$$

Differentiating (8) with respect to Y we obtain:

$$\frac{dC}{dY} = P \,.\, \frac{dC_r}{dY_r} \cdot \frac{dY_r}{dY} + C_r \,.\, \frac{dP}{dY}.$$

Substituting the elasticities (5) and (6) we obtain (4).

Relation (4), which, incidentally, also holds if consumers are not free from money illusion, shows that the relationship between the real marginal propensity to consume and the marginal propensity to consume in money terms is determined by the elasticity of money income with respect to real income and prices, and by the average real propensity to consume.[(2)]

Experience shows that, given money wage rates and productive capacity, the increase in real income which results from additional employment induced by rising effective demand can take place, within a certain range, at constant prices before full employment is reached. Prices begin to rise before full employment is reached when bottlenecks appear in the productive process. When full employment

[(1)] We have

$$Y = Y_r \,.\, P$$

and therefore:

$$dY = Y_r \,.\, dP + P \,.\, dY_r$$

or:

$$1 = \frac{Y_r \,.\, P}{P} \cdot \frac{dP}{dY} + \frac{P \,.\, Y_r}{Y_r} \cdot \frac{dY_r}{dY}.$$

[(2)] We may replace the elasticities ε_P and ε_r in (4) by the elasticity of the price level with respect to real income. We have:

$$\varepsilon_P = \frac{1}{1 + \varepsilon_{Y_r,P}}$$

and

$$\varepsilon_r = \frac{1}{1 + \varepsilon_{P,Y_r}},$$

where

$$\varepsilon_{P,Y_r} = \frac{Y_r}{P} \cdot \frac{dP}{dY_r}$$

and

$$\varepsilon_{Y_r,P} = \frac{P}{Y_r} \cdot \frac{dY_r}{dP}$$

is attained at a given productive capacity real income cannot increase any more, and further increases in effective demand lead to an inflationary gap (see p. 119) and pure price increases, i.e. to a purely nominal increase in income. We may therefore distinguish schematically among the three ranges of an upswing which are depicted in Fig. 78, and which we denote by I, II and III.[1]

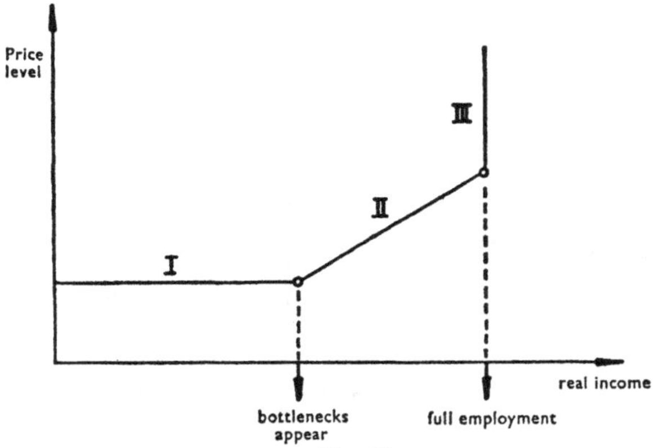

Fig. 78

It is obvious that in range I

$$\varepsilon_P = 0 \quad \text{and} \quad \varepsilon_r = 1.$$

The entire increase in money income consists of an increase in real income at constant prices. From (4) it follows that in range I:

$$\frac{dC}{dY} = \frac{dC_r}{dY_r}$$

i.e. the real marginal propensity to consume equals the marginal propensity to consume in money terms.

Conversely, in range III any increase in money income consists solely of an increase in the price level, i.e.

$$\varepsilon_P = 1 \quad \text{and} \quad \varepsilon_r = 0.$$

From (4) it follows that in this case

$$\frac{dC}{dY} = \frac{C_r}{Y_r}$$

Thus, in conditions of full employment the marginal propensity to consume in money terms equals the average real propensity to

[1] An extremely clear analysis of these three ranges can be found in H. von Mangoldt, *Grundriss der Volkswirtschaftslehre*, Stuttgart 1863, p. 50, Fig. 8.

consume at full employment. In Fig. 79 *AB* is the real consumption function, and tan α therefore gives the average real propensity to consume at full employment. If money income rises above the full employment income the consumption function becomes *BB'*, i.e. the extension of OB beyond B. Consumption in money terms varies proportionately with money income, which means that real consumption remains unchanged.

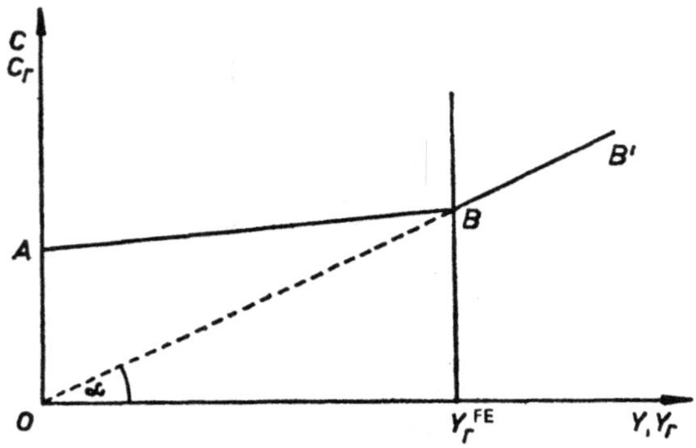

Fig. 79

Finally, in the middle range II $0 < \varepsilon_P < 1$ and $0 < \varepsilon_r < 1$. In this case (4) cannot be simplified.[1]

We can now state the investment multiplier for the three ranges. We simply substitute (4) for the marginal propensity to consume in formula (33b) (p. 114). We then obtain:

$$dY = \frac{1}{1 - \varepsilon_P \cdot \dfrac{C_r}{Y_r} - \varepsilon_r \cdot \dfrac{dC_r}{dY_r}} dI, \tag{9}$$

or, since $\varepsilon_p + \varepsilon_r = 1$:

$$dY = \frac{1}{\varepsilon_P \cdot \left(1 - \dfrac{C}{Y}\right) + \varepsilon_r \left(1 - \dfrac{dC_r}{dY_r}\right)} dI,$$

or, if we substitute the appropriate propensities to save,

$$dY = \frac{1}{\varepsilon_P \cdot \dfrac{S}{Y} + \varepsilon_r \cdot \dfrac{dS_r}{dY_r}} dI.^{(2)} \tag{9a}$$

[1] Some writers neglect range II in their analysis and, to simplify their exposition, assume constant prices up to full employment.

[2] This relation holds both in the presence and in the absence of money illusion.

If we denote the money income multiplier by K_m:

$$K_m = \frac{dY}{dI} = \frac{1}{1 - \frac{dC}{dY}}$$

and the real income multiplier by K_r:

$$K_r = \frac{dY_r}{dI_r} = \frac{1}{1 - \frac{dC_r}{dY_r}} = \frac{1}{\frac{dS_r}{dY_r}}$$

(9a) may be written in the form:

(10) $$K_m = \frac{1}{\varepsilon_p \, . \, \frac{S}{Y} + \varepsilon_r \, . \, \frac{1}{K_r}}.$$

This is a basic relationship in the theory of the multiplier. The Japanese economist M. Shinohara was the first to derive it, and he designated it the fundamental relationship between the real income and the money income investment multipliers.(1) He writes it as:

(10a) $$\frac{K_r}{K_m} = \varepsilon_r + K_r \, . \, \varepsilon_p \, . \, \frac{S}{Y},$$

which shows the variables which determine the relationship between K_r and K_m. For $\varepsilon_r = 1$ and $\varepsilon_P = 0$ (range I) the real income and money income multipliers are equal. For $\varepsilon_r = 0$ and $\varepsilon_P = 1$ we have:

$$K_m = \frac{1}{\frac{S}{Y}} = \frac{1}{1 - \frac{C}{Y}},$$

in which $\frac{C}{Y}$ and $\frac{S}{Y}$ respectively denote the average propensities to consume and save at full employment.(2) (10a) shows that, given ε_r, K_r and $\frac{S}{Y}$, the money income multiplier is determined by the degree of price flexibility as expressed by ε_P.

(1) M. Shinohara, "Real and Money Income Multiplier" *The Annals of the Hitotsubashi Academy*, Vol III, 1953, p. 194. See also the same author's "The Multiplier and the Marginal Propensity to Import", *The American Economic Review*, Vol 47, 1957, p. 608ff. See especially p. 617ff., and appendix II.
See also: H. Reinhold, *Einkommens—und Preiseffekt in der Multiplikatortheorie*. Thesis submitted to the University of Kiel, 1959.

(2) On the basis of measurements Shinohara reaches the conclusion that $\frac{K_r}{K_m}$ is determined mainly by ε_r (*loc. cit.* p. 194).

Let us assume, for the sake of simplicity, that prices and the real marginal propensity to consume are constant up to full employment. We can then represent the effects of the money income multiplier after full employment is reached in a simple geometrical way suggested by Goodwin.[(1)] In Fig. 80 *AB* is the real consumption function or the consumption function in money terms up to full employment. Given this consumption function, investment could take place up to the

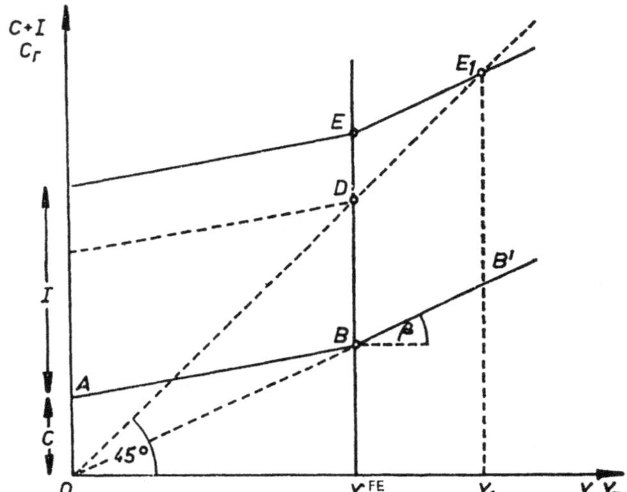

Fig. 80

level *BD* without any increases in the price level. Any investment within the range *BD* would have a multiplier effect, given by the real income multiplier corresponding to the slope of *AB*, which is not equal to the money income multiplier. If intended investment is larger than *BD*, e.g. *BE*, there is an inflationary gap of *DE*. That is to say, at prevailing prices real effective demand for consumption and investment exceeds available resources. Since consumption in real terms remains constant, prices must rise to an extent sufficient to

(1) R. M. Goodwin, "The Multiplier", in *The New Economics: Keynes' Influence on Theory and Public Policy*, edt. S. E. Harris, New York 1947, especially p. 495ff. The reader must be emphatically warned that the inflationary process discussed here is merely a possible, and in practise uninteresting, case of an inflationary process. It is assumed that money wage rates remain unchanged, and thus the problems connected with the wage-price spiral are simply not considered in this model. We also assume that investment decisions are made solely with reference to investment in money terms.

reduce investment in real terms to its full employment level. This is achieved at the level of income Y_1, since effective demand in money terms is now given by EE_1, which cuts the 45°-line at point E_1. Thus, a process of cumulative price increases, i.e. an inflationary process (see p. 121) develops, which, however, converges and stops at the level of income Y_1. Prices and incomes have risen to that extent at which households maintain the same real consumption as at the income Y_r, and real investment absorbs exactly the available free resources. At the new level of income Y_1 the full-employment money income multiplier applies, i.e. the multiplier $\frac{dC_m}{dY_m} = \frac{C_r^{FE}}{Y_r^{FE}} = \tan \beta$.[1]

The figure shows that the full-employment money income multiplier is larger than the money income multiplier (= real income multiplier) before full employment is reached. The figure also shows that the more is consumed at the full employment income (i.e. the less resources are available for investment) the larger is the full-employment multiplier. If the entire full-employment income is devoted to consumption, the marginal propensity to consume in money terms becomes 1, and the full-employment money income multiplier becomes infinite. If now expenditure on investment takes place a non-convergent process of price increases develops.

[1] The *process* of rising prices and money income can, of course, also be traced in terms of dynamic analysis. Such an analysis shows that real investment increases temporarily before the new equilibrium position is reached (see R. M. Goodwin, *loc. cit.*). An inflationary *process* can be treated *only* in terms of dynamic analysis.

APPENDIX II

(to Chapter III, Section A, § 7.)

Wage Rates, Commodity Prices and Employment

We use the following notation:

Y_r real income
Y money income
C_r real consumption
C consumption in money terms
I_r real investment
I investment in money terms
P price index
l money wage rate
M stock of money
N employment, measured in hours of work

We have the following relationships among these variables:

(1)	$P \,.\, Y_r = C + I$	income equation
(2)	$C = P \,.\, C_r(Y_r)$	consumption function
(3)	$I = P \,.\, I_r(i)$	investment function
(4)	$M = P \,.\, L(Y_r, i)$	demand for money
(5)	$Y_r = \emptyset(N)$	production function
6)	$\frac{dY_r}{dN} = \frac{l}{P}$	firms' demand for labour as a function of the real wage rate[1]

We also assume that the money wage rate is given:

(7) $$l = l_0.$$

Furthermore, the stock of money M is fixed by the central bank:

(8) $$M = M_0$$

If the central bank fixes the rate of interest, (8) is replaced by $i = i_0$.

The 8 equations (1) to (8) contain 8 variables: P, Y_r, C, I, i, N, M and l. If we insert for l and M the values l_0 and M_0 in (4) and (6), equations (1) to (6) determine the variables P, Y_r, C, I, i, and N. Full employment prevails if the resulting demand for labour is equal to

(1) We assume that firms behave as quantity adjusters in both the product and labour markets.

the supply of labour at the prevailing real wage rate. Let us assume that the supply of hours of work is a rising function of the real wage rate. If we solve the system (1) to (6) for a given money wage rate and stock of money the three cases shown in Fig. 81 may result:

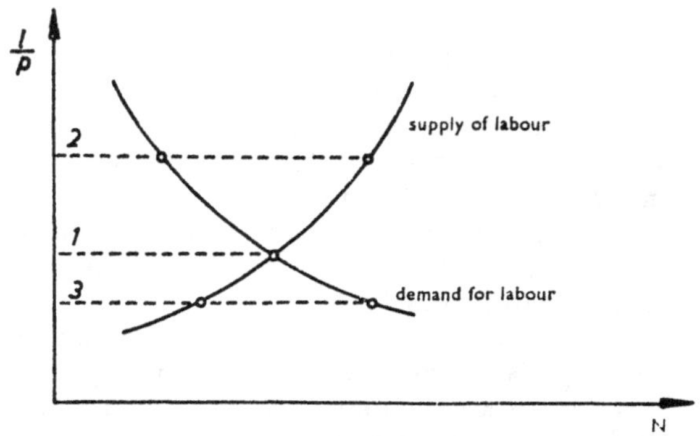

Fig. 81

Case 1: full employment.
Case 2: involuntary unemployment.
Case 3: excess demand in the labour market.

The situation resulting in the labour market depends on l and M, or l and i, and on the forms of the consumption, investment and liquidity preference functions.

The system of equations (1) to (8) can be easily reduced to the three fundamental equations with which we worked previously. Thus the three equations (1), (2) and (3) reduce to the well-known equation:

$$P \,.\, Y_r = P \,.\, C_r(Y_r) + P \,.\, I_r(i)$$

or

(I) $$S_r(Y_r) = I_r(i).$$

(4) and (8) yield the equation:

(II) $$L(Y_r, i) = \frac{M_0}{P}.$$

Finally, equations (5), (6) and (7) assign a particular price level to each level of real income:

(III) $$P = \psi(Y_r).$$

If we make the usual assumption that we are in the range of diminishing marginal productivity of an hour's work, the price level P rises with rising real income, given a constant money wage rate.

The three equations determine real income, the commodity price level and the rate of interest. If we assume that the central bank, instead of fixing the stock of money, fixes the rate of interest, (I) determines real income, (III) the level of prices and (II) the required stock of money.

We can use the reduced or the original system of equations to investigate the comparative-static changes in the dependent variables resulting from changes in the rate of interest (the stock of money), or the money wage rate, or the consumption function. Let us, for example, consider the case in which the propensity to consume increases, the money wage rate and the stock of money remaining constant. As we know, an increase in the real propensity to consume leads to a rise in Y_r (assuming unemployed resources are available) and thus to an increase in N and P.

The effect of a change in the money wage rate on employment and the price level is of special interest. We assume once again that the central bank fixes the stock of money, and that under-employment prevails. The fall in the money wage rate can lead to an increase in employment only if it brings about a fall in the rate of interest. But this is not a sufficient condition. To see this, let us write the system of equations (1) to (8) in a reduced form:

$$\text{(A)} \qquad C_r(Y_r) + I_r(i) = Y_r.^{(1)}$$

Using (5), (6) and (7), (4) can be written as:

$$\text{(B)} \qquad \frac{M_0 \cdot Y_r'}{l} = L[Y_r(N),i].$$

The two equations (A) and (B) determine employment N and the rate of interest i as a function of the money wage rate. Differentiating N implicitly with respect to the money wage rate l we obtain:[2]

$$\text{(C)} \qquad \frac{dN}{dl} = \frac{-\frac{1}{l^2} \cdot M_0 \cdot Y_r' \cdot I_i}{L_i\left[Y_r'\left(1 - \frac{dC_r}{dY_r}\right)\right] + I_i\left(L_{Y_r} \cdot Y_r' - \frac{M_0 \cdot Y_r''}{l}\right)}.$$

Usually:

$$Y_r' > 0, \quad 0 < \frac{dC_r}{dY_r} < 1, \quad L_{Y_r} > 0, \quad Y_r'' < 0.$$

Usually also

$$I_i < 0 \quad \text{and} \quad L_i < 0$$

[1] Combining equations (1) to (3)

[2] $Y_r' = \frac{dY_r}{dN}$; $Y_r'' = \frac{d^2Y_r}{dN^2}$; $I_i = \frac{\partial I}{\partial i}$; $L_i = \frac{\partial L}{\partial i}$.

and therefore usually

$$\frac{dN}{dl} > 0,$$

i.e. a fall in the money wage rate is associated with an increase in employment. It is also easy to prove that

$$\frac{di}{dl} > 0$$

i.e. that a fall in the money wage rate leads to a reduction in the rate of interest. We have:

$$\text{(D)} \qquad \frac{di}{dl} = \frac{-\frac{1}{l^2} \cdot M_0 Y_r'^2 (1 - C_r')}{L_i \left[Y_r' \left(1 - \frac{dC_r}{dY_r} \right) \right] + I_i \left(L_{Y_r} \cdot Y_r' - \frac{M_0 \cdot Y_r''}{l} \right)}$$

It follows from (C) and (D) that

$$\text{(E)} \qquad \frac{dN}{dl} = \frac{I_i}{Y_r'(1 - C_r')} \cdot \frac{di}{dl}.$$

Since I_i is usually negative and the denominator $Y_r'(1 - C_r')$ positive, $\frac{dN}{dl}$ is negative only if $\frac{di}{dl}$ is positive, i.e. only if a fall in the money wage rate leads to a reduction in the rate of interest. In the exceptional case of $I_i = 0$, i.e. when investment is completely interest inelastic, a fall in the money wage rate has no effect on employment. The same is true if $L_i = \infty$, i.e. if the speculative demand for money is perfectly elastic with respect to the rate of interest.

We obtain the following results if we assume that, instead of fixing the stock of money M, the central bank fixes the rate of interest i, i.e. if instead of equation (8) we have

$$i = i_0.$$

In this case equations (1) to (3) determine real consumption, real investment and real income. Equation (5) determines the level of employment, and, given the money wage rate, equation (6) determines the commodity price level. Finally, equation (4) determines the required stock of money.

A rise in the real propensity to consume leads to an increase in N and P also on these assumptions.

According to (5) and (6) a fall in the money wage rate leaves employment and the real wage rate unchanged. That is to say, the fall in the money wage rate is associated with a proportionately equal reduction in the price level. (4) shows that the required stock of money falls.

BIBLIOGRAPHY

Chapters I & II

1. E. Brehmer, *Struktur und Funktionsweise des Geldmarkets der Deutschen Bundesrepublik seit 1948*. Tübingen 1956.
2. W. Ehrlicher, *Geldkapitalbildung und Realkapitalbildung*. Tübingen 1956.
3. C. Föhl, *Geldschöpfung und Wirtschaftskreislauf*. 2nd ed. Berlin 1955.
4. H. Gestrich, *Kredit und Sparen*. 3rd. ed. Munich 1957.
5. H. Gestrich, *Neue Kreditpolitik*. Stuttgart and Berlin 1936.
6. G. Haberler, *Prosperity and Depression*, 4th ed. London 1958.
7. A. Hahn, *Volkswirtschaftliche Theorie des Bankkredits*. 3rd ed. Tübingen 1930.
8. A. Hansen, *Monetary Theory and Fiscal Policy*. New York 1949.
9. A. G. Hart, *Money, Debt and Economic Activity*, 2nd ed. New York 1953.
10. H. Höpker-Aschoff, *Geld und Gold*, Jena 1939.
11. H. Höpker-Aschoff, *Geld und Währungen*, Stuttgart 1948.
12. J. M. Keynes, *A Treatise on Money*, 2 vols. London 1930.
13. E. Lukas, *Aufgaben des Geldes*. Stuttgart 1937.
14. E. Lukas, *Geld und Kredit*. Heidelberg 1951.
15. F. Lutz, *Das Grundproblem der Geldverfassung*. Stuttgart and Berlin 1936.
16. F. Lutz, *Das Zinsproblem*. Tübingen 1956.
17. R. Nöll V. D. Nahmer, *Der volkswirtschaftliche Kreditfonds*. Berlin 1934.
18. J. Pedersen, *Pengeteori og Pengepolitik*. 2nd ed. Copenhagen 1948.
19. E. Preiser, "Sparen und Investieren," *Jahrbücher für Nationalökonomie und Statistik*, Vol 159 (1944).
20. *Readings in Monetary Theory*. Allen and Unwin, London, 1951.
21. D. H. Robertson, *Money*, 4th ed. London, 1948.
22. F. Sarow, *Offenmarktpolitik zur Konjunkturregelung*. Munich and Leipzig 1937.
23. R. S. Sayers, *Modern Banking*. 5th ed. Oxford, 1960.
24. F. Somary, *Bankpolitik*. 2nd ed. Tübingen 1930.
25. R. Stucken, *Geld und Kredit*. 2nd ed. Tübingen 1955.
26. R. Stucken, *Liquidität der Banken*. Schriften der Akademie für Deutsches Recht Nr. 3 Berlin 1940.
27. R. Stucken, *Deutsche Geld- und Kreditpolitik 1914–1953*, 2nd ed. Tübingen 1953.

28. *The Federal Reserve System. Its Purposes and its Functions*. 2nd ed. Washington 1954.
29. "United States Monetary Policy: Recent Thinking and Experience." United States Government Printing Office. Washington 1954.
30. V. Wagner, *Geschichte der Kredittheorien. Eine dogmenkritische Darstellung*. Vienna 1937.
31. A. Weber, *Geld, Banken und Börsen*. 5th ed. Munich 1955.
32. K. Wicksell, *Interest and Prices*, London 1936.
33. K. Wicksell, *Lectures on Political Economy*, Vol II, London 1934.
34. H. Withers, *The Meaning of Money*. 6th ed. London 1937.

Chapter III

Section A

The bibliography for this Section contains only works published in book form; the relevant journal articles are indicated in the text.

35. W. Baumol, *Economic Dynamics*. 2nd ed. New York, 1959.
36. W. Beveridge, *Full Employment in a Free Society*. London 1944.
37. P. Binder, *Die Schalthebel der Konjunktur*. Munich and Berlin 1939
38. J. M. Clark, *Alternative to Serfdom*. New York 1948.
39. D. Dillard, *The Economics of J. M. Keynes*. New York 1948.
40. H. Drahota, *Sparen, Horten und Zins in der modernen Geldtheorie*. Jena 1941.
41. *The Economics of Full Employment*. Studies prepared at the Oxford University Institute of Statistics. Oxford 1944.
42. W. J. Fellner, *Monetary Policies and Full Employment*. Los Angeles 1947.
43. *Deutsche Geldpolitik*. Berlin 1941.
44. G. N. Halm, *Monetary Theory*, 2nd ed. 1946.
45. A. Hansen, *Fiscal Policy and Business Cycles*, New York 1941.
46. A. Hansen, *Business Cycles and National Income*, New York 1951.
47. S. E. Harris, *The New Economics; Keynes' Influence on Theory and Public Policy*, New York 1947.
48. R. F. Harrod, *The Trade Cycle. An Essay*. Oxford 1936.
49. R. F. Harrod, *Towards a Dynamic Economics*, London, 1948.
50. J. R. Hicks, *A Contribution to the Theory of the Trade Cycle*, Oxford 1950.
51. *Income, Employment and Public Policy. Essays in Honor of Alvin H. Hansen*. New York 1948.
52. N. Johannsen, *Die Steuer der Zukunft*. Berlin 1913.
53. W. A. Jöhr, *Die Konjunkturschwankungen*. Tübingen 1952.
54. M. Kalecki, *Theory of Economic Dynamics*. London 1954.
55. J. M. Keynes, *The General Theory of Employment, Interest and Money*. London 1936.
56. K. Kurihara, *Post-Keynesian Economics*, New Jersey 1954.

57. L. Klein, *The Keynesian Revolution*, New York 1947.
58. W. Kraus, *Wirschaftswachstum und Gleichgewicht*. Frankfurt a. M. 1955.
59. O. Lange, *Price Flexibility and Employment*. Bloomington 1944.
60. W. Lautenbach, *Über Kredit und Produktion*. Frankfurt/Main 1937.
61. W. Lautenbach, *Zins, Kredit und Produktion*. Tübingen 1952.
62. A. P. Lerner, *The Economics of Employment*. New York 1951.
63. E. Lundberg, *Studies in the Theory of Economic Expansion*, London 1937.
64. W. Mieth, *Das Akzelerationsprinzip*. Berlin 1954.
65. P. Nørregaard-Rasmussen, *Intersectoral Economic Studies*. Copenhagen 1956.
66. B. Ohlin, *Penningpolitik, Offentliga Arbeten, Subventioner och Tullar som Medal mot Arbetslöshet*. Stockholm 1934.
67. B. Ohlin, *The Problem of Employment Stabilization*, New York 1949.
68. D. Patinkin, *Money, Interest and Prices*. New York 1956.
69. A. Paulsen, *Neue Wirtschaftslehre*. 3rd ed. Berlin 1954.
70. A. C. Pigou, *Employment and Equilibrium*, London 1941.
71. A. C. Pigou, *Lapses from Full Employment*. London 1945.
72. A. C. Pigou, *Keynes' General Theory. A Retrospect*. London 1950.
73. E. Preiser, *Grundzüge der Konjunkturtheorie*. Tübingen 1933.
74. *Prices, Wages and Employment. Postwar Economic Studies Nr. 4*. Washington 1946.
75. *Die Problematik der Vollbeschäftigung*. Schriften des Vereins für Sozialpolitik, New Series, Vol 3. Berlin 1951.
76. J. Robinson, *Introduction to the Theory of Employment*. London 1937.
77. J. Robinson, *Essays in the Theory of Employment*, Oxford 1947.
78. J. Robinson, *The Rate of Interest and Other Essays*, London 1952.
79. J. Robinson, *The Accumulation of Capital*. London 1956.
80. P. A. Samuelson, *Foundations of Economic Analysis*. Cambridge Mass. 1948.
81. J. Tinbergen, *The Dynamics of Business Cycles*. Chicago 1950.
82. J. Tinbergen, *Econometrics*, London 1951.
83. T. Wilson, *Fluctuations in Income and Employment*, London 1948.
84. H. J. Witteveen, *Loonshoogte en Werkgelegenheid*. Haarlem 1947.
85. *Economic Progress:* Papers and Proceedings of a Round Table Conference held by the International Economic Association in 1953, edited by L. M. Dupriez with the assistance of D. C. Hague, Louvain, 1955.

See also items, 3, 4, 6, 8, 9, 10, 11, 13, 14, 17, 18, 25, 33.

Section B

86. E. D. Allen-O.H. Brownlee, *Economics of Public Finance*. 2nd ed. New York 1954.

87. O. Donner, "Die Grenzen der Staatsverschuldung". *Weltwirtschaftliches Archiv* Vol. 56, 1942.
88. H. Fick, *Finanzwirtschaft und Konjunktur*. Jena 1932.
89. C. Föhl, "Steuern und Staatskredit". *Finanzarchiv*, New Series, Vol. II, 1949.
90. C. Föhl, "Das Steuerparadoxon". *Finanzarchiv*, New Series, Vol. 17, 1956.
91. J. Gelting, "Finansprocess og Konjunkturmodel", *Nationaløkonomisk Tidsskrift*. Vol 81, Copenhagen 1943.
92. J. Gelting, *Finansprocessen og det Økonomiske Kredsløb*. Copenhagen, 1948.
93. T. Haavelmo, "Multiplier Effects of a Balanced Budget". *Econometrica*, Vol. 13, 1945.
94. H. Haller, "Möglichkeiten und Grenzen finanzwirtschaftlicher Konjunkturpolitik". *Finanzarchiv*, New Series, Vol. 12, 1950–51.
95. A. Hansen, "Three Methods of Expansion through Fiscal Policy" *American Economic Review*, Vol. 35, 1945, p. 382 ff.
96. A. Hansen, *Economic Policy and Full Employment*, New York 1947.
97. Bent Hansen, *The Economic Theory of Fiscal Policy*, London 1958.
98. W. A. Jöhr, "Das Problem der Schuldentilgung." *Finanzarchiv*, New Series, Vol II, 1948.
99. R. v. Keller, "Ausstattung, Konsolidation und Tilgung staatlicher Arbeitsbeschaffungs—und Investitionskredite." *Weltwirtschaftliches Archiv*, Vol. 53, (1941).
100. A. P. Lerner, *The Economics of Control*, New York 1947.
101. R. A. Musgrave, "Alterative Budget Policies for Full Employment." *American Economic Review*, Vol. 35, 1945.
102. R. A. Musgrave, "Fiscal Policy in Prosperity and Depression." *American Economic Review*, Papers and Proceedings, Vol. 38, 1948.
103. R. A. Musgrave, I. I. Carroll, L. D. Cook and L. Frane, "Distribution of Tax Payments by Income Groups: A Case Study for 1948." *National Tax Journal*, Vol. IV, 1951.
104. R. A. Musgrave, *The Theory of Public Finance: A Study in Public Economy*, New York, 1959.
105. F. Neumark, "Grundsätze und Arten der Haushaltführung und Finanzbedarfsdekkung." *Handbuch der Finanzwissenschaft*. 2nd ed. Vol I, Tübingen 1952.
106. J. Pedersen, "Einige Probleme der Finanzwirtschaft". *Weltwirtschaftliches Archiv*, Vol 45, 1937.
107. K. Philip, "Finanzpolitik und wirtschaftliche Aktivität" *Weltwirtschaftliches Archiv*, Vol 57, 1943.
108. K. Philip, "Finanzpolitik und Zins". *Weltwirtschaftliches Archiv*, Vol 62, 1949.
109. T. Schelling, *National Income Behavior*. New York 1951.

110. E. Schneider, "Zur Frage der Wirkung finanzpolitischer Massnahmen auf die wirtschaftliche Aktivität." *Finanzarchiv*, New Series, Vol. 10, 1945.
111. G. Schmölders, *Finanzpolitik*. Berlin 1955.
112. H. M. Somers, *Public Finance and National Income*. Philadelphia 1949.
113. Ph. E. Taylor, *The Economics of Public Finance*. New York 1949.
114. H. Timm, "Gedanken zur Staatsverschuldung." *Finanzarchiv*, New Series, Vol 8, 1943.
115. *Vollbeschäftigung, Inflation und Planwirschaft*. Editor, A. Hunold, Erlenbach-Zurich 1951.

See also items 3, 8, 41, 42, 45, 46, 51, 62.

Index of Authors

For Product Safety Concerns and Information please contact our EU representative GPSR@taylorandfrancis.com
Taylor & Francis Verlag GmbH, Kaufingerstraße 24, 80331 München, Germany

www.ingramcontent.com/pod-product-compliance
Lightning Source LLC
LaVergne TN
LVHW011117300926
849160LV00008B/426
9780415607124